MAKING IT
in high heels

MAKING IT
in high heels

EDITED BY
KIMBERLEE MACDONALD

Published by BurmanBooks Inc.
260 Queens Quay West
Suite 904
Toronto, Ontario
Canada M5J 2N3

Cover and interior design:
Jack Steiner Graphic Design

Editing:
Kimberlee MacDonald

Distribution:
Trumedia Group
c/o Ingram Publisher Services
14 Ingram Blvd.
LaVergne, TN 37086

ISBN 978-1-897404-07-2

To Lisa Drew

Behind her smile, were so many tears.

Acknowledgments

The publisher wishes to thank the Project Manager, John Manikaros and the editor Kimberly Macdonald. We would also like to acknowledge all the young girls who suffer in silence. We hope you will gain the strength from this book to continue, seek mentors or friends and strive for the greatness you deserve.

Go to www.makingitinhighheels.com for blogs, dvd's and to be part of the new books!

Introduction

Welcome to *Making it in High Heels*. A recent statistic showed girls aged 16–18 had a 12% increase in suicide due to bullying, peer pressure and drug abuse. This was alarming and we decided to use our resources and friends to help lower the statistic. Calling out to women of all ages, we were delighted to see how many wanted to participate by revealing personal stories of loss, sadness, victory and strength.

We felt, as did the authors, that from every bad experience comes a larger lesson. And from that lesson, comes a stronger person. It's not okay to be a victim, and we hope this book will help you find your way and help you deal with whatever situation you have to endure.

If you wish to ask any author a question, email your question to www.BurmanBooks.com and we will make sure to send it to them.

Thanks and enjoy!

www.foxyoriginals.com

This coupon entitles you to

☆ 20% off

of Foxy Originals Jewellery

Enter the coupon code 3699
at **www.foxyoriginals.com**
to redeem your discount

* Discount applies to pre-tax total
* One time use only

Table of Contents

Making It in High Heels

Andrea Pressburger

I've just celebrated my 28th birthday. I guess that makes me a grown up. Doesn't it?

When I was little, I remember thinking, "When I'm in my twenties, I'm going to be set. I'll have a beautiful house, kids and the man of my dreams; and I'll have a successful career!"

Well, aside from my super cute bachelor apartment and a job I really enjoy (in a field drastically different from my childhood aspirations), I've yet to meet the man of my dreams and I still have much to accomplish before I even *think* about becoming a mom. In short, I'm still growing up and I'm pretty sure I'll be growing up for the rest of my life. It hasn't always been easy, but I'm grateful for every step of the journey; every challenge that has contributed to making me who I am today.

I was born the youngest of three, the only girl, seven and nine years apart from my brothers. It was my mom who wanted another baby. I guess she was tired of being outnumbered and wanted to see if "three times a charm" was really true. Until I was born, everyone was convinced I would be a boy. They had even picked out my name and were preparing to enroll me in football, hockey and soccer. Well, much to my mom's delight, she got her wish. When I came into the world, I became the absolute light and sunshine of her life; her little bundle of joy.

The first few years of my life were typical for any little girl growing up in a middle-class, suburban family. I was happy and healthy; I loved to smile and laugh, in spite of feeling excluded by my older brothers. They were two years apart; instant buddies, and I was the annoying kid sister. That's why I was close to my mom. She absolutely loved to spoil me with attention and gifts. We were often at the mall and my mom would always buy me whatever I wanted. She was big on retail therapy.

These were the good years; then I began to notice a change in her. Suddenly my mother didn't have as much time for me; she was distracted and seemed sad all the time. My parents weren't spending much time together, either. Dad had a long commute, to and from his job in the city and Mom stayed home, teaching piano lessons and caring for her children. Whenever my parents were together they seemed stressed. Although they tried to put up a good front, I sensed that things were not well, especially when I compared them to my friends' parents. My mom wasn't like my friends' moms; baking cookies or greeting me at the door when I got home from school.

This pattern continued for the next few years and my mother seemed more and more desolate and despairing. She was lost in her own world, paying little notice to me and my brothers. I remember watching her devour tubs of ice cream and bags of cookies, noticing how she was gaining weight. I was frightened, but fascinated; having no real understanding of why she was acting that way. I began to feel unsafe whenever I was alone with her. In addition to binge eating, she chain smoked, and as I learned later, was taking numerous anti-depressants. I could sense the stress that my father was going through, trying to keep our family functioning as he struggled to help my mother too.

One evening, as he often did, my father took my brothers to soccer practice, and I, as usual, stayed home with Mom. Something felt different on this particular night; something wasn't quite right. Mom seemed anxious and agitated. She began acting strangely, saying things I didn't understand. She was talking to herself out loud about things that didn't make any sense. My mother had become a stranger to me, and I didn't know what to do. Petrified, I hid in my brother's closet, hoping she wouldn't look for me. I stayed there in silence for what seemed like an eternity until I heard a giant crash downstairs. I knew something was terribly wrong. I crept out of the room and stood at the top of the stairs, looking down toward the kitchen.

"Mom...?" I called out tentatively. My heart began to speed up as I anxiously awaited her response.

"Mom?" I called again. Not a sound. I rounded the corner into the kitchen, terrified of what I was about to see. My mother was sprawled on the floor, unmoving, the table overturned beside her.

The next thing I remember was chaos. My dad and brothers rushed in, the paramedics arrived shortly after and our front entranceway seemed full, with everyone trying to revive my mother. Around 3am, my dad came back from the hospital and told us she was gone. My mother had died of cardiac arrhythmia; an irregular heartbeat that turned fatal as a result of all the prescription drugs she was taking.

It's an absolutely surreal moment to be told that your mother isn't ever coming home. I don't think I truly understood or believed what that meant at the time; I didn't want to understand- I was only 8 years old.

In the days leading up to her funeral, I decided that it would be my job to be as happy and as cheerful as I could, in an effort to make everyone feel better. I wouldn't let myself cry. I was the happiest little hostess, serving drinks and entertaining guests any way I knew how. The day after the funeral, I put on my most winsome smile and asked my dad if we could go see a movie.

"Your mother just died!" he retorted back in a way that made me feel as though I had been slapped across the face. That brought me back down to earth pretty quickly. I couldn't hide from reality anymore, and all the pain that came along with it. My tears finally started to flow. All I wanted was for life to be normal again; I wanted my mom back. I didn't understand that I was supposed to be grieving; I didn't know what grieving was.

The days that followed were a real challenge. As well as coping with the loss of his wife, my poor father had to commute an hour each way for work everyday. It was a tough go for him, working at the office all day only to come home and work all night, cooking, cleaning and maintaining a home with three kids.

Two years later, when the four of us were beginning to regain our equilibrium, another shocking event rocked our family. My eldest brother, a talented athlete in the prime of his life, died suddenly of an undiagnosed congenital heart defect, just after his 18th birthday.

At this point, I really went into shock and even deeper denial. How could my brother, a healthy athlete in top condition, die? He was only 18. How was this fair? Was he being punished? Was our family being punished? Losing my mother had been a huge blow, why did I have to lose my big brother too? I had grown up going to church and Sunday school, but now I wondered why God would let this happen to us; for awhile, I had a hard time coming to terms with what life and spirituality really meant to me.

Now it was just the three of us. I was 10 years old and didn't know what to expect or believe in anymore. I just wanted to find some sense of security and happiness again. Slowly, but surely, our family regained its footing, relying on each other and the help of good friends to get through the hard times. Quite often people would marvel at how well we were handling everything. My father did a phenomenal job; keeping it all together, being both mom and dad to the two of us. He is still my hero and always will be. There are times when I look back in amazement at everything we went through and wonder how we survived it all. It took a long time for me to release the pain of those years, but as I got older, I started to regain my faith and understand that there is a greater Divine plan for each of our lives and that everything does happen for a reason. I was forced to grow up fast, but my childhood gave me such a strength, humility and appreciation for life, and for family, that I never took anything or anyone for granted again. I never could have developed that kind of maturity on my own. For that, I will always be grateful.

In retrospect, if I could have done one thing differently, I would have asked for help with my grief when I was young. It is only recently, that I have become aware of all my emotions; buried when we buried my mom and brother. It was far too painful at the time to recognize and express those feelings, so I locked them away and fooled myself into believing that I had dealt with them. That was my own personal journey and I under-stand now that it had to happen that way. But there is no shame in asking for help. If you don't deal with your pain, it will always be there.

At this stage in my life, I see healthcare practitioners, coaches and heal-ers to help me release the emotions I never acknowledged when I was young. These outlets have helped me move forward in my life; they've helped me remove destructive beliefs and unconscious negative patterns from my life, and they have helped me embrace and appreciate the perfec-tion of my journey. For every challenge I was faced with, there was always support. In my case, it was often the support of the two men who I will always admire and respect; my dad and my brother.

There is definitely something to be said for being raised by men; it has made me much more down-to-earth, driven and grounded than I ever would have been otherwise. Although I wouldn't call myself a tom-boy, I am definitely comfortable hanging out with "the boys" and no amount of dirt, mess, crudeness or loud and smelly body functions can faze me—I've lived through it all! I think I may have taught my dad and brother a few things about women along the way too.

I'll never forget the day my father taught me my first lesson in woman-hood. One day in grade 7, I was waiting for the bus when a popular older girl standing behind me chuckled loudly to herself in a way that she clearly wanted everyone to hear;

"Ugh—gross! Look at that hair on your legs. Don't you shave?!"

I was mortified. I looked down and saw for myself that she was right; my legs were really hairy! It had never occurred to me to shave them; when you grow up with men, shaving hairy legs is the last thing you think about. When my dad got home from work, I asked him shyly if he could teach me how to shave. We went up to the bathroom and he gave me a full step-by-step demonstration of exactly how to do it. He was very gentle and patient; showing me the proper technique for holding the razor. To this day, that is one of my fondest memories of my dad.

At age 12, I had to come to terms with not being the only woman in my father's life anymore. He met a woman through a local community theatre group and they really hit it off. That was a big blow to my little ego. Why should I share him all of a sudden? I had had his attention all to myself for the last 4 years and had gotten quite used to it, thank you very much. Well like it or not, I had to deal with it. When I was 14, my father remarried; and like any angst-ridden teen, I thought my life was over. Not only did I have a new stepmother, but I had a younger stepbrother and stepsister too. They moved into our house and we became an instant family. As we all got settled in, I started to enjoy our new life together. It was nice having a woman to care for us again, and although I was green with envy at times, I liked seeing my father happy. It wasn't long afterwards that I stopped relying on him so much; I decided it was time to focus on my own happiness.

Despite the sometimes obsessive over-protectiveness of my dad and brother over the years, it has been nice to feel so safe, loved and cared for. I know they would do anything for me and will always be my most loyal supporters. They have always encouraged me to live my own life and do what makes me happy. According to many of my friends and peers, its rare to have parents who will support you unconditionally, who don't encourage you to live the life of *their* dreams.

One thing I have learned in my 28 years, is that the only path to true happiness is to live your own dream. You have to be willing to acknowledge your dream, honestly admit to yourself and the world what you really want, and fearlessly go after it. It can be scary; especially when it seems to go against everything you've always known or thought you wanted.

Heading into my twenties, I fell absolutely crazy in love with a guy. It was one of those love-at-first-sight stories with instant fireworks and chemistry. I was convinced that this was the man I was destined to marry. Never before had I felt such excitement or passion for anyone. Our friends got along and I adored his family. We had so much fun together; everyone, myself included, thought we were the perfect couple.

When we finished school, we moved to the city together. We finally had a place of our own. For many couples, this might have been the breaking point but we were very happy together; we rarely fought. We enjoyed spending every spare moment together and we shared the household duties with ease and minimal effort.

About a year into our domestic bliss, I got a fantastic job in my field that enabled me to do what I love, but took me out of the city a lot. I really enjoyed my new lifestyle, traveling, touring, fulfilling my dreams. While, of course, I missed my boyfriend at times, it wasn't anything I couldn't handle. I was just so happy to be traveling, doing something that gave me such joy. But I knew every time I went away, he would suffer; I knew he just wanted me at home.

Six months later, he got a new job. It was unionized, with a better salary, great schedule and full benefits. It was the kind of job people keep for life, if they're lucky enough to get it. There was only one problem; it was almost an hour out of the city.

One day he came home from work and asked me,

"What do you think of moving away from the city? We should probably start thinking about a house, don't you think?"

At that moment, I felt like the wind had been knocked out of me. Why did I feel sick to my stomach? I immediately got upset. I tried to contain my emotions, but I couldn't hide my disappointment; I realized I had no desire to move. I did my best to smile and I told him we'd work it out. I was confused; I adored him so much, and I knew we were meant to be together. So why did it feel so wrong?

I finally did some soul searching; I thought long and hard about what I really wanted. It took a lot of courage for me to acknowledge to myself that I didn't want the life he wanted. I didn't actually want marriage or kids, at least not yet. I couldn't bear the thought of leaving the city at that point and finally realized that although I loved him dearly, I was staying in the relationship more for fear of disappointing him and our friends and family. Talk about a 'eureka' moment! I had convinced myself for years that we were supposed to be together because of the sparks I felt when I was 19. I finally opened my eyes and heart to the recognition that I wasn't the same person almost seven years later.

Breaking up with him was probably the hardest thing I have ever had to do, but it was also the wisest. I saved us both a lot of future pain and heartache. I knew I had made the right decision because my spirit felt lighter in the days that followed. I felt like I could breathe again; I felt reborn. It was strange, because although I was never unhappy when I was with him, knowing we were two different people on different paths was taking its toll on me, more than I realized.

This experience reinforced my belief that if you follow your heart and go with your gut, you can never go wrong. The more we listen to our inner voice and follow our own guidance, the happier we will be.

I believe that if you dare to dream it, it can be yours; you are wiser than you think. You know what's best for you; you just have to learn to listen to your heart. If I can do it, you can too. It's going to take courage, a lot of honesty and self-respect. I promise you, it's worth it.

Today, even though I am a 'grown up', I often still feel like daddy's little girl. But I have come to terms with the fact that it's okay to grow up. For the longest time, I rejected the idea of getting older; another step closer to thirty. Recently, I've come to appreciate what it means to be in my late twenties. To me, it means freedom, possibility and unlimited choices.

Do I feel like I've 'made it'? Some days, I do and some days, I don't. It's all a state of mind, anyway. 'Making it' implies that you've arrived; that you're accomplished, settled. While that may sound appealing, I think it's also limiting. I intend to keep dreaming, keep striving, and keep reaching for the next goal; always appreciating where I've been and expressing my gratitude for the multitude of experiences and relationships that have led me to every incredible moment.

You may never feel like you've 'made it' until you stop, take a good look at your life and see how far you've already come. Look at all the people whose lives you have touched, and continue to affect on a daily basis. Think of the last crisis you went through, remember feeling desperate and helpless when you thought things couldn't get any worse? You're still standing, right? And I bet you learned a thing or two. If we can look at every challenge we're presented with and ask ourselves how we can grow from it, we will continue to grow for the rest of our lives, and we will keep 'making it' every day.

It doesn't matter if your pants feel tight, your roots need a touch-up, or you ate that whole piece of cheesecake after you swore you would only have one bite. What matters is that you remind yourself of one thing: You are loved. Despite the mistakes you may have made, the people you feel you've let down and that critical voice in your head, you are worthy of all the love and joy you can handle. Life is supposed to be fun. Everyone's had a tough life in their own way. Everyone has experienced regret. The gift comes in the realization that each experience has helped to shape you into the strong, wise and beautiful human that is you. No one on the planet has experienced life in quite the same way you have. You are unique and special and you have a gift to share with the world...yourself. Recognize yourself for the fabulous person that you are- exactly as you are, and never be afraid to live your dream.

Emily Hunter

As an environmental activist from as early as five years old, when I made 'save the trees please' buttons for a small grassroots eco-group, it's hard to say that one has ever had success. Success seems to be for movie stars, business executives, traders and real estate agents. Success is usually not part of the vocabulary of individuals fighting for not just their own life, but the life of the whole planet. For an environmentalist, the victories tend to be small, the fights large and there are more losses than gains. I also wouldn't say that I made it in high heels, as I've owned about one pair of black high heels since I was thirteen. If anything, I made it in hiking boots or flip flops; take your pick. The only reason I would say 'I made it' at all was because I survived the death of my father and went on to fight in successful (and I would use the word successful here) environmental campaigns to save whales in Antarctica.

But being a relatively happy-go-lucky girl and the daughter of Bob Hunter, Greenpeace founding father and leading Canadian environmental 'shit-disturber,' people have assumed that life has been easy for me; that everything has been handed to me on a silver platter, that I only became an environmentalist because I followed my father's path instead of my own and that my only real hurdle in life was losing him. However, this is not the true story of my life. That's not to say that the latter was not a great hurdle, but rather this is not the whole picture. Let me explain…

When I was a young girl, I had a learning disability which meant that I was unable to learn in the standard fashion. I had difficulty communicating my thoughts which made it difficult to ask questions and understand what was being taught. I needed one-on-one time with teachers to work around this or I risked not being able to understand anything as the class progressed; leaving me still puzzled by previous lessons. To the school board, this meant more time and money, so instead of the greatly needed one-on-one time, I was placed in the 'special' category. A dreaded vague category that mixed children like me who simply have a different style of learning with English-as-a-second-language students and students with mental or physical disabilities. All the students placed in this category are essentially placed in a 'black hole' of education. We were taken away from some or all of our 'normal' classes and put into 'special needs classes' with one or two teachers to deal with a group of special needs kids. As well intentioned as the education system might have been, I found, as I'm sure other 'special needs' students did, that the program only hampered my educational progress. This compromised my ability to carry on to the next grade and integrate with the general school population. I was no longer learning the basics, like grammar and spelling; instead I was doing a lot of drawing in colouring books waiting for a teacher to attend to me; by which I mean giving me more activities to do to pass the time. Not only was I unable to read and write, my sense of self-worth was crumbling; I was being told that I was 'special,' which meant different, and made to feel inferior. I began to feel isolated.

This sense of otherness permeated my soul and later, my body. As a special needs kid, I didn't win any popularity contests by being special and instead was left with a lack of friends. Food became my companion and my friend; it was there for me when I was sad, lonely and bored or even when I was happy about something. As the years went by, I became the fat girl, adding to my sense of otherness and inferiority.

One night, while eating an extra large bag of chips and a dozen donuts in front of the boob-tube (TV was my second-best friend), I made a decision. I knew that I wanted more for myself than junk food and TV; I had bigger dreams for myself and I owed it to myself to try to achieve those dreams. I didn't quite know what those dreams were yet, but I knew that there was something great I wanted to do. I wasn't going to let society, teachers or teasing kids stop me. Sure, I was different, but I wasn't inferior. I realized in that moment that I believed in myself; that love for me would be the engine to drive my life. If I didn't get my life going, no one else would.

Soon after, my parents sent me to a Montessori school; a private school designed to teach students like myself with different learning styles. It was terribly expensive, with private, one-on-one lessons and wonderful, patient teachers. But my parents, especially my mother, made it happen by taking on extra work to have the income to afford the school. After years of one-on-one, at ten years old, I was finally able to read and write. I was still behind in basic math, French and a few other courses that the 'normal' kids in the public education system were excelling in. But I knew that just being at this new school and finally learning to read and write would be the bridge that got me back to public school. With the help of a kind public school Principal, I was integrated back into the same grade as my peers. That same kind Principal later made sure that I got into the high school I wanted to attend, in spite of the fact that my grades still weren't that great. Time moved on and I formed a group of friends in high school. They weren't the most popular kids in the school; in fact, they were the social rejects, the 'Goth' kids, but they were my essential others.

However, in spite of getting over a big learning curve and finally making friends, the feeling of being different and not quite belonging anywhere constantly dogged me. This otherness later became my blessing; I decided that if I never quite belonged or felt part of anything in Toronto, then maybe Toronto wasn't the place for me; perhaps the place where I belong is somewhere that wasn't decided for me by my parents. Maybe I needed to go out and find where I belong. Thus, I began to travel independently.

With the support of my parents and my own research, planning and stubborn determination, I got myself on a student tour tripping around Europe for a couple of weeks when I was sixteen. I didn't really connect with the students I was traveling with, but I connected with being out in the world. I was always leaving the tour group and finding my own adventures. I drank beer in Germany with a fake ID, I danced in the streets in France, I swam in a water fountain in Italy and I climbed a mountain in Switzerland. I had so many adventures that I enjoyed and thrived on, that by the time I got home, I was already planning and saving for my next trip.

That next trip came when I was seventeen. I became an exchange student and lived in Japan for half a year. I learned intermediate Japanese, made tons of friends, ate well, learned how to take care of my body, felt healthy and beautiful. By the time I came home, I found that my place was in the world and not just a city in Canada. I took the skills and knowledge that I gained out in the world back to Toronto. I dedicated myself to school and my marks increased, so that by the time I received my diploma from high school, I was on the honour roll and had been accepted at university; something I never thought was an option for me. I also focused on getting healthy and I was able to get down to and maintain a healthy weight. I now had more friends in Toronto than I had ever had before.

I finally felt like I had made it and had surpassed some major hurdles in life. I continued on with what had become my passion; traveling and discovering the world and my place in it. So, at age 19, I decided to take a year off between high school and university, to teach English-as-a-second-language to college students on mainland China. I was going to be doing something I'd never have dreamed possible, teaching English to college students in an 'exotic' and far-off place like China. It was a milestone for me. I was to teach when in the past, I had struggled to learn. I was to teach in Guangzhou, a capital port city of China.

But, from the moment I got off the bus, it wasn't what I had expected. There were no lush green, grassy mountains with Pandas frolicking or small villages, peopled with hospitable citizens on bicycles, which is the idealized version of China. Instead, I saw more debris from garbage being burned into the atmosphere than greenery. The trees and greenery that I did see looked terribly sick and the environment was massively degraded. The few Panda bears that I saw in China were cruelly kept in zoo cages. I saw very few bicycles and lots of cars, trucks and motorbikes.

There was a real economic divide between the rich and the poor in China. The impoverished majority are separated from the small minority who own everything and dwell on the eastern side of Chinese cities like Beijing and Shanghai. In some areas, like the small town where I was to work and live, the division between rich and poor was dramatic.

On one side there was dirt and pollution everywhere, babies and children getting washed in the streets and monster trucks rumbling through the town every minute like thunder. People lived extremely close to major highways as lack of space was a real issue. In the marketplace on the poorer side of town hung almost every kind of animal imaginable on bloody hooks with flies and maggots swarming around their dead carcasses because refrigeration wasn't affordable. There were families of ten or more living in shanty shacks.

On the other side the school grounds, which was like an oasis, with green grass and trees, although sickly looking; new, large complexes for the school and the dorms; small stores and restaurants full of all the food and merchandise one may need; idyllic ponds and lots of open spaces for the children of the wealthy. Between these two worlds stands a barbed-wire topped wall to punctuate this economic and social divide.

During my stay in China, I witnessed poor people being killed by cars because their smaller bicycles couldn't keep up on the road. I have seen beggars being beaten because they were viewed more as nuisances than valued human beings. I saw more livestock dead than alive and I saw more degradation of the environment than I had ever seen before.

The social and environmental injustices I witnessed in China shook me. Before, my travels had always taken me to high-income countries or I had stayed in the enclosed tourist areas in lower-income countries; creating misleading images of those countries. I had never really been exposed to this kind of reality before. I began to take notice of the fact that, like much of the world, the poor in China were living in impoverished conditions due to an unfair power structure. The poorest members of society were being oppressed by the rich, the government of their country and even the so called 'developed' nations. I also realized that both the rich and the poor exploit the environment in an effort to get ahead. These direct observations changed me and opened up my sense of the world. It was no longer about me and my problems. There was a big world out there and most of the people and the environment were having a pretty rough time; my problems paled in comparison.

In the midst of my social and ecological awakening, I was summoned one day by the Principal's assistant to the track-yard, where I was ecstatic to discover my parents happily waiting to surprise me. They had come all the way from Canada to see me, just when I was in desperate need of a hug and some familiarity. Before I knew it, they whisked me away to Beijing. We got to do everything I had wanted to do, but hadn't had the chance in Guangzhou; we visited the Forbidden City, the Great Wall of China and we ate pizza (not exactly a Chinese custom, but still delicious nonetheless). I was so happy and thrilled about the whole adventure in Beijing that I was blind to a quiet sadness that hung over my parents

On our last night together in Beijing, my Dad told me he had something to tell me. Before he could say anything further, both of my parents started to cry. My Dad looked like a ghost as he voiced the horrible words: terminal cancer. All I could do was instinctually hold my father the second he told me; hold him as he cried and maybe hold myself in this act.

My sense of the world had already been turned upside down by my experiences in China and now my family was being turned upside down. But, I knew I had to be strong for my family facing terminal illness and for this unjust world that faces many injustices. I held my parents and drained a waterfall of tears with them, before we gathered my things from Guangzhou and went home.

I now had two goals: To try to help my Dad and save the world. Ironically, it was my Dad who made my second goal possible. He told me about a group called Sea Shepherd who fought to save marine wildlife and that their ship would be leaving in a week from Victoria, BC. He bought me a ticket, I packed my bags and headed off to sea for the first time in my life.

It was hard work and I was sea-sick most of the time. After a grueling two-week trip, we arrived in the Galapagos Islands where we helped protect the indigenous species, both on land and at sea, by arresting three illegal fishing vessels and implementing a spay and neuter program of non-indigenous invasive species on the islands. By the end of the trip, I was passionate and charged with a purpose in life, to be an eco shit disturber.

Back home, I spent a lot of time with my Dad; talking, hugging, swimming and making him take his vitamins and pills. He seemed healthy and we were all committed to beating his cancer with alternative medicine.

My Dad and Mom went to an alternative medicine clinic in Mexico that summer as the conventional medical system had failed him since they only offered him chemo, radiation or death; which was really more ultimatum than options. In Mexico, he had options with alternative medicine. There he saw his cancer levels lower than they had been in a long time. He seemed healthy, fit and full of life. Things were looking good and I was feeling optimistic about my dad's health. So I was to start my first year of university that following September.

But, by September, 2004, my Dad was in a Toronto hospital and his cancer levels had crept up higher than they had ever been. Dad was still committed to alternative medicine and we were all still hoping for a cure. He went in and out of the Mexican clinic for much of that year. He would have some progress and then he would relapse. As much as I wanted to be with my father, it made him happy knowing that I was going to university; he was always telling me that he'd rather I was there.

The following April was a month I dread to recall. I was studying for exams one night when my Mom called. She was crying and frantic on the phone, telling me that we (my brother and I) had to get down to Mexico immediately. My father was in critical condition; he had blood clots in his brain and pneumonia. They were taking him for surgery to remove the clots and nobody knew whether he would survive the operation. My brother and I were on a plane the next day early in the morning and soon after, my half-sibling arrived too. We all arrived to learn that he had survived the operation.

I realized then that my Dad didn't have much time left; the glimmers of hope for Dad's survival that we had been nursing the past few months had been hit hard by the cold, stale reality of death. There was no time to listen to my Dad, who always wanted me to follow my dreams; instead I needed to listen to my intuition and be with him. After my siblings left, I stayed behind with him and my Mom for several weeks.

During this time, any trace of youthful spirit in me ceased to be as I forced myself to become an adult. I had to do things no child imagines having to do for their parent. I took my shift after my Mom and helped my father with eating, drinking and mobility as he struggled with these issues. I'd stay up all night, sitting beside him in case he needed anything. I had to be a bright, positive, shining aura for both my nearly dying father and my fatigued mother, when all around me was a storm. But I did shine, even when I was hiding my own tears, I shined for them. I helped my mother with greatly needed breaks, as she worked the harder day shifts and had been there on her own helping my father for months before. I put every ounce of energy into helping my father with his health.

Soon, exams were calling me back to Toronto. I didn't want to bother; I wanted desperately to stay with my father. But Dad said it would make him happy if I completed my exams and I listened to him, stupidly again.

I left regretfully and sat for my exams back in Canada. Just as I was to take my last exam, my father decided it was time for him to come home. He barely made it, looking like a faint image of his once marvelous self by the time he arrived. His spirit was almost completely gone; all he knew was pain and a need to be in his own home. He knew he was near the end and he didn't want to be in a hospital in a foreign country but instead with his loved ones in a familiar place. But by the time he made it back to Toronto, he was only able to spend ten minutes at home before we had to get him back to a hospital in Toronto, as his health became so poor on the trip over. It was almost too much to bear; he had made the whole, grueling trip only to find himself back in another hospital.

I was determined to see him improved enough for home care so that he might pass away there; as was his wish. But, it didn't turn out that way. I was no match for Canada's great wall of bureaucracy and I underestimated its unreasonable power. Because Dad had spent time in a 'third world country,' he had to be quarantined before he could get any proper care and due to a series of bureaucratic red tape and processes, they left my father without being fed intravenously for too long; he starved and fell into a coma on the fifth day. By the ninth night, his body was shutting down and we knew he was leaving us. My Mom, my half-sister and I, refused to leave him. I slept like a dog on the floor rather than leave. I hadn't eaten for days and I was in more emotional and physical pain than at any other time that I can remember. But I tried to say strong and be there with him. I kept whispering that I loved him and I was sorry that I hadn't saved his life or got him home.

I had failed him; I had failed at fixing his health and giving him his one last wish, dying at home. I felt it was somehow my fault. I hated myself more than at any other time. I was completely empty; my soul was battered, and the spirit and love for myself that had always gotten me through in the past, was gone. All I knew was that I needed to hold tight to whatever I had left of myself and stay by his side. I spent that morning watching over him, wiping the sweat from his brow and giving him little kisses. I knew this was it, he was going. I gathered the rest of the family. We circled around him, I holding his hand, and all of us said our goodbyes. At ten that morning, my beloved father breathed his last breath.

I lost it a little after that. There is nothing like it in life. Watching helplessly as someone you love so much dies in your arms. A big part of me died too.

It's hard to explain why my father's death affected me so strongly. Part of it was because he was not at all the chauvinistic, dominating father that so many other fathers seem to be. Instead, he was my best friend. He supported every stupid little dream of mine since I was a little girl, from wanting to be an actress or director, to a world traveler, later an eco-activist and university scholar. Whatever I wanted to be, whatever I wanted to do, he was there backing me up. He loved me unconditionally. Even when I made wrong moves and stupid decisions, he loved me and knew I was just finding my own path. There was never any pressure to be one way, only to be myself; whoever that may be. He always treated me like an equal and never looked down on me. He was my protector, my teacher, my co-warrior and most of all, my friend. What was truly illuminating about his passing, was how much he was the center of my universe. Whenever I had a problem, we would talk it over and find a solution together. Whenever I was suffering a philosophical or existential crisis about life and the cosmos, he was there to be my Plato or George Orwell and help me find a foundation again or ponder new avenues of existence. Things made sense when he was around. Without him, the central Jenga piece was missing and the whole tower seemed in danger of crashing down. There was always so much of myself in him and so much of him in me. He was my twin and without him, I didn't know if I was ever going to feel whole again.

Nothing made sense any more. The world should have stopped; I stopped. But, everybody else kept on going. Within hours, my family had gone their separate ways. My mom was making arrangements for the cremation. That night, there was a gathering of friends, with music and pizza to celebrate the life of my Dad. Drama sprouted, some people dealt with his death in negative ways, others positively. But, I just felt dead; I felt like I should have gone with him. There were no real words to utter, moments to be had or thoughts to ponder; so I just slept and slept a lot.

The following summer passed quickly. I kept mostly to myself and barely talked to any of my friends. Food and television became my best friends again. I went back to school in September because I wanted something to keep me busy and distract me from constantly feeling utterly empty and dead inside. I smiled for my Mom and tried to be that sunshine for her so that she wouldn't be burdened with how low I felt; she had her own depression to deal with. I rarely saw my brother as he was dealing with his own depression too. My half-sibling was living on the other side of the country and wasn't there either.

But I had a friend, Kalifi, whom I'd known since I was three years old and she, four. She had lost her Dad to cancer two years earlier. He had been a friend of my Dad's and also a leading Canadian eco-shit disturber and she had been extremely close to her father, as well. She was now a volunteer activist with the same eco-group I had been an activist with, the Sea Shepherds. Kalifi wrote me in the fall and told me that her mother was going to be visiting her in the Galapagos Islands, where she was working on conservation efforts, and my mother and I should come along, too. So, with nothing better to do than be utterly depressed, my Mom and I jumped on a plane and went to visit Kalifi and her mother.

I had recommended Sea Shepherd to Kalifi originally, and she had made me so proud of her; she was now bosun, which is the leader of all the deckhands on the ship. After plenty of drinking at the various dilapidated bars on Santa Cruz Island with Kalifi and some of my old crew-mates on the Sea Shepherd ship, Kalifi convinced me to join Sea Shepherd again in the winter for a big campaign to go to the Antarctic waters and help save the whales. Devoting my time and energy to bigger problems, like helping to save the highly intelligent whales, would be better than continuing to dwell on my own problems.

Before I knew it, I was back on the old Sea Shepherd ship, heading for the other end of the world to go against a Japanese six-ship fleet that was set to kill over a thousand whales. It was ironic that a culture and country that had once breathed so much creation and healing into my life was now destroying so much life in the world. Well, the time had come for drawing lines and standing on one side or the other; I was defining myself and was willing to go up against an entire nation for their criminal unjust actions. Don't get me wrong, there are many beautiful aspects of Japanese culture that I adore. But mass slaughtering intelligent whales was not one of them and I was willing to stand up against this.

It was very empowering; maybe my other half was gone, but the rest of me was still here and kicking. I was passionate about doing what I could to help save the whales. Although I was only one person, at the end of the world surrounded by glaciers, I had a certain amount of power. For, I had my weapons; my mini high-8 videocam and a satellite telephone. I was communicating with CityTV, a newstation in Toronto about the whale campaign in Antarctica, doing live stories via telephone and capturing everything that was happening with my camera. I captured the pursuit of the illegal Japanese whalers and our confrontations with them, our blockading, ramming and stopping them. Sea Shepherd may be considered the radicals, even the detractors, of the environmental movement by both the public and environmentalists themselves, but we saved nearly a hundred whales that year and put the whalers on the run; a first for Antarctic whaling.

Back in Canada, I was able to publicize Japan's illegal whale hunt and the Sea Shepherd's success in fighting the hunt. I got an hour-long show on CityTV and later spoke about the issue at different schools. As a result, I became aware of other young people that I had inspired by being a young activist and speaking out publicly. The power of the media dazzled me and I realized that I could make a difference in this world by being a role model, getting these environmental issues known to the public by working with the media and standing up for what I believe in. I had found my dream.

I was out campaigning with Sea Shepherd again the following winter to help save the whales in Antarctica. It was the most successful campaign I had been on to date. We had put the fleet on the run again, but this time we actually stopped one of the Japanese ships, making a citizens arrest, which slowed their operation down. Later, the engine room on the Japanese fleet's flagship caught fire; their whole operation was halted and the dead whale catch was a loss. I captured everything on film, up until the fire as we were nowhere near it. I have since been bringing the issue to Canadians. I have written articles for newspapers and I have appeared on CityTV, Canada AM and MTV. I've been working with directors and authors who are trying to capture the events of the Antarctic whale wars in films and books. It's become my passion. I'm now finishing my degree and I've become an eco-shit disturber in my own country and abroad.

At the end of the last campaign with Sea Shepherd, I ventured to New Zealand and met a Maori tribe. I was honoured with a Maori tattoo and stood at the top of the North Point Mountain where the souls of the deceased Maori are believed to ascend from. I stood there and knew that there is life after death, and that I am alive again. I know who I am. I'm not the young girl I used to be, but who I was always meant to be; I am sure of this.

Life isn't easy. There are hurdles we must overcome, loved ones that we will lose and pains we must endure. But, surviving all of it makes life that much more valuable. Because you've earned that next day, you've worked for life and you deserve that next chapter. Life is a gift; that much I know. Whether it's the whales I helped saved, a microcosm in the universe, or you and me, it is precious. But it isn't going to be handed to you on a silver platter. Life is going to test you, challenge you and make you work hard for it. But if you keep jumping hurdles, you'll find out just what you're made of, how strong you really are and what your dreams and passions really are.

Losing my father was my biggest hurdle to date. I thought that I was dead, too; a big part of me did die. But, something else has woken in me; a stronger, wiser more dedicated person who found her dream and is working toward it. I am an eco-shit disturber; I fight to protect other life around me. I fight to protect the environment. I will keep fighting every day to earn that next day of life for myself. Life is a battle, but it is one worth fighting for.

Fight!

Amrit Maghera

I have many memories of events that have shaped me into who I am. Particularly, I recall an event that occurred when I was 15 years old.

At school, my teachers and I were confident that my strengths lay in the more creative subjects; dance and art, and although I didn't realize it at the time, I was also quite clever academically. But, my parents were divorcing, and this was having an affect on my concentration at school, especially in the academic subjects. Upon reflection, it's easy to see what was wrong; back then it wasn't so simple. I was the naughtiest girl in my class with demerits and lunchtime detentions happening frequently.

More specifically, I remember my biology lessons as being completely mind numbing. I would regularly fall asleep, only to wake up having no idea what the lesson had been about. The lessons continued without my learning anything and soon exams were looming. These exams, according to my teachers, were a matter of life or death and they never failed to remind me that my results would stay with me for the rest of my life. With six months to go before the real exams, we were given a trial run. I approached the mock exam with an extremely blasé attitude; ticking boxes at random and answering questions using any long words that came to mind; in the hopes that this would impress my teacher. Realistically I had absolutely no idea what I was talking about because I hadn't paid attention to the classes.

A week later, the results were posted. I remember feeling a bit nervous at this point. I was still confident of a passing mark, but I didn't expect the grade to be amazing. My name was second from the bottom. I hadn't even passed. I was embarrassed; afraid of what I was going to tell my parents. They were already worried about how my home life was affecting my schoolwork. Well, my mum was furious. She immediately met with my teacher. Mrs. Bale told her that there was no way I would ever be able to turn the situation around in time for the real exam. She was sure that there was far too much work for me to catch up on in only five months. I was told that I just wasn't very good at Biology and that I didn't really have much hope.

To be told that I, Amrit Maghera, had no hope, made me feel something that I had never felt before. I was outraged! I couldn't believe how discouraging my teacher was being. I knew I was going to make something of my life, even if no one else thought I would. I decided that I was going to show Mrs. Bale that I was capable of passing biology with a good grade. I was suddenly on a mission. It was going to be hard work, but not impossible. I was going to show this woman that she was wrong, wrong, wrong! Suddenly, all the things that had previously occupied my mind; which boy I fancied that month or something similar, were overshadowed by visions of proving my teacher wrong. So, I taught myself the entire syllabus from beginning to end. I dug up my mum's old biology books and studied with a vengeance.

A few months later, I took the exam and answered every question to the best of my ability. When the results came out I got an A. Wow, I felt so happy with myself. Not only had I passed, I got the highest grade possible! It was such a good feeling!

It was at this point that I realized the depths of my determination. I learnt that when I wanted something badly enough, anything was possible. That lesson gave me a lot of confidence. It proved to me that with a bit of hard work and discipline, I could achieve things. I have drawn on this determination many times in my life and career. I just think about what I want and go for it with all my energy.

My teacher's words provoked a positive reaction in me because I didn't accept what she said. Thankfully, it fuelled a desire in me to succeed. My hard work has paid off and I learnt, and am still learning, that success is sweeter when you've worked hard to achieve it. So, in a funny kind of way, thanks Mrs. Bale!!!

Antonia Adamopoulos

Mommy, you're my best friend."

Those words, coming from my four-year-old son, are like gold to me. If you were to tell me, ten years ago, that I would be raising this perfect little boy on own I would have laughed in your face. My first thought would have been, 'yeah right, my family would kill me if I came home pregnant.'

By the time I was in grade eight, I hadn't developed yet. I had never kissed a boy and I had no idea what it was like to wear a bra. I wore big dorky glasses, had teased puffy bangs and wore my hair long to hide my ears. My ears were so huge that I could just about use them to wipe the tears off my face when the other kids teased me. I was called Dumbo so often that I would react as if someone was calling me by my name.

There wasn't a whole lot that anyone could say to comfort me, because I just didn't believe they could understand. My family tried to console me, telling me that kids are just kids and they don't mean the things they say. Nothing they said would comfort me though; I just felt so alone, always. I did a bit of research and decided to get my ears fixed; I figured I could get my ears fixed, stuff my bra and BAM! I would have friends and people would have no reason to make fun of me.

The day of my appointment with the plastic surgeon arrived and it felt like the happiest day of my life. I wasn't even frightened; I was way too excited for fear to be a factor. After the surgery, I took one painkiller and then I swear I didn't take another, because I didn't feel any pain. To this day, I believe it was the happiness of having little ears that drowned out the pain (if there was any). I wore a hideous headband for about six weeks after that, but I didn't care how much people made fun of it; I knew that I had beautiful, small ears underneath. I was right; they were perfect.

Little did I know that those rotten kids would still find a million other things to make fun of; things I couldn't just 'fix'. Eventually, I realized that no matter what I did, there would always be someone making fun of something. It was inevitable, but I had to believe in me.

When I was fourteen, the boy I had a crush on asked me out and I officially knew what it was like to be on cloud nine. We started dating; by which I mean we held hands for about fifteen minutes after school every day and wrote silly notes to each other between classes. We never even properly kissed, but I was in bliss and thought life couldn't get any better. About three weeks later I was heartbroken. I realized he wanted to do a lot more than hold hands; things that I wasn't interested in doing. So, he found some other girl who was more willing. I thought I would never date again. I wanted to hide in a hole and disappear. I was embarrassed and angry, but very lucky to have a few good friends to help me through the worst. I eventually got over him and slowly let go. By let go, I mean, at night I would secretly curse him; it was very healing.

By the time I was in grade ten, I had a gained a little in popularity and found myself throwing little parties at home and drinking all my parents' alcohol; I actually thought that I had so many friends because they liked **me,** not my parents' free alcohol. One night during a party there were about forty kids in my house. We had an old stereo with the bass so heavy you could feel it throbbing through your clothes. I was arranging to meet my girlfriend in the basement so I could talk to her about getting some people to leave. When I had parties, I always chose a friend to stay sober with me, so I would have help later with the throwing up, clearing up and drunk removal.

As I waited in the basement, the boy I had dated back in grade eight showed up. I got sort of giggly with him; he had broken my heart, but I still thought he was cute. He told me he had overheard me telling my girlfriend to meet me in the basement. He had rushed to get there first because he wanted to tell me how much he liked me and how sorry he was. He kept trying to kiss me. I was pushing him away and laughing at the same time. I was shocked that he wanted to kiss me, but also repulsed because he had been drinking. He got more aggressive and my giggling stopped and turned into fear. I was asking him to back off and to stop being so pushy with me and it made him more pushy.

Suddenly, he grabbed me and dragged me down the hall into a bedroom. I started to yell and hit him as hard as I could. He wasn't much taller than me, and he wasn't muscular, but I was thrown to the ground with such force that the back of my head smashed into the floor and I saw stars. He mounted me while laughing sadistically. With both hands, he picked up my head and smashed it on the hard floor repeatedly. At that moment I thought I was going to die in my own basement. I was yelling as loud as I could, but that damn bass-driven stereo was blaring at its loudest. My clothes were being ripped off and I was kicking and screaming and punching and clawing. He was inhuman. Over and over again I continued to think, 'I'm dying, I'm dying, I'm going to die' until my pants were ripped off and at that point, all I thought was, 'I want to die, I want to die.'

There was no stopping him; he was a monster. I was no longer a virgin. I was covered in blood. He got up, wiped his hands on my shirt and left me there, lying alone. I lay there really wanting to die for a very long time. After a lifetime, my girlfriend came in. All I asked her was, "Am I dead?" She kicked everyone out, ran me a bath and stayed with me. I still wanted to die.

I never wanted to go back to school again. People started finding out what had happened and I was mortified. Some people actually made fun of what happened! It was the most horrifying thing ever. One day, a few weeks later, I was in the hallway after school, picking up my daily home- work assignment. I heard there was a fight going on outside; it was my sister and **him**. She had heard what happened and started kicking the snot out of him; I couldn't believe it. I ran outside and there was my sister and most of the school. She asked me if it was true in Greek, so that nobody could understand her. I told her, "yes." Shortly after his face had been cut open and his blood was on my sister's knuckles, a teacher broke up the fight. Usually, when you get caught fighting on school grounds, you get suspended for three weeks, no exceptions. We had a female principal; she was very understanding; my sister got a handshake, not a suspension.

Then I had to have a meeting with all of my teachers and three police officers in one big room; I wanted none of it. I just wanted that night to go away, but it was more prominent than ever. I explained to the teachers what happened and the officers asked if I wanted to press charges. 'Yeah, right,' I thought, 'and have to go to court and deal with more drama? Not a chance.' I said, "No, I just want all this to end." My schedule was changed so we didn't have any classes together. My teachers were very understand- ing and my principal was amazing. The hardest part wasn't coming back to school, though, it was the times I was alone, replaying the event in my head, over and over again. But walking down the same halls as he did everyday took its toll on me.

After about a month, I dropped out of school. I started seeing a coun- selor who helped girls in my situation. I made myself a promise after I dropped out of school; this guy was not going to beat me. He had raped me, but I'd be dammed if I would let him hurt me again; it was just that simple. I began having nightmares, reliving the rape in my dreams every night. Every night, I would wake up at the same point in the attack. I kept telling myself to fight back harder in my dream and end it. For weeks I was waking up in a cold sweat every night. Finally, one night about eight weeks later, I had the dream as usual, but this time I fought back and killed my attacker in my dream. For the first time since that boy had taken my life away, I slept through the night; I never felt better. Since that night, I feel better able to help people who have been through the same thing; I can talk about it without wanting to throw up. I wanted to close that chapter in my life, so I did.

I grew up in a very strict home, filled with rules. I didn't think I should have to abide by these rules, though; I often felt like I was choking and just had to get away; so I did. When I was fifteen, I met a guy I liked who was 21. I lied to him and told him I was eighteen and I decided to run away from home to be with him. I grabbed a few bags filled with my 'important' possessions, like CD's, shoes (all of them) and of course my makeup; the essentials for a fifteen-year-old with no money and nowhere to go. I met my boyfriend at the theater and when the movie was over he asked what I wanted to do, unaware that I was now a runaway. I suggested we go to his house, as it was freezing outside and it had just begun to snow. When we pulled up at an RV Park, I'm pretty sure I almost peed my pants; I thought, 'great, he lives in a box run by a generator!' I was pretty relieved to discover that in fact his family owned the RV Park and he lived in one of the cabins on the grounds; it may as well have been a fifteen-room mansion!

Eventually, we fell asleep together and I woke up in the morning feeling completely liberated and positive that I could do this 'on my own' thing, no sweat. When I told my guy the truth, that I was a runaway, he took it pretty well; although he still thought I was eighteen.

After hiding out for two days, I contacted a friend of mine and was blown away by her reaction; she could hardly speak, she was so upset at the thought that I may have been dead. I met up with her at a coffee shop to find that she had already written a eulogy for me. I was touched, but I was fifteen and didn't concern myself too much with the feelings of other people. I made her swear not to tell anyone where I was and promised to stay in touch. Later that afternoon there was a knock at the door. As I sat on his bed, my boyfriend walked in and told me my dad was at the door. At that moment, I saw my life flash before my eyes. As I walked toward the door, my dad grabbed me by the hair, dragged me down the stairs and threw me into the 'getaway car', where my mom was waiting to strap me in. I got in kicking and screaming and banging the car windows, hoping one would break so I could jump out. While my dad was driving, I heard them mention taking me to the hospital to have me checked out for drug use. I thought, 'yeah, take me to the hospital and I'll escape from there. I'll find a way to run away again.'

There was a balcony outside my second-floor window; an easy escape route, I thought. But, my dad was way ahead of me. He had put new locks on my window and door. I was in a little prison also known as my bedroom. For good measure, he handed me a bucket and told me I could use it to relieve myself. At this point, I was too angry to see how much I was hurting my parents and two older sisters. I was so wrapped up in what they were doing to me.

For a while after that, I thought I was in hell; I spent my days plotting my next escape. I had been home for just over two weeks when I decided it was time to get out; they didn't understand how suffocated I felt; I needed my space. I went to stay at my girlfriends' house for a few days, until her parents had had enough of me hiding out there, so I lied and said I had somewhere to go, but asked if I could keep my things there for a bit longer. Off I went to nowhere; I was so determined to not go home that I slept in a park across the street from my house. I used my teddy bear for a pillow and a huge towel I had for a blanket. For some reason I was not afraid of these places at the time, but I certainly would be now!

I continued to live on the streets for over a month. I remember there were times that I would walk into a grocery store and steal baby wipes just so I could clean myself. It wasn't often that I was able to shower; when you don't have a home, it's embarrassing to have to ask someone to use their facilities. I lived a very low key existence and withdrew from my friends. To this day, I have never used drugs; I've never even smoked a joint. I stayed away from home, simply because I didn't like the rules; not because I wanted to party and do drugs. I remember sleeping in Stanley Park in downtown Vancouver a few times. I think of it now and get goose bumps; I have no idea how I avoided being raped or killed in places like that. I had no fear and must have had a guardian angel watching over me.

I soon found a job in a little deli and rented the attic of a house. All I had to furnish my new home were some stuffed animals, some towels and my clothing. The towels served as my blankets, one of my stuffed animals was my pillow. I managed for about three months before I was fired from my job. When I couldn't make the rent, I swallowed my pride and asked my dad if he would help me out. He gave me one condition; if he paid my rent for the month, I would come back home at the end of that month. I agreed in a heartbeat. Deep down inside, I was dying to come home, but again I had this stupid pride thing.

I think that first night back in my bed at home was the best sleep I ever had in my life. The next day, I sat down and had a talk with my dad.

I explained that I had never done any drugs, I just didn't want to live in a house where I felt everyone was angry and the rules were suffocating me. I never ran away to hurt my parents or anyone, I was just feeling trapped. I had never realized how ill I made my mom and how much I hurt my sisters and family; I was just too wrapped up in me. After I spoke with my dad and he realized I didn't do anything but simply try to survive out there, he told me something that I will always remember; he actually had some respect for me for standing firm to my convictions. My life changed after hearing that.

I was living just up the street from my parents, in a cute little basement apartment, when I met this guy in the summer of 2002. We dated for a while and took our time with everything. We would watch movies together and go for dinner; it was a very simple relationship that got complicated when I took that pregnancy test. My first thoughts were, 'oh my God, I'm going to be a mom,' which pretty much sealed the deal on my choice. My entire 'big, fat, Greek family' had different plans for my life, and I hadn't yet told them that I would be going it alone, as the father had left the building. I was terrified. I had two cousins and one aunt on my side; the rest of the family was very much against me. I had made up my mind and it was the hardest thing ever because my parents and sisters weren't going to be there for me. Putting away my fear of being a single mom at 25 was a little hard to do, but I did it. I never stopped believing in myself and constantly reassured myself that this would be wonderful thing. I had never felt so alone and scared, though. I would lie in bed at night and pray that everything would work out, that I could afford to clothe and feed this baby and that the baby would be healthy.

I went through most of my pregnancy with my dad scowling and my mom and sisters not talking to me. Slowly, as they realized that my tummy was growing and the baby was on its way, they began to come around. My dad was the hardest to soften up until I went into labour. It was a very tough labour and my dad was my knight, speaking to the doctors and making sure that I had all I needed. My sister didn't sleep for the two days I was in labour; after which, it ended in an emergency c-section. The doctors came in and asked me who I wanted to take in the room with me and I chose my dad. Coming from the 'big fat Greek family' I thought if I have a boy, my dad needs to be the first to see him!

From that day on, my dad has been one of the biggest supports in the lives of my son and me. When I was a teenager, if you had told me that my dad would eventually come around and be any sort of support for my unwed pregnancy; again, I would have laughed at you. The family I wanted to get away from and didn't understand; now I could not do with out. My mom and sisters are there everyday for us. And as you see, things when you are younger, become so different, it's like a twilight zone. The people you thought judged you; can become your best friends, the ones you think are against you; can become your biggest supporters. I'm almost 30 yrs old and my closest friends are 2 people, 68 & 71 yrs old, I know I could not do without my Papas. You never know how things will turn out; you just have to trust that there is a plan that you may not see right now, but one day you will step back and say, "That's why this happened."

Belinda Brady

I f yuh want good, yuh nose haffi run." In Jamaica, that said it all; nothing comes easy and life is hard, but hard work will get you ahead. As a woman, in the midst of my life journey, those words resonate for me. Through my confusion, as I continue my journey, I have looked to a higher power for guidance and comfort. I have lost myself many times over and my God has brought me from the brink of suicidal thoughts and self-destructive behavior.

I'm the youngest; my mom's third and my dad's eighth (as far as I know). Carl Brady had four children with his first wife, one in the middle, and three from my mother, his second wife; now divorced. We were the Brady Bunch! I felt like I didn't exist to anyone; I yearned for a little bit of love and acceptance. I often felt in the way; not truly loved. As a woman in my thirties, I've chosen to live alone. At times it gets lonely, but it has been therapeutic too. I'm getting to know Belinda Brady. I'm learning to love myself more and more. I'm beautiful inside, and I'm learning to believe that without having to hear it from someone else.

As a child, it was easy to dream. My single mom did everything it took so my siblings and I felt that we could achieve our goals. I dreamt of becoming a singing superstar or a famous actor. This seemed like destiny; my sole purpose in life. My parents were professional artists who had toured the world with *Byron Lee and the Dragonaires,* a renowned Jamaican *soca* band. Entertainment is in my blood. It was my duty to continue the legacy, on a larger scale. I knew exactly where I wanted to be; I just had no idea how I was going to get there. My feelings were so intense; I wanted my poster plastered all over the walls of my legions of fans.

Working as a background singer with artists like Shaggy and the late, great Bob Marley's son, Julian, showed me a side of the industry I wanted for myself. The lights, the adoration of thousands of fans, the glory, the money, it all combined for a lifestyle that I wanted. The struggle to reach that level of success as a solo artist has been one of the most painful challenges of my life. I started my career in this industry full of naivety. Like many aspiring female artists, my experiences have left me with the bitter realization that talent may not be enough. As I get older, managers and record companies are looking at other options for their rosters. It can feel like a heartless world.

Did I stop dreaming? After a while, the dream turned bitter. I'd endured years of excruciating financial and emotional hardship. I'd invested so much money and time in the studio; only to get hit on half the time. The dream of becoming a megastar, once a bright journey of excitement and hope, had turned into a struggle of anger and disappointment.

My relationships with men never worked because I never made them a priority. If I wasn't spending time away from them with my music, I was spending time with another musician. I've hurt many people along the way, but mostly myself. I thought music was the only thing that made me happy; the truth is, I had no clue how to make myself happy. I didn't know myself well enough to know what made me tick. I always had feelings of insecurity about my physical and mental demeanor. I suffered from a 'victim mentality'; to escape, I turned to music, then boyfriends. When one boyfriend neglected me, I turned to the next candidate. I was constantly seeking someone who could fulfill the dark hole inside with love and acceptance.

When I reflect on the past, I feel more secure about the personal and professional choices I've made. I'm not perfect though; everyday continues to be a struggle. I realize that wanting to be a superstar was not so much the desire to become a *Janet Jackson, Britney* or *Madonna*. Instead, I believe I wanted to be loved and accepted by everyone. Subconsciously, it made sense to me that if the world loved me, the pain of my neglected childhood would vanish.

So, I'm an artist; I will always be an artist. I realize now that in all the years of struggling and chasing a dream, I almost missed the 'true dream'. I, Belinda Brady, am the dream I have been chasing. I have all the love and acceptance I'll ever need….from ME!

Andrea Lewis

Two of the constants in my life have been the support of my family and an early exposure to the world of entertainment. My father was a huge music fan, with diverse tastes, enjoying everything from country and rock, to pop, R&B and soul. Almost from my mother's womb, I was hearing all kinds of music and really taking it in. My mother loved fashion shows and award shows; anything that she felt was glamorous. I grew up in a world filled with music and I preferred a Michael Jackson music video or glamorous movie on TV to an episode of *Sesame Street*.

When I was about six months old, I was with my mom in a shopping mall when we were approached by a talent agent. She told my mother that she thought I was very adorable and had no doubt that I would do very well in commercials and print work. My mother took the agent's card and told her she would think about it. My mom wanted to weigh the pros and cons of a baby in the business; she wasn't sure if it was the life that she wanted for her daughter. So, it was a year later before she called the agent back and agreed to have me do a screen test. Many babies are cute, but not all of them are still cute after spending hours in front of a camera and under hot beaming lights. Apparently I loved it, however. I was a tiny toddler with crazy Diana Ross-like hair and I loved being in front of the camera. From that moment on, my life was set. I quickly started doing print ads and commercials. At a very young age, I had found my lifelong dream.

As a child, I was simply expected to be cute, but once I hit my teens, it wasn't that easy. I became more serious about my craft. I began taking voice and acting lessons and paying close attention to anything that was relative to performing. Like many black entertainers before me, I realized that the path I had chosen was not going to be easy; I was even more determined to be successful.

The entertainment industry is tough and requires very thick skin; particularly for a black girl. Nothing that I have accomplished has come to me easily. I still have to prove myself constantly and fight for parts more challenging than the neighbor, the best friend or the stereotypical "black girl". This is the card I've been dealt however, and God doesn't give you anything you can't handle.

Recently something happened that I thought I couldn't handle. After twenty-two years of marriage and thirty years of being together my parents were separating. When I was younger, some friends' parents got divorced and it affected them very badly; forcing my friends to split their time between two homes and two parents who were constantly fighting with each other. I never imagined that would be my parents.

My mom and dad immigrated to Canada from the Caribbean as teens. They met in high school. Although they are polar opposites; mom is outgoing and fun, and my dad is quiet and reserved, they found a way to make it work. They lived together during college and worked together at a local hospital. They were ambitious and worked hard; saving their money to buy a home and start a family. They married in April, 1985, with their first child already on the way. Eventually the family expanded; I had a brother. My parents bought a beautiful home in the newly developing town of Pickering and made the move to the suburbs.

By the summer of 2007, my mom had worked extremely hard for most of our lives developing careers for me and my brother. My brother is honing his skills as a chef. I now live in LA and am currently working on my second album while writing and reading scripts. My mother and I are best friends and I was shocked and devastated when she told me my father had packed his bags and left. My parent's relationship wasn't perfect, but I couldn't imagine a life where they weren't together.

I know my brother and I aren't babies anymore, but we still rely heavily on our parents. It was going to be very difficult to deal with the prospect of a separation. Over the next couple of days, the reality of the situation hit hard. My father had abandoned us and my mom was now taking on the responsibilities of managing two homes by herself. She also had ongoing health problems to deal with. It soon began to look like we wouldn't be able to afford both households. Los Angeles is a very expensive city and we didn't know if we could continue to keep my home in LA, as well as the family home in Pickering.

By now everyone, including my dad, was telling my mom that I should return to Pickering, to help my mom and give up on what they thought were unrealistic dreams. Those words hurt me more than anyone could imagine. I felt like all my hard work had gone unnoticed and no one in my family believed in me. But, I've come a long way in my career and I've gained a lot of confidence; I was not about to give up. This industry can really work a number on your self-esteem and even though I've been in it my whole life, I still had a lot of personal demons to overcome. This unfortunate situation with my parents was devastating but it was making me more determined to succeed.

Although I've gotten a lot of work in movies and on television, I've never had the opportunity to appear in a movie or TV show as the lead character. I'm confident that if the opportunity presented itself, I would prove to be a strong lead actress. I had a part on a hit TV series, but I've never really gotten the chance to expand as an actress. So I decided to move to Los Angeles where I would have a better shot at lead roles.

When it came to my singing, I was very shy and didn't always have much confidence. I would only allow certain people to hear me. I always tried to sound like someone else and worked very hard on imitating others, instead of just embracing my own voice and style. I'm also a songwriter; I started writing songs at about twelve and it's one of my favorite ways to relax. I can express my true feelings and tell stories about what's happening in my life through songwriting. But I never had confidence in my songwriting and I always kept it very private. I struggled with demons for years, telling myself that I believed in my abilities and working harder to prove it.

Everything changed for me when I took on the lead role in the stage version of *Dreamgirls*. It was my first stage musical and it was a completely new environment and a great learning experience. We were doing eight, two-hour shows a week, and we had only three weeks to learn a show with almost fifty songs in it. The task was exciting but overwhelming. I learned a stage motto, "go big or go home", which I took very literally. This adage really resonated with me. I started to learn a lot about my own determination and it was the beginning of a transformation of sorts. Something inside me woke up and I knew that no matter what insecurities I had, this was the way I was going to be spending my life! Today, I feel I possess a God given talent and I want to share it with the world.

I knew that although my family was telling me to give up on my dreams and return home, I couldn't do it. My mom had also come to this realization and supported my decision. My mom has always been my biggest supporter and I'm grateful that I have her on my side. Although we didn't think I should call it quits, we didn't know how we were going to afford for me to continue living in LA, pay off the rest of our mortgage and feed and clothe her and my brother back in Pickering. My dad had cut off the family on all levels, not only emotionally but also financially. I had managed to cut down all my living expenses in LA, but I was still concerned about my mom and my brother. My brother was taking the divorce really hard and he was expressing his anger by distancing himself from the family. My mom and I spent a lot of time talking to my brother; with the help of some friends and family members, we were able convince my brother that he shouldn't give up on life. All of our problems were distracting me from my work.

I was in the studio working on my next album, but my mind was elsewhere; I found it hard to channel positive thoughts into my songs. I began writing songs about what was going on in my life and the way it made me feel. I started to feel a lot better about my situation. I'm normally a very guarded person; it can be frustrating for anyone trying to get to know me. It's become easier for me to express myself through my craft. When I'm dealing with a negative situation, I can't let it get to me; I just have to be as optimistic as possible and turn my negatives into positives.

At the end of the day, my parents are no longer together and there is nothing I can do about that. Our financial situation isn't the best, but this only motivates me to work harder. My brother has realized that my mom and I love him more than anyone in this world and he can look to us for support. As a family, this awful situation has brought us closer together and we're taking it one day at a time as we turn to God and attempt to turn all the negatives into positive learning experiences. As they say in Jamaica, "What don't kill you will make you stronger".

Antonietta Robino

My parents, Sebastian and Pierina, lost their vision of a loving family. After many years, I've been able to come to terms with that fact. I assume they had a vision of what they wanted from family life, because this, as with many other things, was never expressed in my family home. The simplest things, like hugs or affection, weren't expressed during most of my childhood. Children are great observers; they know only what is presented to them. When I would come home from grade school, my welcome at the door would be the loud voice of my mother, screaming at me to make sure that my shoes were clean. How could I make sure my shoes were clean when I was just a kid coming in from being at school all day? I wasn't asked about my day, or the math class I was failing and nobody sat down to help me with my homework. Growing up was learning from the TV, pressure from the other school kids and a non-existent father most of the time. I knew I still had a father because I would see him on Sunday mornings, watching Italian soccer; he would be around to participate in big family gatherings and of course, he was the target of many of my mother's outbursts.

It was very difficult growing up in that kind of family environment; I learned early that my friends weren't going through the same thing, or at least not to the same extent. I was saddened to observe that when the neighbourhood kids came around and heard my mother scream, they would get really scared. I was envious of the kids who seemed confident enough to do a spelling test. My family life at home made it really hard for me to concentrate at school and focus on the important lessons that a kid should be learning.

I got through grade school all right; I was a popular, pretty girl who chased the boys at recess. Why was I chasing the boys so much? Well, I'm sure you'll recognize that I was chasing the affection and approval that I was missing at home.

High school brought my darkest days. Having pretty looks and many friends didn't help me in the halls of Pope John Paul High. Entering high school, I got a lot of notice early on as a pretty, white girl with a lot of pretty friends and a popular older sister who had just graduated. Yes, I prettied myself up as it was a constant focus in my life and my friends were good looking as well and because of an older, pretty sister many of the seniors knew me. All of this combined to cause resentment with some of the mostly black and Filipino student body. Racial tension and escalating violent crime rates were a problem at the school at the time. My girlfriends and I were looked at hard with looks that could kill or with looks that horny boys couldn't control. It was hard to walk through the halls and have girls hissing derogatory comments and to have guys participating in the same behavior or labeling me because I may not have given them the time of day.

We were able to get through the first year thankfully with no real physical problems, because I had friends in the older grades who respected my sister and took care to make sure nothing happened to my girlfriends and I. Some of the good choices I made growing up have been my good friends. My closest friends, who remain in my life to this day, come from good families, are well focused and have good heads on their shoulders.

Though I had great friends and the popularity that many girls wanted, it couldn't make up for the unhappiness I was feeling. My parents were constantly fighting; I never got along with my brother and sister, being the middle child; I continued to harbour dark, guilty thoughts from a family battle with our neighbours a few years previous; high school kids picked on my friends and I was plagued by insecurities about not being as smart as those around me.

Academically, I'd always gotten by in elementary school, but I had often been reminded that I wasn't progressing well. Of course, I wasn't given the help to change that at home; I never got help with my homework or any school lessons by my parents. Going into high school, I had no confidence about my academics and I did everything in my power to hide that fact. I had to; the pretty, popular girl had to be smart enough. The pretty, popular girl couldn't be getting special tutor help! No way, that wouldn't be cool. I pretended everything was fine, but little did everyone know, how much I hated it. I hated the fact that I was struggling in some of my subjects and I was too embarrassed to get help. I hated that I had to try extra hard to pass my courses while my some of my friends were passing tests without studying or had parents that cared for them enough to sit and do homework with them. There were days that I got so depressed that I wanted to scar up my face and I wished I was blessed with great intelligence.

Near the end of my first year, I met a boy who was in grade eleven. He was two years older than me and he had shown an interest in me for some time; that in itself piqued my interest. Our budding relationship took my mind off the pressures of school and my family. It was the first emotional relationship that I put much energy into and we spent as much time together as we could. As comforting and fun as the relationship was at first, it turned dark for me.

In grade ten, being in a relationship with a boy two years older than me, brought nothing but more problems and stress. If it wasn't the problems he was going through in his life at home and with his friends, then it was our relationship at school. The high school kids seemed a lot meaner and more aggressive that year. They hated the fact that I was dating a boy from an older grade. There were many reasons they had to pick on us, including our race, our public relationship, our popularity or just because of our confidence to stand up for ourselves; they just fed on making our relationship miserable. My boyfriend and I got into many fights with the other high school kids. On many occasions, it got physical and my boyfriend's car was vandalized in a couple of cases.

It was all tough times that troubled me more and brought nothing but intense arguments between my boyfriend and me, the one person I had a comfort zone with. I spent far too much time sitting in the Principal's Office, getting suspended and sometimes even having police reports filed. I cried tears of shame at being caught up in such trouble so often.

I bottled up so much trouble, insecurity and stress that eventually, it was like the bottle cap popped off. I woke up one day with dark clouds hanging over my heart. I probably woke up to the sounds of my parents yelling; I can't remember as it happened so often. During my geography class, feelings of frustration and helplessness swamped me. I got up, went to the girls' washroom and used my school uniform tie to try and hang myself from the top bar of the cubicle stall. I had simply lost the battle between my conscience and my exhausted emotions; I felt empty. I was sick and tired of the rotten relationship my parents had; of hearing arguments; of who was doing what and my parents stressing about money. I was sick and tired of the non-support or lack of love in my home and of worrying about my academics. I was sick of my boyfriend relying on me so heavily, emotionally and I was tired of trying to break free of him. I was sick and tired of the fights and problems with other school kids and I was sick of pretending and tired of my life. I wanted out, so I tied the tie around my neck and onto the bar and slipped off the toilet seat. Fortunately, a girl came into the washroom and realized what was happening. She called for help and they crawled under the stall to stop me. As I was being helped down, I was angry. But I knew that if I had really wanted it to happen I would have tried harder. I knew that wasn't what God wanted; that wasn't my path.

The counselor of the school took me to her office and sat with me, trying to get me to open up. I was too disturbed by everything and I just didn't know how to express myself. She contacted my parents and we all sat down together to look for answers. I told them what they needed to know, but I never really explained how I really felt. I just wanted them to go away; I didn't want to deal with them. My parents then sat down with my boyfriend's parents and discussed my suicide attempt and my attempts to separate myself from their son.

It was a long week of talking to counselors. They seemed interested in helping me, but I never believed them; I just gave them the short answers, intended to shut them up. If they really cared, they would have noticed and talked to me sooner, I reasoned. Returning to school just heightened the stress; I knew everyone would have heard. I could sense the morbid curiosity of others; the hidden truth that no one speaks of, but all are aware of.

If there was a silver lining to that episode, it would have to be the concern that I finally sensed from my parents. I decided it was time to change my life. I realized a miracle would have been needed to change the troubles with my family and that I wasn't magically going to wake up the nerd that I secretly wanted to be, so I set myself to focus on my schooling and avoid any trouble.

Things settled down for the next two years; I was doing better at school as I focused on the subjects I was good at. I was working two part-time jobs, as money stayed a constant issue for me, but I enjoyed providing for myself. My parents were always stressing with their own problems so, I learned to be independent quickly. My friends stayed the same and we were having more fun than ever and I was in another relationship with an older boy from a different school. Things were fine for a bit until again things seemed to fall apart.

In the winter of 2002, my aunt tragically passed away in the middle of the night from a massive heart attack. This was my first experience with the death of a close family member. She was a lovely, 51-year-old woman who enjoyed the season of Christmas more than anyone I know, which made the timing so sad since it was just a few weeks away. Christmas was usually a most wonderful and exciting time with my big, Italian family. My mother had been quite close to her aunt and didn't take her death well. I mourned my aunt, while trying to be a comfort to my family. It was a trying time for me, staying up late with crying relatives, making funeral arrangements, facing friends with sadness.

In my last few months of high school, I ended my relationship with my boyfriend and began applying to universities and colleges. I didn't know what I was going to study but I was happy that I was at least applying. My older sister had chosen not to pursue a postsecondary education , and I had made it my mission to be the first member of our family to graduate from college or university. The fact that there wasn't much attention or confidence shown toward the subject only made me more determined.

In the summer of 2003, I met a caring Italian guy through my best friend. That led to a great summer of fun, double dating with the boy, his friend and my girlfriend. The four of us did everything together. It was a great relationship that quickly turned into love and acceptance by my family. I fell really hard; I was in love for the first time. I dreamt of a future with this guy, envisioning a family with him. I put so much energy into the relationship that I started to lose motivation and focus in school. At the time, my relationship was fulfilling my needs of comfort, love and attention.

During my first year of university, my grandfather passed away from Alzheimer's disease. He had fought a long battle against his horrible illness and my mother had been there every step of the way. I understood that my grandfather had lived a long life and it was his time to go, but my sadness about his passing just seemed to add to the pressure of adjusting to university life. It was too much for me to deal with and I failed some of my courses. Only two months later, my Godfather became the eighth fatal victim of SARS in Toronto. That hit me hard, since my Godfather was a role model and the only person who had instilled any discipline and taught me some of the lessons that I should have been getting at home. I was hurt, but my pain was nothing to that of my Godmother and her children. It angered me that a beloved father was taken from his family.

I was sad for some time. My mother saw it in me and did show me concern by offering to take me to see someone about my struggles. But I wasn't good at talking about my feelings. Deep down, I still blamed her and my father for my emotionally weak state and lack of parenting. I constantly blamed them for my struggles and those of my brother and sister. I felt that if my father had been around more, I wouldn't be looking for my male role model in boyfriends. I felt that if my mother had treated her children more equally and lovingly, I would have more confidence and less relationship difficulties.

It was a difficult period, but I wasn't about to attempt suicide again. I guess I didn't have the balls, or I didn't want to deal with the embarrassment of failing and having to face people again. So what did I do? I did what I knew; I pretended. I played off that I was fine and I hid the fact that

I was on academic probation at university. I played my role of the pretty girl everyone wanted to be like or date. But, deep down I was unhappy with my life; I felt nothing good was going to come of it.

With blame and resentment about my family fuelling me, it was my goal to prove that I was better. So I worked more jobs to save for my OSAP loan. I was already bartending on weekends and doing a reception job part-time for Chrysler. I had my second year of university to get off academic probation; which I did. I started to think more about what I wanted to do for a career. The fact that I was a bartender and giving up much of my social life and my weekend nights to make money never sat well with my boyfriend. We started to have many disagreements; once again my relationship was on the rocks.

Slowly, I started to sense a change in my perspective and the way I thought. I believe it was a combination of the training I was receiving in university and maturing as an adult. Early in 2005, I made the decision to leave the charming Italian boy that my family adored, the boy that I had envisioned settling down with. But I knew it was time to let go. Although it was my choice to separate, I still did not have the strong emotions to deal with it smoothly; it was damn hard.

Four months later, on the day of my sister's birthday, my grandmother was killed by another resident in her nursing home. My spry, alert grandmother of 94 was wrongfully beaten into a coma and passed away. My family was devastated. The case garnered a lot of media attention and calls for investigating nursing home abuse in the city. It was disturbing to see my father, a man who had never shown any emotion, break down in tears. I started to let go of my resentment toward my father. I realized I was lucky to have parents who tried in their own ways to provide for my family. It may not have been in the best way, but I had to appreciate and accept what I have.

This is when I started to believe in angels. A few days later, I sat back and analyzed everything that was going on in my life and it seemed clear to me that I have angels watching out for me; that I was being tested time and time again but there were angels waiting to pull me through. I knew I couldn't give up and that I had to be there for my family. It was time to give back to my family for what they had given me: A roof over my head, clothes on my back, siblings, and hard love.

Though my inner faith was building, I still had a lot of insecurities and sad emotions. I desperately wanted to get my mind off things, so I made myself as busy as possible. I worked two, even three jobs, went to school and went out often. During this time I got involved with the night club scene and I started working for one of the best promotion companies; I went to a lot of parties and met all kinds of people. I was introduced to a percussionist who was working the clubs as well. At first, I didn't think much of the meeting, as my mind was still jumbled with the other events in my life. But, with slow steps and a mature attitude, I started to see something I really liked and was able to connect on a different level. The more time this gentlemen and I spent together, the more I was appreciating his life and everything he was about. He was well educated, set in his career and enjoyed many of the same hobbies that I had interests in. It was a bonus that his hobby allowed him to perform in the same night clubs that I worked.

It all seemed too perfect; I believe I wished for it all too soon. They say, 'careful for what you wish for, that it may come true.' Well, it comes true; it may not come in the form you wish for, though. With my wish, I was forgetting about my emotions and time I needed to heal. I've learned this is important; everyone needs time to heal. We are all human and it takes time to mend wounds. Without giving myself enough time to focus on myself, I really put a dent into my independence and self-confidence. I've had many emotional events occur and I've always made sure that I had a boyfriend to lean on.

Well, the very smart guy I was dating saw this and helped me to see it as well. We decided to part ways for the best. During my time with this man, I learned a lot. He inspired me in areas that I didn't know I was interested in. I learned from him that it takes a lot of self-discipline to find your way in life. I learned that no one is going to do anything for you, that you have to make it happen yourself. One of the great life lessons he taught me was that everyone comes into your life for a reason; find that reason and appreciate it.

Though we decided to separate, I know he was a blessing that came into my life for a reason. He has helped me to see the unseen and given me the time to polish myself. For that I thank him and hold him as my first mentor in life.

I had never had any mentors in my life. Most people looked to their parents for mentoring or idealism, but mine were the last people I was likely to look to. Instead, I resented and blamed them for all the struggles and stress in my life. I made it my mission to prove that I can do better. I had always wanted so much from them that I was blind to what I already had. My mother always told me that I had to stop blaming others; she's right. I have stopped blaming others; I have looked at underlying reasons and I'm an adult and I do take responsibilities for my actions and choices.

I'm sure I would have had an easier time if there had been someone I could have really talked to, someone who really listened to me. But instead, I had sparks of faith and hard lessons that made me realize that I was being challenged in life. There is no manual on life; you have to find your lessons in your own journey and take them as blessings. The times when people who care about me came in when least expected and showed concern, the times I was appreciated for who I am and the times when I envisioned dreams so real that I felt I could fly on top of the world are the times that brought me the comfort and motivation to live my life.

At this point, I take nothing for granted. I enjoy and appreciate my education more then ever, and I now love learning. I see the possibilities I have opened up for myself as I have gotten myself involved with volunteer work by being part of two school councils on leadership and giving back to the community. Every day is a new day that may come with a struggle, but I face it by reminding myself of the life lessons I've been taught and that I deserve to do better for me and for the people around me. I surround myself with good respectful friends and lastly, my family. Family will always be family. What you make of that is up to you.

Bev Isla

O n a cold and dreary autumn night, I was sitting at home, alone. I felt emotionally drained; utterly depressed. It was October 2004. I had just lost my job of two years at a pharmaceutical company, and the man I had become involved with was going back to the States. I felt lost and alone. The girls I lived with were nice but they had been close friends with each other before I moved in, so I felt like an outsider. Just a few weeks ago, I had been comfortable in a downtown condo with my best friend, until she decided to set up house with her boyfriend. So within a matter of weeks, everything that I had become accustomed to was gone. What was I going to do now? How could I get my life back on track?

Initially, my goal was to be a police officer. After graduating from university, I took the required examination, but didn't make it by a mere few points. Maybe it wasn't for me after all. To make ends meet, I became a Research Specialist with a pharmaceutical company. I disliked the boring, mundane duties of my position, and didn't get along well with my boss. Eventually, my dissatisfaction began to affect my work, and led to my lay-off.

Prior to the layoff, I met a man there. Bob was in the city on a work contract. I thought he was here indefinitely from the States. We spent a lot of time together, and became close. I was falling for him. For six months, we acted as a couple, and I thought that when his contract ended, we'd find a way to keep it going. Then I got laid off. We were out having dinner and he told me he was due to leave the following week; he didn't want a committed relationship. I was shocked. I was fighting back tears at the dinner table. The next day, he left.

It was some time before I felt at peace again. I realized that things happen for a reason. I hated that research job; it was never going to be my career. Bob tried to keep in touch, but my respect for him was gone. So, things started to calm down. I moved back in with my best friend at a new apartment downtown and I started focusing on what I really wanted to do. I began looking for volunteer opportunities. I was bartending at night, leaving my days free to pursue something more meaningful.

A few weeks later, I walked into a dingy-looking building that housed a production company. The producer and cameraman of a car television show told me they were looking for a PA intern, available to travel to America. They said it could lead to a paying job. I was interested. So, by early 2005, I was exploring a new field. The next few months at the production company were eye-openers. Having no knowledge of television production, I had to learn how to do everything from the ground up. I was quite proud to see my name in the credits.

To add to my feeling of rejuvenation, I met a man on vacation at around this time. Richard treated me like a queen; he soon had me jetting back and forth between Toronto and Jamaica. The relationship helped me stay positive. I traveled to Jamaica frequently that year but didn't consider moving there permanently. There were no prospects for my industry in the Caribbean. His career in the resort business was more profitable in Jamaica than it could be here in Canada, so he couldn't consider relocating either. Nevertheless, the relationship flourished while I strived to find myself in the workplace.

By the fall of 2005, my experience at the production company had started to sour. The paid job lasted for only two cheques before the show was off the air. Members of our crew were leaving and we were all feeling unappreciated. I left; feeling lost once again. But now I had a desire to pursue a career in the television industry.

The pressures were mounting, though. By the summer of 2006, in spite of some additional training, I was becoming all too familiar with job rejection. I was also feeling pressure from my family. My parents were disappointed in my career choices, three years out of university. To my traditional mother and father, pursuing a career in television was ludicrous. They didn't consider it stable. Being a family oriented person, disappointing my parents caused me great guilt. They had helped me with my living expenses while I was in university, and I wanted to pay them back. The pressure and responsibility on my shoulders felt heavy. It was becoming very hard to keep a positive outlook.

Inevitably, my relationship with Richard started to feel the strain. We fought more often; I felt pressured to establish a career as soon as possible so that we could relocate to a mutual location. For much of 2007, the relationship took a beating. It was a struggle to stay positive. The fights grew more heated; it was obvious that his motivation was waning. I was feeling neglected; he was feeling that he could no longer make me happy. What had once been so special had became a series of misunderstandings, miscommunications and misinterpretations. In September, an intense fight resulted in the breakup. I was devastated and heartbroken. For weeks I cried, with no effort on his part to reestablish our connection. But, day by day, I picked myself up again.

With 2007 at an end, I'm starting to feel that I'm establishing a career. I'm volunteering at a radio station in a major news market, and my on-air skills have improved tremendously. I've also formed a partnership with a good friend in an entertainment & marketing company.

As for Richard, he has mentioned wanting to work things out. There are moments when I feel strong enough to let him go, but there are other times when the pain of the breakup feels like it happened yesterday. Perhaps if I really make an effort to let go of Richard, we'll both achieve some peace. Perhaps we can become good friends, or at least, less hostile toward each other.

I've started to question myself in order to gain clarity and untangle my emotions. What will it cost to release my anger, or to hold onto my sadness? Will I find peace if I let go of my need to control situations? How can I change my negative reactions and become more accepting? Choosing happiness means finding victory from within. That can only be accomplished with confidence and a strong sense of self-esteem; then a career and partner that reflects well on me is possible. I have to trust that challenging experiences are not meant to destroy, but to build. Focus on positive thought and move from disbelieving to believing, and you'll shape your dream future. Everyday, I make the choice to do exactly that.

Taylor Valencourt

A s I sit here in the Copenhagen airport, I find myself struggling to hold back the tears. I am returning home, having just spent the past four months living in a world far different from anything I had ever experienced. I will be leaving behind people who have only known me for 120 days, but know every thought I have; all of my faults and quirks and most of all, how to make me smile. I have been lucky enough to meet people from all over the world; people who have touched me in many different ways. I was fortunate to find a great group of friends who stuck with me through thick and thin and always managed to laugh. I met someone who has touched me for the rest of my life, someone who reminded me who I really am and helped me define who I hope to be.

My name is Taylor Valencourt and I am currently going into my fourth year of political science at Wilfrid Laurier University. I am twenty-two years old, I have wonderful friends from high school that remain close to me and I have great friends from university. I have two wonderful parents who love me and support me in everything I do, even when it's questionable and a sister who is kindness itself; not only toward me, but to the world around her.

I grew up in a city of 100,000 people; there were five high schools in my town, all with reputations of their own. I was nervous going into high school because instead of going to the French high school, my parents wanted me to go to the English school as they felt it would help me get into university. Some of my fondest memories took place in high school, but there were times when it was unstable and scary.

In grade 10, I befriended an older, fellow student. 'Barry' appeared to suffer from some social anxieties. What started as an innocent friendly overture on my part, quickly escalated to the point where I was feeling stalked and threatened, both online and in the hallways at school. Eventually, it was necessary to involve the school authorities and the police. No charges were laid, but I ended up staying away from school for a couple of months until I felt safer.

Later, I went on a weekend retreat up north with my high school sports association. During some lighthearted play on a trampoline, 'Craig,' a 200-pound rugby player, landed badly and broke his back; he would never walk again.

I've had the more typical teenage issues to deal with, as well: I fought constantly with my mom from age fifteen to eighteen; I had a high school boyfriend who left me heartbroken; I ran away from home and thought no one in the world understood me. I can remember being seventeen years old and my parents were constantly telling me how lucky I was, but I didn't understand. I would get in petty spats with my friends, my boyfriend and my mom; sometimes I wished I could just disappear. I had thoughts that I believed were abnormal for someone who had 'so much.' I wished some nights that I could just fall asleep and wake up somewhere else, or not at all. I've screamed at my mom and told her I hated her; I've said hurtful things to people who love me, not realizing until recently how much my family cares.

I graduated from high school, but wasn't ready for the next step; so I went back for my fourth year and tried to figure out what I wanted to do next.

I began university in September, 2004. My roommate was a good friend from high school. My first year was filled with exciting, sometimes scary experiences. For the first time in my life, I was independent. My roommate and I were inseparable; we were an unstoppable pair, just eager to find the next party. I made some wonderful friends; we shared many laughs, many parties and tons of reality TV. In the middle of all that, I met a boy who would eventually turn my world upside down.

At first, I was head over heels in love; I had found the man of my dreams. By last year, however, I had become someone I was not; I had lost myself. I had become insecure, constantly comparing myself to other girls. I was no longer the excited, outgoing person I used to be and I was not a good friend; I had put friends and family aside for this person. When he broke up with me I thought I would never get over him. This was the person I was supposed to be with forever, this was the person who gave me butterflies every time I saw him, even after he had been my boyfriend for ages. I tried to move on, but couldn't; it didn't help that we still hung out, although we were just 'friends.'

Last February, I decided enough was enough; it was time to move on with my life and get back to my old self. So, I went on a spring break holiday and had the time of my life. Back home, a job posting came up for a flight attendant; my parents called me immediately and said I should go to the open interviews. I didn't want to go because I didn't think I stood a chance of getting the job when over ten thousand people across Canada would be applying for the position.

I decided to go on the interview and I was given the thumbs up for a second interview. I wasn't excited yet because I was still up against thousands of applicants. I went to the interview and gave it my best, but it was almost three weeks later, when I had given up, that I got the call. *I was hired!* I had been chosen from a field of thousands of people; I couldn't believe it! I immediately accepted the position and was informed that I would be sent to Montreal for two months of training. I would be living in a hotel and going to 'flight attendant' school.

After I finished my exams, I headed to Montreal and my new home for two months. My roommate during my training period was to become a lifelong friend, along with a wonderful group of Flight Attendants I met there. Together, we helped each other get through the training and we helped one another realize how special we were. We were a group of eight girls, between the ages of 21 and 25, lucky enough to be training as flight attendants for a wonderful company, and to connect so well with each other. We shared our relationship war stories and discovered that in many ways, all of us had faced similar situations. When we graduated from flight attendant school, we went our separate ways and each began our individual adventures.

I flew to New York, to Japan, to Trinidad and to Vancouver; I met hundreds of people, both passengers and co-workers and I was very happy. I would walk through the airport, thrilling to the sound of my clicking heels and suitcase wheeling behind me. Life in the sky was perfect; when I looked down from the sky, everything with the world felt right.

As the end of summer neared, I was getting ready to head off to Denmark on an exchange program; I was going to study abroad for a semester. Initially, when I was accepted by the university in a town called Arhus, I was thrilled. But now, I didn't want to go. I had already delayed my departure by a week because I was enjoying my job as a flight attendant so much. I didn't feel ready to leave my family and friends behind. With much convincing from my parents, I boarded a plane; this time, I would fly as a passenger and stay away for the entire semester.

The first week in Denmark was extremely scary. I was in a country where English wasn't the first language and I was surrounded by unfamiliar faces. But, within two days, I met a great group of people who were to become what I called my 'Danish family.'

There are no 'sure things' in life. I am only twenty-two years old, but when I think back to when 'Barry' was my biggest fear, or when I watched 'Craig' take his last step, to running away from home and losing my self-confidence and worth, I never thought I would be where I am today. My future isn't going to be all sunny-filled happiness, but I know there are reasons for the hard times; they make me stronger. Life is a series of adjustments and constant change. I don't know what I will choose for a career, I don't know if I will attend grad school, but I do know that I am constantly changing, and life will only get better.

Cheryl Anne Meyer

I grew up in a small town in Northern Ontario. Both my parents are well-educated professionals and our family is well-known in the community. I have an older brother who got top marks throughout his school career and was destined to be the electrical engineering Ph.D. student that he is today. Then there's me.

In high school, I liked everything and tried it all, but could not commit to anything for long. In my adolescence, I was a member of every group and sports team that would have me. I would rush from volleyball practice to dance class to guitar lesson to play rehearsal. I had no distinct direction, but I was determined to impress everyone. I tamed, as well as I could, the rash adventurous creature within and decided to 'grow up'.

When I was sixteen-years-old, I planned out my whole life in my pink notebook. My life's 'to do' list was less than a page long and in chronological order. I had decided my life path with the help of an elaborate career test, beyond that provided by the school's guidance department; I had sent away for mine. It was twenty-five pages long and took several weeks to be analyzed before it was returned with my results and a conclusion: Medical Science 97%; Law and Business 94%; Arts and Entertainment 92%; with all other career possibilities in the eightieth percentile. When the time came to pick a university and field of study, I chose to apply for science at three of the very best universities in Ontario.

Unfortunately, I was only sixteen; I had to wait three years for my glorious journey towards higher education to begin. To prepare for my career in the field of medical science, I took co-operative education at the local hospital, I chose only science related courses and I read the Merck Manual (a compendium of medical diagnostic reports) as a pastime. I had smothered the unruly, spontaneous me for so long that it had finally gone dormant.

The year of my graduation was the year of 'the double cohort', when the last OAC (grade thirteen) class in Ontario and the first of the grade

49

twelve graduates applied for university admission the same year, thus significantly increasing the competition for university entrance and programs. I was accepted by my second choice. In spite of this, graduating from high school was a sweet victory and the summer was going to be even more glorious; my friends and I were going to party all summer before we embarked on our new, exciting lives as undergrads.

During that summer, I had a steady boyfriend. I knew that when I went away to school we would break up; this was mutually understood. So when the time came, we ended it nicely and were ready to be friends. I was on my way, with all my loose ends wrapped up.

While partying with friends, I met someone new and, while he definitely did not fall into my notebook plan; there he was. We fell in love very quickly and soon became inseparable. He was already in university, but his school was nine hours away from where I would be. Suddenly, my excitement about university was being tested by my longing to stay with my boyfriend; this made my departure a less joyous occasion than I had always dreamed it would be.

University life was less than sweet when I discovered the size of my room. I had never been in a dorm room, but had imagined it would have a little more privacy and charm. I had envisioned dorm life as a very long slumber party, but it seemed more like prison with day-pass privileges. I was determined to look past the living arrangements and see the good points of school, such as its exciting, new courses and helpful, informative professors. But as the weeks progressed, I began to feel duped.

Thankfully, from the first week of our separation, my boyfriend and I decided that we would do whatever it took to make our relationship work. Every month I would escape on a nine-hour train trek to his place, and he would drive to my campus once a month as well.

As my well-laid plans deteriorated before my eyes, so did my marks. I was getting much lower grades than I had in high school and definitely not the kind of marks that would get me into medical school. As the year wore on, I was finding my number-two university less than captivating; with my parents' permission, I applied to a different school for the following year. My boyfriend applied to the same school and we were going to move in together. I had to use a lot of white-out in my pink notebook, and I added a new section of 'to-do's'. When my predetermined life plan began to falter, that reckless beast deep inside me began to whisper again. I tried to ignore it, but I knew it was there.

As part of my honours-science program, I was allowed elective courses and I had taken a full-year film class. It became the highlight of my week; I was fascinated by the subject of filmmaking. I started doing extra research and explored scriptwriting and acting. I was mainly interested in scriptwriting, but I was also curious about acting.

I came home to work for the summer and spent four months with the guy I loved. However, he had bad news; although I had been accepted at the new school I applied to, he had not and we could not live together. By now, I had dumped a whole bottle of white-out on my list and was finding myself quite directionless again. Although I had decided I would attend the new school, I could not decide what program to take or where to live once I got there; I definitely didn't want dorm life again.

One day, as I skimmed through the website for course options at my new school, I opened my film auditions website; a reminder of my 'field of dreams'. I began videotaping myself practicing monologues from my favourite movies and began chattering incessantly to my parents about films, auditions and scripts. Finally, my parents offered to support me if I wanted to take a year off from school and pursue acting and scriptwriting. I was surprised by the offer; I'd always thought they wanted me to be a doctor or scientist but, as it turned out, they just wanted me to be happy.

I had to think about it; although it was what I really wanted, I was not sure if I had the guts to carry it through. I would have to admit to everyone that I was dropping out of school; I wasn't going to be a doctor, but possibly a starving artist. But my adventurous monster finally broke free and I had to go for it. I took my pink notebook and ripped out the section about school and career and stared at a blank page. It was quite liberating; especially since the section that dealt with love and marriage was still intact. I felt security in that.

I decided to move in with my boyfriend, near Montreal, and try to get an agent. As the summer ended, my parents and I moved all my stuff to Quebec. Before moving there myself, I was to spend a week in Toronto, acting in an independent film. I was to stay with a friend in Markham, who had offered me his living room futon.

That week stretched into two weeks, then stretched even further; it quickly became apparent that it would be necessary to my career for me to stay in Toronto, as more auditions were rolling my way. To enhance my acting skills, I enrolled in several classes, which further extended my stay. It was a challenging and exciting time for me although I was alone and living out of a suitcase. I was in a new city and it was so much bigger, busier and brighter than my home town. I walked the streets everyday armed with a map and a notebook filled with addresses. I was getting a lot of auditions for student films and television pilots and I kept taking classes, until my resume was full enough to get an agent. My day consisted of waking up on the futon, catching the GO bus to Union Station, running around to auditions and classes, then catching the GO bus back to Markham, eating some canned food and back to the futon to sleep.

Occasionally, I would take the train to Montreal to visit my boyfriend. Our relationship was becoming strained because it was difficult for him to relate to me; our lives were so different. He was a student with all his friends around him on campus; I was an actress alone in a big city six hours away. But he had promised me that when he graduated he would move to Toronto so that we could be together; I looked forward to that day. We had talked about marriage and I believed he would propose to me after he graduated. So I plugged on.

By the following January, I had upgraded from my friend's futon in Markham to renting a room in Etobicoke with friends of my boyfriend's family; a woman and her daughter who were very nice, but whom I rarely saw due to my busy schedule. Time was flying, and by March I was lonely and desperate to see my boyfriend. He drove up with his roommate to see me and I decided that I would go back with them to Montreal so that we could have a longer visit.

On the drive back, my boyfriend got a phone call from his father. When he hung up, he excitedly announced that he had been accepted into graduate school in Virginia for the following September. At that moment, my last pink notebook plan disappeared before my eyes. I had thought that we would be moving in together in May, engaged by July and happily married the following year. The car ride back to my boyfriend's apartment was the longest six hours of my life. I debated what I was going to say to him once we were alone and finally decided not to try to influence his decision to go to America. Who was I, to tell him how to live his life? He had dreams just like I did, but they were pulling us in opposite directions and straining our relationship. We could not spend another year and a half away from each other and we were growing more apart with every month. When he did decide to go to Virginia, I knew our relationship was over.

I waited until I was able to move out of his family friend's place before I ended it. It was the hardest decision I have ever made but he was destined for great things in his career and I was destined to find what it was that I wanted most. I found a cheap apartment that had mice, clogged plumbing and foundation problems. I lived there for a year with another girl whom I seldom saw.

Soon I was able to find work in acting and related fields, such as promotional jobs for different products at different venues. Through these jobs I started meeting friends and eventually I had a social life. I met a guy who I dated for most of the summer. The money he spent and the expensive restaurants and lounges we frequented caused me to think about my financial future; I decided that I wanted to be able to take care of myself, without relying on a man. As a result, that summer I decided to go back to school. I wanted to get a bachelor of commerce degree and I would start online courses in September. My parents were very happy that my long journey had led me back to education; of my own choosing this time. Both my practical side and my adventurous side had agreed on a path. I was able to pursue an education and an acting career simultaneously.

Two years have passed and my life is heading in a direction that I love. During those two years I have had another failed relationship, filmed a failed television pilot, and failed a mid-term; but I kept moving forward and learning from my experiences. Currently, I am still acting and am in my third year of a commerce degree program at Ryerson University, with a strong academic standing. It took me a while to figure out what was right for me, but the trip was worth it. I have performed in some television shows and dinner theatre productions, and I have successfully auditioned for a supporting role in an independent Hollywood film. I have partnered with a friend to develop our own IT company and I have found someone that makes me very happy and with whom I hope to have a future.

These are my rewards for taking risks and following my inner beast, which longed for more. It was a demanding journey with a lot of hard decisions to make along the way. I learned several things from my experiences: First, only make 'to-do' lists for the week and make 'wish-lists' for the future, and write them both in pencil. Second, you can only suppress your true desires for so long before they overwhelm your whole being. Third, taking risks and experiencing failures are necessary parts of the pursuit of real happiness. Finally, don't try to live your life to please other people; as Shakespeare so aptly said, "To thine own self be true."

Kate Todd

Growing up in the country and being discovered at a young age, I went from small town girl to the bright lights and working on film sets quickly. The rural landscape I grew up in offered me fresh air, open spaces and the freedom to express myself. I also developed an appreciation for the seasons and all of Mother Nature's glory. Whether I was nursing a small bird that had fallen from its nest or watching butterflies emerge from their cocoons, life was simple, yet never boring. It is from these humble beginnings that I developed a vivid imagination. With no immediate neighbourhood children nearby to play with, I was constantly singing, writing stories and skits that I would perform for my family and our friends. Although we lived somewhat isolated from the outside world, my rural roots contributed to the uninhibited, healthy lifestyle and stringent fitness regimen that I continue to maintain.

My father, Glenn, jump started my love for music at the tender age of six when he bought me a **Cranberries** CD. While most children were into sing-a-longs, I was amassing a CD collection of artists such as **Annie Lennox**, **Amy Grant** and **Sheryl Crow**. At nine, I begged my older sister, Kelly, to take me to a massive outdoor rock concert starring **Alanis Morrissette**; I was certainly the youngest person there by a long shot. Music became my passion; I couldn't live without it. Dad says it's my grandmother, Fern, who I inherited my musical talent from; she still enjoys playing piano and singing in our local church choir. I believe it was the unconditional support of my family, my rural roots and my insatiable desire to succeed that helped make me who I am today.

I was always presenting my parents with spontaneous and sometimes outrageous ideas, but I was rarely given a disapproving eye. Once, when I was thirteen, I came to the conclusion that I wanted to visit Spain. So off I went, with my parents' blessing, to live with a Spanish family for the summer, where I was completely submerged in a foreign culture. It must have come as no surprise to them, as my love of traveling stems from my family's tradition of visiting different areas of the world annually. I was fortunate to experience many different cultures and observe first hand how other people of the world live.

Throughout my youth, with the support of my family, I have taken karate; figure skating; dance and piano; performing in many recitals. I attribute my love of performing anywhere and everywhere to these early childhood activities. In high school, I chose to play the trumpet and French horn, little realizing a monumental change in my life would soon lead me to take up another musical instrument altogether!

I discovered at an early age that I had the ability to make people laugh; I like to think I still do. Laughter, it's said, warms the soul; having a sense of humor can lead to friendships and take you almost anywhere. At fourteen, I presented another outrageous idea to my parents; I wanted to act. I say outrageous because no one in my town really knew how to get into acting. I didn't even know what happened on film sets or what a film set was, but I knew I wanted to be part of the 'action.' My mom, Cheryl, gladly and without question, packed up our truck and drove me to Toronto to find an agent. After being turned away by one of Toronto's top agencies because, as I was told, they had too many blonde haired, blue eyed girls on their roster, I politely corrected the gentleman, explaining, "I actually have green eyes." Sadly, that didn't make a difference. Although I was discouraged, I decided that nothing was going to get in the way of what I wanted to accomplish. I returned home and found myself a local acting class. I studied for two years and after I was finished, I came back to my parents with yet another proposal. I was ready to go back to Toronto and see the same agent that had turned me down previously. I had my monologue audition prepared for him and I was ready for anything else he might throw at me. He was very impressed by my dedication and, over-looking my lack of prior experience, he decided to take me on as a client. The next thing I knew, I was standing outside my very first audition, without a clue what to expect.

Within six months of signing with an agency, I found my next musical instrument was to be the guitar, as I had landed the lead female role on the TV show, **Radio Free Roscoe**, to be aired on the **Family Channel** in Canada and **The-N network** in the United States. I play a down-to-earth rocker chick who is an aspiring singer/songwriter! At this point, I had no idea just how huge this was and how it would change the next few years of my life. I went from attending a 700-student public school in the middle of a field, to bright lights and camera crews.

My mother was there every step of the way. She would get up every morning at 5am and come to the set with me, where she would sit, knitting, in my dressing room or by the set monitors, waiting for me while I worked. My father was able to support the family by changing his schedule so he could drop by the set before going to work. My family and I had to work together like a well-oiled machine. Suddenly, I had autograph-signing mall tours, public appearances, photo shoots and script readings to deal with; life was moving pretty fast. My parents were always there to keep me grounded and to keep everything in perspective. I would come home every night to my country home, away from the spot light, and remember that this is truly who I am; this is where I come from.

I was always doing my own thing. In high school, I could be found playing my guitar in the halls with my guy friends, writing songs and jamming. After graduation, I was faced with some very difficult decisions. In addition to working 70 hours a week on set, I worked hard at school. I graduated as a designate 'Ontario Scholar' with honours. I was eligible for scholarships at several universities, but wasn't sure that was what I wanted to do. I know I will return to school one day; I do love learning and I feel it's essential for my happiness, but for now I am studying my craft as an actress, singer and songwriter. I eat, sleep and breathe these subjects and continue to hone my craft by enrolling in clinics and workshops, studying the various techniques and methods relating to each art form.

The most important thing I have learned in dealing with the pressures of this business is how to breathe deeply and think positively. I take care of myself and I listen to my body; I am acutely aware of its needs. I suppose I was destined to be a fitness and health food advocate because my parents would never take me to fast food restaurants as a child and you would be hard pressed to find chips, cookies or junk food in my cupboards. I really look forward to my workouts. I know it can be hard in the beginning to stay motivated, but exercising actually gives me motivation. I use exercise to envision success and it gives me time to reflect on my dreams. It becomes a little chunk of time where I can connect with my body and my mind, while also staying in shape!

One of the concerns an actor must face in the industry, is how you are going to be viewed. There are elements of yourself that are beyond your control, but ultimately make you the unique person that you are. For instance, I have been turned down for roles because of my height; I'm 5'8" and the leading man may be only 5'6"; I can't control that. I can't control it when the casting directors and producers want to see a brunette, blonde, or red haired actress. If I got upset over every audition that wasn't successful, I wouldn't have the motivation to continue. It takes a strong person to stay committed to this industry.

As I've matured, I have learned to embrace the flaws or differences I may have been conscious of in the past. It is my belief that if you recognize your strengths, everything else will follow. You will reflect a more positive outlook and the confidence you display will gain you respect and better treatment. It's important to stay true to yourself and not apologize for any of the quirks that have made you who you are.

Success doesn't come without sacrifice. Everyday, I am doing something to advance my dreams, my goals and my career. In the entertainment industry, you have to be prepared for anything. That's what makes my career so rewarding; I am constantly being physically, mentally and emotionally challenged. It can be very taxing rushing to auditions, vocal coaching, band rehearsals and recording sessions, all booked back-to-back. Time management and relaxation methods are absolute keys to success; I make sure to set aside time to myself to decompress and regroup before switching my focus to my next undertaking. Striving to maintain balance in a world of such extremes can sometimes be a daunting task.

In life, there are always high and low points. Sometimes you feel like you have the world in the palm of your hand and then, just as fast, everything falls apart and you feel like you have to start over. Not everything in life is fair, but you have to make the best of your situation. It is necessary to envision yourself being successful and taking control of your life. Ask yourself what it is that you want and work towards getting there even if it means stepping out of your comfort zone or doing something you have never done before, you have to go for it. You have one life to shape for yourself in any way that you want. It may not always feel like it, but you've really got the world at your fingertips.

Having a supportive family and a strong desire to succeed has made me who I am today. Who would have thought that a small town girl would become a working actress in the entertainment industry? I certainly haven't accomplished everything I've dreamt of, but I am continuing to climb higher and higher and I won't give up. Always remember that you hold the power to your future and your success; if you can dream it, you can do it.

I know it's common for kids and teens to sometimes feel different. I know it can feel extremely lonely when you have different goals and aspirations from the people around you; I've been there. Everyone has a different story and different circumstances, but at the end of the day, we're all in it together.

Throughout my teen years, I was rarely at school; I did much of my schooling on set with a certified tutor. As soon as the director yelled "cut," I was whisked to the schoolroom trailer to complete an exam or finish the last sentence of an essay. By the time the weekend rolled around, I was too exhausted from my seventy-hour shooting schedule and completing my homework assignments to hang out with my friends. Quite often, they didn't know when I would be around or if I was even available. Luckily for me, I have many true friends who have stuck by me and have supported my career from day one, recognizing that I couldn't always attend the dances or go to their parties; I will always appreciate them for that. My family, my friends and my loyal fans from around the world remain my most gratifying and motivational forces.

Peace and Love,
Kate

Stacey McKenzie

Who knew a picture in a magazine my sister brought with her while visiting us was going to be my motivation to pursue a newfound career. I was six years-old when I came across a picture of Jean Paul Gaultier and Madonna. I thought they were just as funky and weird looking as me and I wanted to know everything about them. My sister read the article and by the time she was finished, I knew that was my calling; I was going to be a model.

Growing up in Kingston, Jamaica was pretty rough. It was just my mom and me; my brother and sister were grown and had lives with their own families. My mother was a typical Jamaican and she was very protective of me because I was always being teased. There was a time when she was being made fun of as well, because people actually thought she was walking around with a white doll when she was with me. Other than school, I was only allowed to go to church. My mom wanted me to be a nurse, or better yet, a doctor. When I told her I wanted to be a model, she dismissed me like I was crazy.

I knew I had something special and I knew there was a place for me out there and I was going to go all the way to find it.

I didn't have anyone to help me become a model. It was just me and my mom and she surely didn't have a clue! Because I didn't have a guide or mentor, I took it upon myself to do what I could with what I had. I taught myself everything!

To learn how to dress like a model, I started off with my school uniform. I would roll up the sleeves of my shirt and pin the waist of my dress to give me some shape. To learn how to walk, I exchanged my regular black school shoes and white socks for my mom's wedge heels as soon as I was out of my mother's sight; every time I showed up for school, I was immediately escorted out to change my shoes. To learn how to pose, I would sit in front of the mirror for hours and do different facial expressions, pretending to be shy, happy, nervous, surprised, mad and any other emotion I could imagine.

For years I trained myself, but as I grew, the teasing grew. There were moments when I felt that negative people out there might try to block me from making it. I started thinking about all the attention; I couldn't go anywhere in peace. It was negative attention, but it was a lot of attention. Right then and there, I knew I was blessed with a different look and a quirky voice for a reason and I needed to be seen on a bigger scale. When my mother told me, at thirteen, that we were moving to Canada, I thought, "this is my chance and I'm going all the way."

I thought Canada was going to be a lot easier for me, but that wasn't the case. I was teased even more, but I didn't let it get to me and I kept my focus. At the age of fifteen, I started to research agencies in Toronto. I approached each and every one of them and they all said no. I tried a few more times and they all said no every single time. At the age of sixteen, I got kicked out of my mom's and dropped out of school with the goal of pursuing my dream career in New York City. I got a second job and researched agencies in New York while living in my small studio apartment. I got on a Greyhound bus and went to see all the agencies, and again, every single one of them said NO!

I couldn't believe it, but I didn't take it personally. All I needed was that one person to give me a chance, just to let me get my foot in the door and then I would blow them away. I got back on the Greyhound and planned another trip to come back to New York. I ended up trying a couple of times and always came home empty handed.

Then one night, while at a club, a young guy approached me and asked if I was a model. Without hesitating, I said I was. His name was Roger Larose and he was an aspiring agent. He told me that he was driving a few girls down to New York to get them signed with agencies and I immediately told him I was going with them. Within days, me and about seven girls were stuffed into a big old Buick, driving to New York!

When we arrived, we had one day to see all the agencies, so we had to hustle. I went to them all and they were all saying no again. Toward the end of the day, we went to see a well known agent who claimed to want to represent me as soon as she came out to look at us. She told me I should go home, pack my bags and get my butt back to New York.

I couldn't believe it. All my hard work was finally paying off! I had found someone to take a chance on me. I went back to Toronto, packed my bags and headed back to New York. But when I walked into the agency, the same woman told me she wasn't interested, she walked into her office and closed the door in my face. I couldn't believe it. I gathered my wits and decided to try my luck with the other agencies since I was already there.

I went to all the agencies again and at the last agency I went to, the booker liked me a whole lot. She had to get the owner's approval first, so she had me wait outside his office while she spoke to him. I sat there and listened to this man calling me ugly and hideous and saying there was no way in hell I would make them any money, she pleaded with him to give me a chance and after a long while, she came out to tell me that I had three months; if I didn't do well, she was going to be out of a job. I hugged her for the longest time, telling her that she wouldn't regret it, because I was going to be big!

I moved into the model's apartment with a couple of girls. My career in New York was short lived the first time around, not because I didn't work; I got my first cover for a local magazine within two weeks, but because I was a young girl living with a couple of other young girls with no guidance whatsoever. I would sit at home and watch as they partied almost every night, going out with rich, old men for dinner. On top of that, a few of my roommates were very spoiled and behaved disrespectfully toward people.

I was in a different country, with no family or friends. I didn't want to become someone who lived too fast, trying to fit in and get ahead in my career. I didn't want to lose my soul, so I decided to walk away from it and come back when I was ready. I knew I was taking a big risk, because in this industry you might have only one chance; it's a short career at best, so if you have the opportunity, you should take it and run with it. At the same time, I felt I was way too young to be out there in this big world of fashion with a lot of eye candy being thrown around; some good and some real bad. If I didn't have my head screwed on real tight I could easily lose my way. I wasn't about to let that happen for anyone or anything and with that in mind, I packed my bags and left for home.

I was back to square one; this time, moving back in with my mom. She wasn't happy at all about my chosen career path and she let me know how she felt every chance she got. It wasn't easy, but I dealt with the pressure until I was able to get out on my feet again. I held two jobs while getting my GED in night school. I even got married, but that's another story. Eventually, I decided to try my luck with Toronto modeling agencies again and, of course, ended up with a no from every single one. But, an agent told me that I should try my luck in Paris or London and suddenly, I had a new focus to work toward.

Paris was going to be a big step; my mom wouldn't be a bus ride anymore, I didn't know anyone there and I would have to master a language that I had hated and failed at in school. But I had to go all the way; if it was meant for me, it would fall into place; if not, at least I knew I took a chance.

I worked my butt off and within eight months I was headed to Europe. I arrived in Paris with $300 to my name and with that I had to find a place to stay and food to eat. I got on the Metro, hoping to reach the centre of the city when I looked around and saw a bald, black girl. An instinct told me to go talk to her and I did; her name is Dawn Leak and she is a model from Philadelphia who was on her way to meet her boyfriend, a photographer named Vincent Peters. 'Thank God, someone who speaks English,' was my first thought. I tagged along with her to a local agency where she was meeting her boyfriend. While waiting in the lobby, one of the bookers spotted me and asked Dawn who I was. Within minutes, I was signed to the agency. I was so excited. I settled into a cheap hotel that Dawn and Vincent took me to and began my career again.

Within two weeks I came crashing back to earth again. When I had been signed, the head booker wasn't in town. When he got back, there was a big agency dinner and that's when he met me for the first time. Right away he hated me. He insulted me, calling me ugly and laughing at me; he made fun of my secondhand clothes. This man was really out to make me feel like nothing. I decided to set him straight and when I did it was a big mistake. The next day when I went to the agency to pick up my portfolio, I was told they didn't have it and they didn't know where it was. I demanded the portfolio that I had worked so hard to put together in Canada and they still didn't give it to me. I was told that I was no longer represented by them and had to leave. I had two weeks until the Pret-a-Porter shows and I was running low on money.

I went back to my tiny hotel room and cried my eyes out, not knowing what to do next. For the first time, I felt like giving up, but I talked myself out of it. I had come too far to give up; I needed to explore all avenues of the business before I could come to that decision. I got myself together and thought about calling some of the people I had become friends with in the industry to ask for help.

I called Vincent right away and he did a free photo shoot for me. I bought a portfolio and was off to look for another agency. Again, they all said no. Vincent then took me to a really small agency and the agent, Gaspard, took a liking to me. He told me to come back and I just blurted out, "No! I'm here right now. I can't afford to come back, so let me know right now if I'm in or not."

I guess he liked my drive and went to talk to the owner. It was New York all over again; she wasn't interested, she thought I was 'strange' and didn't feel that I would make the agency any money. Finally, Gaspard came out and told me I was in, with major conditions; he wasn't allowed to advance me any money if I needed it and the owner made it very clear that if I needed help, it was all on him. It's rare to find someone in this industry who is going to have your back; Gaspard took it upon himself to help me in any way he could and to this day we are still very good friends.

The next day, I began my castings for Pret-a-Porter shows. I went to see Jean Paul Gaultier, the same funky looking designer whose picture graced my wall when I was six years-old! I will never forget when I walked in and there he was, sitting with his entourage. He took one look at me, smiled and said, "Elle est belle."

He was the first person in the business to call me beautiful and I just stood there, crying my eyes out. He had me try on a man's suit with heels and walk for him. I blew him and his entourage the hell away and with that, I was booked.

I ran out of his office screaming. I ran to the telephone booth to call Gaspard and right away he told me that Jean Paul had booked me for his show! I got on the phone and called my mom, then I started telling everyone in the street, in the coffee shops, in the bars, in the café, the bus drivers, the people waiting for the bus and the school kids!

That season, I walked 12 of the biggest designers' shows, including Jean Paul Gaultier. Madonna opened the show, with me walking right behind her with the biggest grin on my face. I FINALLY MADE IT!

Dionysia Katsilieris

Many of us fear the future, the unknown. We use defense mechanisms to brace ourselves for a horrifying experience that's bound to come crashing into our lives. But, what's the point? How do we benefit from living in fear even when something bad does come our way? Isn't that a pretty sad way to live?

Not too long ago, I entered a very challenging period in my life. It was a time of change, fear and a lot of unexpected experiences. It started a little over two years ago. I was living in Canada with my parents. I had a great job in television, friends, independence and security, but for some reason, I was preparing to leave all that to try something new; a move to Greece. My parents are from Greece, my sister had moved there and I felt that it was something I should try also. I thought to myself, "Now is your chance. Try something new."

You might ask why I would leave the great life that I had to move to a country very different from Canada. Well, although I had this great life, for some unknown reason I was unhappy. Or at least I felt like there would be something in Greece that could make me happier. It took me a year to finally decide to make the move. Some days I would be convinced it was the right decision and others I would be convinced otherwise. But finally I made the decision and stuck with it. So I packed my bags, said a very difficult good-bye to my friends and family and took off to start a new life in Greece. I was excited but also really scared. I was so scared that I might have been making the wrong decision.

It was summertime when I got there and I already had an excellent career opportunity lined up. An acquaintance of mine in Canada had proposed that I produce a travel show for Greek television. I was excited and eager to get to work. That summer was especially exciting because my sister was getting married and I would see my parents again when they came to Greece for the wedding.

The wedding was fantastic; better than a fairy tale. It was set in a little village and the festivities left time for sunbathing and socializing. When all the wedding celebrations were over, I returned to Athens and got to work.

The TV project I was working on was exciting at first; I was meeting new people in the industry, negotiating with the sponsors and overseeing the filming. It was a great experience. Eventually, the team started to fall apart. The relationship between my two managers was deteriorating quickly. When the project was over three months later, I wasn't unhappy to see it end. The partnership between my two managers was dissolved, so nothing much ever came of the project.

My plan to be a success in the television industry in Greece had suffered a serious setback. My new strategy was to flood the industry with my knock-out resume, pound the pavement, network with as many industry people as I could come into contact with and search the newspaper daily for new openings in the field. Aside from meeting my boyfriend, not much came from my efforts.

My new boyfriend and I were getting a long fabulously. We seemed to have an instant connection and were spending loads of time together. He was sweet, affectionate and generous and he always wanted to spend time with me. I was on cloud nine. With him, I could be completely myself and I felt very comfortable; which was rare with me.

Time passed and my daily expenses were mounting; I needed a job. A friend of my father's ran a non-profit cultural organization and he was looking for someone to proofread and edit texts in English, French and Greek. I am fluent in all three languages, so he hired me to work for him part-time. This really helped to cover my expenses. The job was boring and a long commute, but I learned a lot from the books that I was proofing and my boss was nice.

A couple of months later, my grandfather passed away. My grandpa, 'Papou' Christos, was the only grandparent I had left from either side of my family, and I loved him a lot. He was a generous and funny man who always made me laugh. 'Papou' Christos had been getting weaker over the years, which we attributed to old age, but it turned out he was in the final stages of prostate cancer. I had gone to visit him one week before he died and we had had a really nice conversation. It was as if we had both known it was the last time we would see each other. That night, as I was saying goodbye, I gave him one last hug; he was so fragile it felt like I was hugging a newborn.

The process of death has taught me to be strong, to enjoy life and to remember the good moments; otherwise, you're bound to fall into a dark hole of negativity and depression. After my grandfather's death, I was determined to create a family tree and document the lives of my ancestors so that I had something to remember them by.

My mom flew over from Canada for the funeral. That was one of the most difficult experiences of my life. My parents had always been my pillars of strength, my motivators and my refuge. But a few days after the funeral, I went to my grandpa's tomb with my mom and my aunt and my mom was a mess. She was crying uncontrollably and could barely cope with her despair. I remember having to gather all my strength to hold her up and console her. It was hard for me not to cry, but I had to be strong for my mom. I felt like I had truly grown up, because while my mother was grieving for her father, I had taken on the role of the consoling parent. It was an especially trying time for my mom because she had lost her mother when she was only two-years-old; my grandfather was all that she had left. It helped me to know that my father would help my mom get through her difficult time. My father has always been the strong one in the family.

After months without any news about a job in television, I was hired by a production company as a director of research for a documentary. I kept my proofreading job to be on the safe side. That turned out to be a wise decision; the documentary project was scrapped when it was learned that the subject had died. My boyfriend and I rode out the ups and downs.

Five months after that, I got a job on a TV talk show. The catch there was that I was actually competing for the job with seven other applicants, and working on a trial basis (unpaid) in the meantime. That was the last, demoralizing straw.

After that experience I became extremely discouraged. I began thinking that I had made a big mistake moving to Greece. After all the put downs, rejection and tricks, I was exhausted and I felt like I had lost my independence. I was depending on my family for financial support while I struggled to achieve my dream and I was depending on my boyfriend for a lot of emotional support. I didn't want to burden anyone, but I didn't want to give up my dream, either.

I was so angry that I couldn't get into the small world of TV that I decided to give it a break. I decided to step back and really try to figure out what was important in my life. I was discouraged and disappointed. There I was, a young woman with lots of experience and the willingness to do the job, but nobody wanted to hire me. Now, all this time, my older sister has been telling me to just find any job. I didn't want just any job, though. I knew what I wanted and it bothered me that she couldn't understand that. But I would soon realize that big sisters may know a little something about life, after all.

I felt like no one valued me. I decided to take my sister's advice and applied to various jobs in various fields; I even went to a few head hunters. I tried for a while, but then that old longing to become a TV producer crept back in. I tried for about two months to find a job, then I gave up altogether because I got no calls. No one in TV wanted to hire me and now it seemed that no company in Greece wanted to hire me. I was told by many people that it was extremely difficult to find a job in Greece, especially for women my age. Apparently, in Greece, many companies take gender and age into consideration because they want to avoid hiring women who may get married and start having babies. Many companies prefer hiring younger women with little experience; it's cheap and there are no strings attached. Women with university degrees and years of experience were not widely sought after.

A couple of months passed and a good friend of mine came to me with an offer. This friend had also moved to Greece from Canada and was also pursuing a career in television. She had an idea for a documentary series and found a production company interested in developing it. She wanted me onboard to develop and organize the project. I was so happy to have finally found a job that I wanted to work on. The company could only pay me a small amount but I had all the resources I could need at my disposal and my own office. I was working long hours, but I felt so good; like I had finally found my calling in life. Three months later, filming was ready to begin. I packed my bags and, with the crew, flew to Kosovo and Montenegro for a week of location filming.

Before the trip, I was afraid to go to Kosovo. I had heard and read so many stories about the dangers of Kosovo and I was becoming preoccupied with fear. I was especially scared because of the unrest in Kosovo being broadcast on the news. I was afraid because I didn't know what to expect. I thought I was heading into a place full of landmines, poverty and people on the hunt for potential enemies.

Some people in our original crew even backed out of the project because of this fear. But I was determined to go and make the best of the situation. Shortly before heading off to Kosovo, I was also having relationship problems. My boyfriend and I were clashing more and more frequently. He wasn't communicating, he was spending less time with me and I was exhausted trying to hold our relationship together. I thought this trip would do us both good. It would give us time to reflect on our relationship.

The fear I had built up in my mind was a waste of time and energy because Kosovo turned out to be the experience of a lifetime; it was fabulous! The cities are modern, the country is natural and clean and the people were kind and friendly. I met several natives and they were very hospitable, welcoming us into their homes and offering us their delicious, traditional meals. I was very impressed with the number of people who spoke fluent English; it gave me the opportunity to ask both opposing sides about their experiences during the war and about their point of view on the conflict between Albanians and Serbians, as well as life in general. One young Albanian woman in particular stood out. She was 18 years old and had lost her brother and sister during the Kosovo conflict. Instead of dwelling on her hatred and fear of Serbians and war, she had vowed to promote peace to children in Kosovo.

The production crew was amazing too. We worked very hard and experienced several challenges along the way, but I can't remember the last time I've laughed so much. The only negative thing about the trip was the feeling I had that my boyfriend and I were on the verge of breaking up. I was torn; I loved him, but we had grown apart and I was afraid of letting go. I was afraid that if we broke up I would be making the biggest mistake of my life and I was afraid of having to do it all over again if I were to ever find love again. But I knew, more than ever, that he and I were not meant for each other. Our interests were very different, as were our personalities. My brother-in-law once said to me,

"Take a moment and think; in this relationship, have you been happy or sad most of the time?"

Bang! What a red flag. In the beginning of the relationship, I was happy. But then, most people are happy in the beginning. After the first few months however, I was sad more often than not. That wasn't entirely his fault, though. I allowed it to happen; too often I made compromises and didn't set my standards high enough. Every woman should know what she is and isn't willing to put up with and if she sees signs of things that she doesn't want in a relationship, she has to be strong and willing to let him go. She has to love herself first.

All my life, if there is one thing I've wanted most, even more than a successful career in television, it's to find the love of my life. The man who would be my best friend, who would love me unconditionally, make me laugh and share similar interests with me or at least support my interests; my soul mate. Sometimes, I secretly feared that I may never find this man and that my clock was ticking away. But I realized that time is not impor- tant. The important thing is to love myself, be happy and have faith that my heart's true desires will come my way.

When the fantastic trip to Kosovo and Montenegro came to an end, it was time to go back to Greece to finish the project and face the problems I was having with my boyfriend. My first week back, I tried to get close to him, but I guess it wasn't enough; by week's end, we just stopped calling each other. I didn't have the strength to try anymore. I thought that he might try to make things work; to tell me that he loves me and we would get through this, but he never called. Everyone told me to move on and not to contact him, but I needed closure. I needed to let him know that I still cared and wanted him to be happy even if we weren't together. A month and a half later, I contacted him and expressed this to him. He replied in a similar vein, but he wasn't willing to make things work. But I got my closure and I could now move on. I've never had a more difficult time getting over a boyfriend.

By this time, the documentary project was coming to an end and my sister gave birth to a beautiful baby boy. Where one thing ends another begins. My nephew is the light of my life; sweet, funny and innocent with eyes full of hope, wonder and love. No fear. I guess you could say he's my role model. The documentary was completed and then it was simply a waiting game. Waiting for the next project to come along; a project that has yet to surface. So once again, I was on the hunt for a job.

Fortunately, I was approached by an old acquaintance with a job offer to teach English to adults. I wasn't very eager, but I decided to give it a try. Somewhat to my surprise, I found I really enjoyed teaching. It turns out, everything I've learned through experience and education could be applied. I had to be organized, creative, dynamic and communicative while learning about various subjects. Most importantly, I was helping people achieve their goals and that made me feel like I was making a contribution to the world.

As I was settling into the teaching job, my ex-boyfriend got in touch with me after four months of silence. He wanted to meet and talk; basically, he wanted to try again. Deep down, I knew I shouldn't, but I agreed to give it another shot and it was worse than ever. Once again, I went through an emotional roller coaster. It was less intense than the last time, but nevertheless, I was allowing myself to be his emotional punching bag again. He would make plans, then not call and he would never apologize. I didn't put up with it for long though, because this time I listened to my inner voice; the voice that reminded me of how completely I lost myself with him in the past. I had no friends, independence, security or confidence and I had latched onto him and allowed myself to be consumed. We should all listen to our inner voice when making difficult decisions; we have to learn to trust our instincts. I have no hard feelings toward my ex-boyfriend because he is a good person; he's just not a good person for me. I learned a lot from the relationship, including how important it is to never doubt myself. Sometimes people will try to mess with your head and cause you to doubt the truth, but I advise you to stick to your guns.

Most of the time, we create our own fears. Fear of disappointing others; fear of making a mistake; fear of losing someone or something; the list goes on and on. Our mental state plays a huge role in our happiness. So it's important for us to find peace of mind. You owe it to yourself and I owe it to myself.

Everyone has their cross to bear and some may feel that my experience was not a terribly difficult one. My cross was a heavy one because it was a new experience in my life and now, having gotten through these things, I truly believe that I am a more capable person with a stronger heart and more positive outlook. I couldn't have gotten through this rough patch if it weren't for my family; they are my support system. Taking the time to care for me also helped. Every night, I meditate about my day and the challenges in my life. I give myself a pep talk and refuel with some positive thinking. Sometimes, it's easy to let negative thoughts take over. Getting angry at someone who cut you off while driving, resenting a boyfriend who treated you badly, thinking badly about yourself because you hit a rough patch in life or fearing the future all stem from negative thoughts and negative thoughts usually stem from fear. Fear doesn't have to be powerful, though; we feed its power with negative thoughts. Whenever you find yourself thinking negatively, don't dwell; replace the negative with a positive thought. It's tough, but if you really try, it will become a simple habit that will change your life for the better. This is something that I've been working on for awhile now and it really does make a difference in my life.

View the unknown as friendly. There is no reason to fear it. Happiness isn't found in your environment, it's found within you. I realized that if I was unhappy in Canada, I would be just as unhappy in Greece unless I changed from within.

For now, I am still teaching, making new friends and taking the time to dive back into some of my hobbies. My life isn't perfect, but I am content knowing that I can make it happier, one step at a time.

Jasmin Bir

L ife is full of transitions. We all go through periods of learning and growth until we reach a point when it's time to move on to something new and unfamiliar. One of the biggest transitions in my life occurred when I graduated from high school. I was parted for the first time from all I knew as a child as I moved toward the exciting and uncertain future that lay before me. It was difficult to start over, but I faced my future with strength and courage. I began my journey into the world equipped with compassion, understanding and an eagerness to learn; sure that I would continue to evolve into the phenomenal woman I was meant to become. My journey took me to university.

I was raised by two of the best parents a child could hope for! Along with my two siblings, I was encouraged to be myself and to appreciate the unique differences within the human race. This strong family environment paved the way for an amazing high school career; it was a unique time in my life during which I began to fully express my individuality through intelligence and style.

I am passionate about many things in life, but the two things I cherish most are learning and fashion. I could easily get lost for hours in a book, learning about something new or enjoying the adventures of a novel. I have always cherished the way a book can transport a reader; the possibilities are endless! My dearest friends would tease me about my constant attempts to get a part time job at the local library. But, what could be better than working in an environment filled with the magic of books?

Well, I suppose there is one thing… fashion! I was lucky enough to land a job at my favorite clothing boutique, allowing me to fulfill my other desire; to be chic. I remember seeing Vogue for the first time; the thick, glossy magazine was packed with the latest trends from New York, Milan and Paris. As I scanned the pages a hot rush sent shivers through my body. The luxurious designer clothes, adorned with stunning accessories, creating art on the human form, enchanted me. I could often be found in the school halls dressed in something dazzling while carrying an enormous backpack, bulging with books and notes. My stylish expression brought me much joy, and allowed me to conquer all of my tasks with confidence and a positive attitude. Fashion is an expression of my soul.

I had many friends in high school and was well rewarded for my relentless pursuit of higher learning. I was able to find something in common with everyone I met and that kept me in good favor with all. I was on the honour roll, played varsity volleyball and helped organized Red Cross blood drives. I was President of the National Honour Society; President of Eastern Cultures Society; Activities Director of our Student Council and a member of the Junior Engineering Technical Society, the Latin Club, Letterman's Club, etc. I was given excellence awards for education and invited to take part in academic related seminars for gifted students. I volunteered at two local hospitals, the Special Olympics and various projects for Kiwanis Club, while holding the position of Vice President for my high school's chapter. I even attended a local college during my senior year as a post secondary student. My classmates voted me 'Most Likely to Succeed'. I received many scholarships, including a full academic scholarship to my future university. I was named one of the school's 'Fashion Divas' and was named Prom Queen my senior year. I was respected by classmates and teachers alike for my work ethic and character. I often helped other students with academic problems that were challenging. I was liked and accepted for my intelligence and my flair for fashion.

At university everything was new and no one knew of my accomplished background. Although it was somewhat refreshing to be unknown, I felt a sense of anxiety at the thought of being one nameless face among thousands. Would I succeed? Would I earn the respect of my colleagues and professors as I did in high school? Would any of my previous accomplishments matter in this unfamiliar new place? Will I be accepted for who I am? The questions absorbed me for days before my departure.

I chose my outfit with care on my first day of school. I wanted to feel fabulous and nothing can make me feel more fantastic than looking sharp. I wore stiletto black boots with black tights, a long, cashmere sweater dress and a to-die-for black trench coat. I added a leather belt with beautiful detailing and I tied one of my signature scarves to my book bag for an added touch of glamour.

I walked into calculus feeling extraordinary, until I met the gaze of another female student and that's when it happened. She was sitting in a chair close to the row I was approaching. Her chin was tilted slightly toward the ground, with her lips slightly parted; her eyes, wide, stared at me with disgust. She looked me up and down and then turned to her friend and, to my astonishment, started to whisper! I looked back, trying not to stare, but unable to help myself because I was confused by what was happening. Her friend gawked at me too and they both laughed. They were laughing at me based on my appearance! I obviously didn't fit in with the masses in university sweats and sneakers. Suddenly all those exuberant feelings I had felt earlier that morning disappeared and I was humiliated and hurt. In that instant, all the pride I had felt for my character and accomplishments in high school vanished in the face of ridicule. I looked back again; maybe I was wrong, maybe I had misinterpreted something. Not only did she bulge her eyes at me, she rolled them and raised one eyebrow too. Emotionally, I left class that day feeling a strange sense of displacement. I wondered how someone could deliberately judge me for no reason.

I still have no answer to that question, but that moment was a sign of things to come during my time at university. Unfortunately, the girl who had judged me so harshly was also a student in my recitation class. I was to have the pleasure of seeing her every day, not only in lecture, but also in the smaller recitation class. I continued to be myself, but with a strange sense of uncertainty when it came to fashion. Should I change my look? Mentally I laughed at the idea, but emotionally I was torn. I would blend in better if I looked like everyone else. When I dressed as myself, I stuck out and subjected myself to unnecessary mockery. I tried to brush off such thoughts, too busy with school work to be bothered with all that nonsense.

Ironically, studying for calculus was consuming most of my time. I participated in both lecture and recitation. I would work with other students in class on problems and we would help each other to reach the right answers. My hard work paid off when I received an A on my first midterm! More than 70% of the class had failed the exam. I was happy to have earned my score, but felt compelled to help others in my class do the same. When I received my exam in recitation, I turned to the other students I worked with and told them to speak to the professor. I, along with other students in the other recitations, would attend his office hours for extra help in understanding difficult problems. He would hint at problems that we should pay particular attention to in his office hour discussions. These difficult problems were conceptualized as new problems on the midterm, and all that extra time studying really helped me earn a high grade on the exam. To some students in recitation that day I suggested they meet with the professor to ensure that nothing was graded improperly and ask what they could do to avoid failing the class. All of a sudden, my old adversary turned around and darted her beady eyes at me. She rose from her chair and loudly shouted, "Well, if we all dressed up for class every day and went to speak to the professor, in private, then maybe we would, like, all get A's!" She shrilled in an odd attempt to mock me. "Ohhh Professor, I like don't understand these problems... Can you teach me?" I sat frozen in disbelief as she continued to make insidious remarks implying that I had compromised my integrity in exchange for a better grade.

I looked around to meet the stares of the male students who were gathered. Some of them laughed, while one favoured me with a look of sympathy before turning away. None of them voiced a word in my defense; in spite of the help I had given them with their homework. My cheeks burned red with embarrassment. I was accustomed to appreciation and respect from my peers. This malevolence was something I had never experienced before.

I remained silent for the rest of class; it felt like an age before the bell finally rang. I was angry and confused; I had an urgent need to speak with one of my closest confidantes, someone I could trust to boost my confidence. I called my sister as I stepped from the building.

"Hello, Jasmin! I was just thinking of you!" She exclaimed in a cheerful tone.

A warm teardrop streaked my cold face. "Hi," I murmured.

"What's wrong? Is everything ok?" She asked with concern.

"People in my class judge me! They don't know anything about me!" I said with anger. I related what had happened in class that day.

"All I wanted to do was help. I never expected to be insulted like that! I have worked so hard to earn good grades! She painted a picture of me that's the polar opposite of the truth. I dress the way I did in high school and everyone respected me there. I just don't understand!"

"Don't worry, Jasmin," my sister said a few moments later. "You're right, they don't know you, and even if they did know you, it doesn't matter what they think. All that matters is what you think of yourself! Eleanor Roosevelt said 'No one can make you feel inferior without your consent.' You are an original! I don't know anyone like you! You were meant to be exactly who you are. Don't ever change that. Your style is part of you, and you rock!" My sister enthusiastically exclaimed.

Her kind words were like a breath of fresh air. She reminded me that in life there are going to be people who will judge you harshly with little reason. Regardless of what people say, all that matters is what you think of yourself, and that you carry yourself in a respectable, graceful manner.

During the next recitation class I sat on the other side of the room. I continued to contribute to classroom discussions; I didn't let the negative, unjust comments get in my way. I was more determined than ever to do well in that class, and to do it in style; I continued to wear my most fashionable outfits. I am not sure whether that woman passed that class; many people failed. I, on the other hand, aced the final exam, achieving the highest score in the class. I earned my A, and I did it on my own fashionable terms. I was elated. Hard work earned that grade and I could not have been happier, or better dressed.

Throughout university I came across ignorant people who judged me based on my appearance. They would assume that I was shallow and unintelligent. I didn't fit in with the sea of students wearing sweatpants and pajamas to class, but I remained true to my chic self. Overall, university life was filled with opportunities to learn, grow, reinvent myself and thrive against the intimidation of unfamiliarity. I actively participated in different social settings and dared to be myself against what was considered the norm.

Of course, I met people along the way who shared the same passion and zest I have for style. We celebrated that rare connection we shared. Withstanding the negative judgments and rejections has made me more empathetic toward others and even more tolerant of the differences I enjoy seeing from person to person.

Coco Chanel once stated, "To be irreplaceable one must always be different." We will all face moments when we'll be judged by others who don't know who we are, where we come from or where we're heading. Don't let yourself be defined by what others think of you, whether it be good or bad; define yourself. Don't change because 'they' think you don't belong. You are a gift to the world and are meant to shine just the way you are.

Making It in High Heels

Juliana Vasquez Ruiz

I n Miami, my mother and her friends would often tell me stories about the hardships immigrants had to face in their new country. I was amused by the thought of people sleeping in their car, being lost for days because they didn't know the streets or being reduced to jobs that were beneath them because of a language barrier. Well, their stories may have had humor, but when I had to go through it myself, I realized that it wasn't very funny.

In January of 2005, when I was 17, I moved to Canada. I arrived with only one heavy suitcase, crammed with the warmest sweaters I had in my closet. Days later, I came to the realization that there was no turning back. But I had never in my life felt so alone and defenseless.

The Canadian family I was living with turned their back on me; in their eyes, teenagers are crazy and do crazy 'stuff.' They even had the nerve to accuse me of being a runaway. Their attitude forced me into a shelter; I had nowhere else to go. Conditions there were very poor, but at least it was warm. Life in a shelter makes you feel like there is no place in the world for you; like you were meant to fail. I felt that the staff pitied the residents there; particularly me, as the youngest woman.

In Toronto, I met up with a man I had known before. He took me out of my loneliness and boredom and I thought he was good for me. Too quickly, things got serious.

I remember that night. I waited in the bathroom, while he was in his room. I was worried; he was hoping. That night I felt like my dreams had been crushed. I was pregnant with his baby. I cried and hoped for a miracle. I cried because I was carrying his baby and felt I had to put my dreams on hold. I cried because I was living in a shelter, sharing a room with someone I didn't know. I had nothing for this baby, only my values; what kind of life was I going to give this child?

The days passed and I didn't know what to do. I knew I wanted to keep the baby. I just didn't know what else to do. I had a hard time telling my mother, despite the fact that she was so far from me. When I had finally told my family, the father proposed that we move in together. It seemed like the easiest solution.

By the day of the lease signing, I was still having doubts about us moving in together. We were in his car when I told him I wasn't ready to move in with him. His response was unexpected; he started blaming me, screaming hysterically that I was being unreasonable. Because of me, he told me, he had told his parents about my pregnancy and that he was moving out. He made me feel responsible me for the shame he would feel by going back home to tell them that he wasn't moving anymore; his pride was more hurt than he was. We were both under pressure and screaming, the next thing I knew, he was pushing me and holding me. I wanted to get out of the car, so I fought back. I scratched his arms and got away; I started walking 'home.' But I had no idea were my home was; I was lost. He got out of the car, pushed me in and we talked things through. I felt so desperate and helpless that I went through with the signing of the lease.

In April 2005, I set up house with the father of my child. The first couple of months were hectic. Throughout my pregnancy, I was running from one place to the other, going to doctor's appointments, ultrasounds, blood work and tests for the baby. Being pregnant had become a complex adjustment in my life. I had to learn to deal with morning sickness, back pain, cravings and healthy eating among other things. I know now that it's good to exercise; it really helps during labor. However, during my pregnancy, I wouldn't even sweep the floor for fear that the baby would be born too early.

Every day I would pretend to be happy in front of other people; we acted as if we were the happiest couple in the world. At home, it was more like an inferno. We would argue about everything. I hated to be alone, but I hated to be with my man, as well. In the beginning, our arguments were no more than a loud exchange of opinions, but later it became name-calling insults and then, abuse. My home had become my prison.

He started insulting me in every way he could. He told me how ugly I was, that he was too good for me and could easily find someone better. When I arrived in Canada, I was a confident young woman, determined to succeed. After living with this man for a couple of months, I had low self-esteem, no confidence in myself and my personality was completely subject to his whims. His abusive behavior escalated every day; it eventually became physical.

On one occasion, we were getting ready to go out. As usual, we started to argue but this argument was different from the others; he kept pestering me and trying to hug and kiss me, even though I had told him to leave me alone. To him, I was a complete joke; it was so upsetting. He made me feel disgusting, like I didn't matter. Suddenly, he grabbed both of my feet and dragged me across the floor, setting me on the couch. He looked at me with so much hatred and slapped my face. I was angry; but I felt so weak that I started to cry. The slap did not hurt me as much as the obvious lack of respect. It hurt because I was always taught that men do not touch women in that way. Why did he need to hit me? I still can't understand it. What I do understand is that with that slap he took what little pride that I had left; he destroyed my self-respect.

I was packing my bag to go to a friend's for the night before realized that what he had done was wrong. He begged my forgiveness and unfortunately, I believed him. I stayed, but nothing changed; things only got worse.

At this time, I enrolled in a school for young women like myself, either pregnant or with a baby. I was trying to finish high school and get into university. The school I attended was meant to help young women, but the classes where pretty basic and none would earn me a credit to enter university. If I had said anything about the abusive state of my home life, the Children's Aid Society would have been called and that would have created even more problems.

By the time my daughter was born, my decision-making skills were gone; he was making most of my decisions for me. I wanted to tie him to his responsibility, so I thought it was best to put his name on the birth certificate. Instead, of making him more responsible, however, I just put myself more under his control.

Valentina, my daughter, was four months-old when I decided to leave him for good. It took a lot of strength, but after he pushed me while holding the baby, I knew I had to get out. I kept coming back, though; I was so afraid of my daughter growing up without a father.

In the summer of 2006, I met Andrea page, owner of FITMOM. She had come to my school to give a Mommy Motivator exercise seminar. It was probably one of the best courses I've ever taken. Andrea not only got me back into shape with her tough exercise routines, she also became my best friend, my sister and only family here in Canada. I owe so much to her. She gave me back my sense of worth. Andrea stood up for me when the world seemed to go wrong.

On Christmas Eve, 2006, he came to my apartment and we had one of our typical 'talks' that always went the same way; I would be crying in a corner while he insulted me. That night I ran to Andrea and swore to myself that it would be the last time. Nevertheless, he was back on New Years' Eve, although I had told him never to come back to my house again.

This time was different, though; I was not going to let him push me around or hit me anymore. He ended up choking me and the next day I went to the nearest police station and had him charged. The charge was domestic violence even though we didn't live together because we had a baby.

For six months, he couldn't even see Valentina. I was stress free and focused on myself and my daughter during that time. Foolishly, I thought that getting custody of her would be easy, since he was facing charges, had been separated from my daughter for so long and had never paid child support. Well, it's been seven months since I hired a lawyer and I'm still trying to get full custody. If only I hadn't listed him as the father on the birth certificate; if only. In my journey, however, I have learned that to concentrate my energy on negatives and 'if onlys' is a waste.

My baby's father used to always scream at me that opportunities don't fall from the sky; I was a dreamer if I thought that. As a matter of fact, I do believe that when a person is ready to believe in miracles, they can happen. Until that miracle happens, I struggle daily with an internal battle. I fight for my sense of self worth and struggle against the negative feelings he injected in me.

Through it all, one constant keeps me grounded; my daughter. She has helped me keep standing and has given me strength when it all seems to be gone. Also my dream of a career in chemical engineering has helped me look to the future when it all seems to be foggy. It is important to feel successful in order to be successful

Even when my self-esteem was at its lowest and I didn't believe in myself, I still had dreams and hopes for my future. Andrea taught me to turn those dreams into goals. Who else can change and reshape my future? No one but myself. I know I will be successful and I am proud to look back and say that I, Juliana Vasquez, fought a battle against me and the winner was me. I once read to "aim for the stars to get to the sky."

Kalifi Moon Ferretti-Gallon

My name is Kalifi Moon Ferretti-Gallon and I live in Montreal. In spite of my elaborate and exotic name, I am a 4th generation North American who grew up in a typical, middle-class neighbourhood. Perhaps the only exotic thing about me is my unruly blonde hair. I have spent a lot of time explaining the contrast of my Caucasian appearance to my African name. My name is a tribute to the meeting and subsequent partnership of my parents. Budding environmental activists, they met in Kenya and agree.that the coastal area of Kilifi is where the romance began.

Every time I explain the origins of my name, and these have been countless, I am reminded of who my parents were and what they stood for. My name and its meaning have imbued me with the spirit of my parents' principals. A few years ago, I almost lost that spirit. One of the biggest inspirations in my life, and my great mentor, my father, died. And, for a while, a big part of my inspiration to make the world a better place died along with him.

As I mentioned, my upbringing was fairly typical; my family consists of two parents, a sister, two cats and a dog. I struggled with the usual high school pressures and pangs of adolescence. At fifteen, I was in the middle of high school and life was as good as it can be for a teenage girl. I had good friends, a great family and I was active in school groups and sports. Like most girls, I was preoccupied with my wardrobe and the opposite sex, but my perspective on the world was changing and growing. Our parents felt it was important to broaden our scope through traveling, which we did often. We had just returned from a trip to Mexico when my parents sat my sister and myself down and told us that Dad had cancer. After being assured that proper precautions were being taken and being pelted with numerous success stories, we weren't too fussed and went on our merry way. One year passed, then the next. We were riding a bright steed of hope, and every set back, every relapse, was only a glitch on the road to recovery.

After three years of becoming frighteningly familiar with colon cancer, and witnessing the physical decay of my father, I realized that things were not turning out as we had hoped. A strange new reality was settling in; the idea of life without my father. The panic that began to set in was in direct proportion to the bond I had with my dad. I knew of friends who had had contentious relationships with their fathers, so I was aware of how lucky I was; I was able to confide in my father; I told him everything. He knew about my heartbreaks, my teen angst charged with body image and other social stresses. For all my questions, Dad had answers, and comfort. He made sure that everything he knew about the topic in question was explained. He was my primary resource on life.

By the spring of 2003, everyone was resigned to the fact that Dad's resistance to the cancer was fading; everyone but me. My dad had even decided (as so many others have) that the cure was worse than the disease; he had given up on a trial therapy in California to come back and breathe his last in Montreal, surrounded by his family. I would have given anything to not be part of the family. I just wasn't ready to say goodbye.

I had to assume the leading role of the family. My mum had taken on a new job as Environmental Consultant Leader in a well known international organization and had no choice but to commute to and from DC during the last months of Dad's life. Those months were punctuated with tooth decay, colostomy leaks, swollen feet, frequent trips to hospital and house guests. I rarely dwell on that period in my life; much of April, May and June of 2003 is remembered with a shapeless sense of horror. A few days after my dad received the Canadian Citation of Lifetime Achievement, he died.

His death was felt strongly by everyone in our family and coloured every aspect of our lives. My academic, social and family lives all felt jeopardized. As I became more and more preoccupied, adjusting to a world without Dad and desperately trying to look forward to a different future, I also shouldered the responsibility of overseeing my dad's business affairs. Consequently, my grades suffered and I felt more and more alienated from my circle of friends. All of this was happening while my mum was beginning her new job in Washington DC. My whole family was preparing for our first move in ten years; I was preparing for the dissolution of my family as I had come to know it.

In the months following my father's death, I thought I held it together pretty well. At times, it was difficult, but I began to understand and appreciate the fragility of life. I was in the throes of new independence, with my first apartment. I was soldiering through my third term in university, and presenting an unruffled face for my friends' benefit and an attempt for a semblance of normalcy. I thought I could view the concept of grief as outdated, and that I could exempt myself. However, my grief manifested itself in episodes of hyperventilation, and bouts of both insomnia and extreme oversleeping. Eventually, I began to withdraw completely; both from school and my friends.

Without understanding the far reaching effects of my disillusionment, and not wanting to distress my family in DC, I kept things to myself. I was sure that notifying my mum of my new situation would result in an immediate extraction from Montreal to DC; I wasn't ready to give up my new and exciting freedom. Since normal wasn't working for me, I decided to try filling my life with as much fun as possible, fighting the days of thoughtful solitude with new relationships; a more exciting peer group, and substance abuse.

The following years were fraught with attempts at escapism, but in the end, escape cannot prepare you for the ultimate loss. When you realize that the goals of your teens may change, all is not lost. Life is a dance; you have to match your steps to the beat.

Kate Kelton

There were bits of my father's ashes stuck under my fingernails the night I scattered him from the edge of a cliff on the Great Canadian Shield. I'd dug for a handful of the gritty rubble that was all that was tangibly left of my father and the wind had picked it up. Technically, I'd killed my dad, Joe; but I knew it was exactly what he wanted. I would come to realize I couldn't shake him; little bits clung to me, like his ashes under my nails. I wasn't necessarily wearing heels, but I know this event propelled me more than any other. My father was seventy when he died. I was twenty-one.

I woke up on Boxing Day and went down to the pool without Joe because, as he was wont to do, that morning he had robustly announced that he was constipated. He just wanted to be left alone to smoke his pipe on the john in peace. I came back when he still hadn't joined me, to find him in tears, and excruciating pain, shivering half-naked on the toilet. He couldn't find the strength to stand, so I helped him and got him into an ambulance; completely mystified by what was wrong.

It would be ten hours before I learned that an aneurysm had burst next to his kidney. A doctor finally emerged with the news that he was in a coma. They had tried to replace the stretch of ruptured vein rendered useless after the aneurysm burst but because of its close proximity to the kidney, they couldn't use readily available artificial material; the organ would reject it.

Unfortunately, my father had had his varicose veins removed years before when the swelling started preventing him from being able to walk up a flight of stairs; they likely had to cut right along the scars left on his calves. By this point, Joe had been under for hours. After a reaction to the anesthesia, they pronounced him brain dead. The best prognosis had him hooked up to a machine for the rest of his life; this was the very nightmare existence my father had specifically taken steps to avoid in his living will.

But that living will was written in Canada and we were in Florida, where North America's old come to die; apparently their young come to sue, shortly thereafter. They could not 'unplug him', as per his request, because his living will wasn't recognized as a legally binding document. After three days of trying to figure out a way around it, the doctors managed to issue a 'do not resuscitate' order on his chart, should any further complication arise.

They told me he was brain dead, but he'd been thrashing about violently in his coma, brow furrowed and etched in deep anger. In a crazed display of futile rage, he'd attempt to lift himself out of his prone position, fists pumping. I leaned in close to his ear, calmly reassuring him,

"Don't worry, Daddy. We know what you want and we're doing everything we can to make it happen."

He would immediately stop his fighting. His eyebrows would shoot up, as did the outer corners of his mouth and he would peacefully sink back into his pillow. He had heard me, and he wanted me to know he had heard me.

A day later his heart stopped and, as promised, they did not restart it. I held his big square hand for half an hour, having arrived ten minutes and a missed phone call after it happened. I knew. I watched the colour drain out from his face; even his hands were ashen. He wasn't cold, though. I was surprised that it felt like his hands and face were getting warmer.

Outside the hospital, I saw the sun come out for the first time during my two-week vacation. Joe had just taught me how to drive stick shift. Now it was my car. Driving to a stretch of swampland behind our apartment complex, I sat on a little red wooden bridge that spanned the bit of glassy sludge in the middle of an acre of massive cypress trees. We used to have a place by the ocean, years ago, but this is where I had once seen a wild Manatee floating by. I hoped I'd see its sweet, seal-like muzzle sniffing the air, just one more time.

Five days ago, we'd celebrated Christmas, as Czechs do, on the 24th of December. After our feast for two, during which he spontaneously taught me how to make sautéed, garlic-buttered shrimp over toast, we exchanged presents. Then we got drunk together for the first and last time of our lives, talking late into the night. He told me tales of visiting the Art Gallery of Ontario many years ago with a friend; they'd pack rye bread sandwiches with margarine, raw onions, celery salt, and hashish and run around looking at all the Rothkos until their buzz wore off.

Joe's mother lived to be 99 years old. Alzheimer's meant I never knew her able to tell the difference between my sister's perm and the poodle, but she was a licensed pilot whose father had designed Prague's Central Train Station. After she married George, an engineer, my father was born

August 1, 1925. After the war, the Communists swept in, taking everything, and my ancestors fled the country.

As a young boy, Joe's migraines were blinding enough to warrant heavy adult doses of archaic pain medication. Just before graduating from University of Toronto's School of Architecture, the first of my father's kidneys completely petrified due to the strain; kidneys were never his strong point. He passed so many kidney stones that his urethra collapsed entirely and he became the first Canadian ever to have an operation that replaced his shattered urethra with a piece of his intestine. He was given two years to live post-op, but he wore that 18-inch scar down his gut for more then four decades afterwards. He only occasionally quibbled about the resultant lopsided belly-button.

Joe saw his life as icing on the cake, after being given two years to live before he'd even hit thirty. He saw only the good in his life. When he married, Vera had come to Canada to recover from five years in several concentration camps, Poland and Austria's worst, Auschwitz and Bergen-Belsen included. I cannot imagine what she must have witnessed, but I am sure it was integral to why Joe saw himself as blessed to have known and loved someone so strong. She'd suffered a miscarriage for every child born healthy, and then at fourteen, one of her girls fell into an inexplicable coma. When she woke up, her short-term memory was damaged from encephalitis, and she was epileptic. Vera then fell ill too.

Vera and my sisters Ann, Jane and Mary would spend every summer at the cottage; known simply as 'there'. Standing on the dock, you could see a tree that jutted out at a 90 degree angle over the lake; it had been slowly dying for years by the time I saw it, each year leaving a smaller and smaller tip of evergreen as the rest of the branches lay bare. I looked out at it the last time we closed the cottage for the winter, and I just knew that when it finally died, so would my father. Sure enough, on our first trip up in the spring after Dad died, it was completely barren. We scattered his ashes from the same cliff that Vera and his parents had been scattered from.

That cottage was his cedar love child. There were no right angles in the floor plan and Joe owned the land for over a year before putting pen to paper to begin designing the building. Driving up most weekends, he'd watch where the sun fell throughout the day and the seasons, measuring arcs and angles to determine the best possible play of light and colour over the cedar walls. We watched many lightning storms sweep over the lake in that perfect viewing theatre. The living room's massive ebony bulkheads, ribbed the vaulted ceiling like the hull of a ship. The beams and planks were splattered with the fingerprints of workers. Most clients didn't appreciate fingerprints all over their ceilings as the oil in their hands aged and turned black over time. My dad never did fall into any category beginning with the phrase 'most people', though.

Joe designed the flagship McDonalds in Toronto, opposite the ROM's Crystal entrance on Bloor Street. He got the account because George A. Cohon, the man who had brought the chain to Canada, was so thrilled with the house and country chalet my father had built for him. I always loved that my dad managed to sneak in enough space for a sunken garden with a cherry blossom tree ... at a McDonalds.

In 1980 on the day John Lennon was shot, my parents fell in love in Florida. I remember sitting with them in the garage, listening to the radio in the car for half an hour after returning home from dinner. We could smell Boca Raton's ocean air while we listened to news reports, interspersed with songs from Lennon's new album. Joe and my mom were crying and holding hands. When my mom and I flew back to our little apartment in Hamburg, Germany, Joe came with us. I presided over a makeshift ceremony at our little kitchen table with flowers and tinfoil rings, and married them before they ever stepped into a courthouse.

Four years before he died, Joe suffered a stroke that led to a harrowing ten weeks in hospital. His remaining kidney petrified, necessitating dialysis, and his heart needed a pace-maker. During the operation, his lungs collapsed and nary a breath nor a bite of food was possible without additional tubing. He took ten, twelve pills a day; it seemed at times that he was indestructible.

He fell asleep behind the wheel while driving south, flipped his car and spun out in a ditch, and walked away with nothing but a scratch. He started smoking at the age of nine, but was spared lung cancer; although he smoked five packs of filter-less Gauloises a day, until he switched to a pipe in his forties. The only bad habit he regretted was his lifelong love of tanning in his skivvies. It seemed like every other week another cancerous mole had to be lased off. Now I live in California and make sport of dodging direct sunlight; he'd be laughing.

Four months before he died, I came home to realize I had forgotten to get my dad a birthday present and in twenty minutes, we were leaving to celebrate his birthday over dinner. In a panic, I grabbed a photo of him smoking his pipe in front of the fireplace at the cottage. I grabbed a piece of Bristol board I'd salvaged from a design class with a pool of bright red spilled ink where I began etching out his face and glasses from the photo. It's still the best painting I've ever done; he loved it and thought the red face signified the warmth from the fire.

Two months before he died, I followed my dad to the hospital with a Bell & Howell 16mm camera and some sound equipment. I shot my documentary assignment on how my dad got his blood cleaned every other day. Thankfully, it wasn't one of those days in the dialysis wing where the IV tubes got all tangled up and blood spurted all over the walls. That drama is rare, albeit creepy. He just spent most of his time, when he wasn't pestering nurses, listening to the classical music he loved, as his father had before him. I shot a completely unfair, clichéd long shot of him walking down a dark hallway that just happened to end in a bright light. We laughed about it while we shot it, but I remember a nurse saying that there are those families who talk about it before it happens, and there are those families who don't; it's the families that don't that suffer more when the time comes.

A month before he died, I discovered that the same friend he toured the Art Gallery with all those years ago was my favourite philosophy professor at school. I had been telling Joe about his lectures since September, but it was my professor who made the connection during attendance the first time he saw my last name.

"Kelton? Kelton! Do you know an old barfly named Joe Kelton?"

"That's my papa." I replied with a weak smile, then a big laugh.

He immediately apologized. He hadn't seen him in years, but Joe was pretty much the reason he was now teaching philosophy. Joe had been like a father to him, in many ways. Having chosen Joe as my own father as well, I completely understood. We had a ball when my father ambled into class with his pipe and cane, to sit in on a lecture on his way to dialysis.

I lived with Joe for fifteen years. Moving to Los Angeles to further my acting career would not have been possible without knowing this man's journey. It's incredibly calming to put things into perspective. I know precious few events will ever be as harrowing or frightening as losing him. No big audition, no important director, nor any first day on set will ever compare to the pain of my loss. Keeping the faith in the face of the rejection this industry is famous for, has proven much easier knowing he's out there protecting me; in surprisingly tangible ways.

The first night that I was back in the apartment we shared in Toronto, a storm raged outside. We used to watch from the balcony when a storm hit; just stop whatever we were doing and go outside; my dad and I had done it many times. We lived on the thirty-second floor of Palace Pier, a 46-storey building by the lake in a suburb of Toronto. I loved it when our building got caught in a cloud; from floor to ceiling the windows would be nothing but white outside. When the fog broke, other bits of buildings would float into view like ghost ships.

Tonight was just the thick, pea soup of night with orange city lights glowing below. I stood on the balcony looking out at the lake on my left;

the city stretched out to the north past the airport on my right. Directly before me stood the odd contrast of a cookie factory across the highway from a sewage treatment plant; thankfully, in the fight for our nostrils, the cesspools mostly lost out to fresh-baked goods.

There were three distinct sets of lightning slicing open the sky that night. The first was the closest; the bolt that had brought me outside. Running parallel to our building, it felt like I could have reached out and touched it. I'd never seen lightning so close. It was shocking. It remained lit up for so long that I had time to tilt my head back to see its tip erupt in front of the floors above me; then time to bow my head down again to see it strike the cookie factory below. I looked it up and down, wondering when it would disappear again. The second batch of lightning, on the northern horizon, consisted of long horizontal flashes, sequentially riding along the skyline. They lit up entire cloud formations, suddenly making it day. No discernable bolts of lightning, just pure light; like flipping a light switch. Night, day, day, night; it seemed like a magic trick. I suddenly laughed. Then, occasionally, a third smattering of lightning would hit the part of the lake I could see to the south. They would always start as a single bolt, but would invariably split on the water and scramble across the surface of the lake, like some crazed many-fingered claw.

At some point I realized that the bolt that was the closest was the 'yes', the flashes that kept tweaking night into day along the horizon was the laughter, and the claw over the lake was the 'no'. I had a forty-five minute conversation with my father through lightning that night.

I'm at a loss for the specific words used, but I know that during our talk I probably went through every stage of grief: denial; anger; bargaining; depression; acceptance. I know I probably railed,

"Why did you leave me?" or, "How could you go?' at some point. I know I was questioning my direction in just about every avenue of my life. I know that every time I asked his advice, he answered. Whatever I suddenly thought, said out loud, or screamed out into the night, was answered with a yes, a no, a little or a lot of laughter, or a combination of all of the above. I couldn't deny it. It was happening.

I know that he answered promptly and incredibly forcefully at times, willing me to listen. At other times, for the tougher, deeper questions, the pauses between question and answer seemed appropriately delayed, whether due to thought, tenderness or hesitancy. I couldn't rail against him for that. He spoke in death as in life.

I know that he got aggravated with a particularly fearful train of thought I jumped on, lambasting me with a sudden lash of claws over the lake to snap me out of it. I think at some point I just tried to make a deal with myself that if this was really happening, if they really never leave you, then what would happen if you ignored them? I found I couldn't bargain my way out.

I know that he was frustrated at only having two words at his disposal; he wanted to tell me more. Especially about what happens ... after. It struck me how sad it was to limit such a great communicator to two syllables, even if he had an entire sky to play with. I knew I could never hug him, smell him or look at him again. I felt very small, very still.

We shared some simple peaceful moments where nothing was said at all. Then he'd laugh and I knew he was there. I knew then that he would always be with me. There was a story I'd heard, through some indirect source growing up as an agnostic kid, a lovely turn of phrase about footsteps and Jesus and being carried; maybe there was something to it. The footsteps with me just happen to be a specific pair of size nine Birkenstocks, walking alongside my size seven flip-flops.

Understandably, this was all a little heady and unsettling. I told Joe that I was going back inside, then the rain started. I closed the balcony door, knowing that the last big bolt of light that hit the cookie factory agreed that it was late and that I'd catch my death of cold if I didn't get inside; it was the dead of winter. Shortly after, the lightning stopped.

I know I could have imagined it all, but I find it impossible to reconcile the accuracy of each answer and the timing with mere coincidence. I know what he would say yes to, no to, laugh at; we were best friends. It wasn't as though I was talking to just anyone, I was talking specifically to him. Not a God by any stretch of the imagination, but a damn good man who amazed and inspired anyone who ever met him.

Time really does solve so much more then we give it credit for. In 2005 I was packing my car for the four-day drive to Los Angeles and I wondered if I was insane to attempt to haul everything I owned across the desert, in the middle of the heat wave that had hit that summer. I worried that I should have just paid to have everything insured and shipped there instead. The first night that my friend Julia and I arrived at our hotel after our long day's drive, we found out a plane had been downed in a ravine by Pearson International Airport during a vicious thunderstorm; it was the day after my father's birthday. Julia and I couldn't believe it, but I didn't mention my dad's affinity to communicating with me through lightning until the next night.

Many have described the four-day drive from Toronto to Los Angeles as half thrilling and half mind-numbingly dull. The two days before arriving in Los Angeles are filled with awe-inspiring vistas of mountains and blinding deserts and Las Vegas, but the first two days are flatlands with fields of wheat as far as the eye can see. It was toward the end of the second day when Julia and I felt like we were going to lose our minds; by the time the sun set, it had become clear how uncomfortable sitting in a car for days on end can be.

Then, the same storm-system that had downed the plane over Toronto reached us near the Iowa-Nebraska border. We were an hour out from where we'd planned to spend the night and the sky around the car became an insane light-show all of a sudden. Lightning bolts were practically striking in time with the music, in a full circle around the car. Swirling about, trying to catch them all, we were giddy with laughter. I told Julia about my dad. She sat quietly for a second as the lightning hushed. Then, a huge bolt cracked down right in front of us; instead of finding ground like all the others had, it inexplicably bowed back up to the sky instead, in a huge half-circling arc. Julia, stunned, looked at me and said,

"Oh look. Your dad's smiling at us."

Making It in High Heels

Katrina Hadden

Life throws us obstacles and challenges everyday. Some people overcome their obstacles and come out wiser, others come out weaker and there are those who don't make it at all. There's a reason I'm still here, stronger then ever before.

"Honey, wake up. We're leaving now; get your stuff together and be out in the car in five minutes." Where now? I thought to myself; just when things started to feel right with my new friends and school, it was time to leave again. There wasn't time to say goodbye to my friends and teachers or the boy I had a crush on. That was the story of my life growing up; never knowing where I would be staying or what school I would be attending. Along with my mom and my brother, I spent much of my childhood moving back and forth from city to city; I was always the new kid in school. It was hard for me to make close friends because I knew there was always a chance I'd be leaving soon, without being able to say goodbye.

My dad left when I was four years old. I don't remember him very well during my childhood years, but I do remember the night he left us. I was in my room and I could hear my mom and dad fighting on the other side of my door. My baby brother was trying to see what was going on and I covered his ears so he couldn't hear them arguing. The image remains clear in my mind; I'll never forget that evening. I woke up the next morning feeling a sense of abandonment. What had I done wrong? I must have done something wrong....

My elementary school years were difficult. I was always the tallest kid in the class; I felt like a shy and awkward giant. Grade four was a particularly difficult year. I was living with my grandma because my mom was sick and couldn't care for us on her own. I was petrified to go to school because everyday I had to walk by the older kids' classroom to get to my class and everyday they would yell out,

"Hey, Evil Eyes, where are you going?"

"Green giant,"

"Big Bird!"

Being bullied was such a nightmare! To this day, I fear that playground and avoid it. I think that experience caused me to create an internal wall to shut myself off from the world.

In addition to dealing with the usual girls' issues, I was dealing with something at home that nobody, myself included, understood very well. My mother was struggling with high anxiety and paranoid schizophrenia. I didn't really understand her condition; I just knew that she wasn't feeling well very often. It's hard to understand why sometimes the kindest people get hit with the worst luck and suffer the greatest hardships. My mother is the most loving person. She always thinks of others and wants to help, particularly those less fortunate. My mother taught my brother and I to give generously.

One summer, Mom stayed in bed for weeks while my grandmother took care of us. I remember her terrible withdrawal symptoms; head pressure, paranoia, severe weight loss and an inability to distinguish between fiction and reality. She was convinced that people were deliberately making her sick. One day, Mom was found walking in the middle of the street, narrowly being missed by all the cars, she was in a trance; she thought someone was hypnotizing her. On another day, we were driving down the street and she suddenly increased her speed and began running stop signs, going 180 km an hour because the pressures had become too much for her to handle. My uncles tried to take me away from her by putting her in a mental institution. My family didn't understand her condition and kicked us out of my grandmother's house. We ended up in a woman's shelter for a time. I felt like my schoolmates and my family were against me. It was hard to take in, but I kept my spirits high and continued to have faith that someday my mom would feel better and we'd have a place to call home. I never gave up that dream.

The only person that understood what we were going through was my grandfather. He too struggled with the pressures, but in silence. He passed away ten years ago and I miss his quiet strength. He loved the music of the piano. He would leave me a few dollars by the side of the piano so I would play for him. He loved Beethoven and the classics, but I would compose music for him, as well. I have continued to compose music to this day, in the hopes that my music will soothe those who need it.

In high school, I was involved in many activities, mainly to keep myself occupied and to make new friends. I was the 'most valuable player' of my high school basketball team and nominated 'athlete of the week' from the summer camps; I was on the honour role and was chosen to participate in various leadership camps.

One of my personal highlights of high school was when I scored the two winning points to land the National Ontario Basketball Championship. Right after we won the game, I looked up in the crowd to find my mom beaming at me with pride. I knew she hadn't been feeling well that day, but she had pushed herself to come out to support me. I spent years playing basketball and training; I wanted to continue to play at the university level. During my senior year, I was scrimmaging during a practice and something popped in my left knee. I couldn't play anymore; I knew I was out for the rest of the season. I couldn't believe it. I had invested a lot of time and energy into basketball and now my dream was shattered. I had surgery a few months later and knew I wouldn't be playing again.

Graduation day arrived and I was left to ponder what I would do with my life; what my next step would be. My mom was unable to attend my ceremony because she was ill. Luckily, my brother was there with me; I knew all my classmates would be with their families and I didn't want to be there alone. When they called my name, I made my way up to receive my diploma while thinking,

"I made it this far, I've endured so many hardships and obstacles, so much pain and happiness, what's next?"

University was next, a new adventure and a fresh start. But I was still struggling with my own identity; deciding what to major in was definitely a challenge. I had no firm ideas and switched majors five times. My indecisiveness came to a head during second year. I was sitting in class and suddenly decided that I couldn't continue with university; it didn't feel right. I was lost.

I bought a ticket to Australia and left for a couple of months. I landed in Sydney and had to figure out where I was sleeping that night; I hadn't planned that far; just kind of picked up and left. Traveling for a few months opened my eyes and helped me gain a new perspective on life, love, family and enjoying the moment.

For women, the teens and early 20`s aren't easy. We're faced with self esteem issues, pressures from relationships and budding career issues. I had always worked hard in everything I did, including going from a size 18 to a size eight. For years, I was constantly on yoyo diets and using food as my source of comfort. When I returned from Australia, I had skyrocketed to 220 lbs., my heaviest weight yet. I would walk the streets looking for sweets; as if I were using food to fill a void. Instead, I felt awful; I had no energy and I felt bloated and unattractive.

I decided I needed a lifestyle change and I began exercising regularly. I motivated myself to stick to a routine and protein shakes to lose weight and get fit. Working at a gym made it easier because I could work out on my lunch breaks. I had dropped down to 160 lbs. and people were noticing the change. I kept up the same routine because it felt good getting the attention, but the weight wasn't coming off anymore; I had reached a plateau. I remember having a cousin who struggled with bulimia and thinking, there is no way I could ever do that, it's just not healthy. But, one day it happened. I was overwhelmed by the compliments and stressed that I wouldn't be able to keep the weight off after eating a whole pizza and I self-induced vomiting. I felt so good afterward; my stress was gone. I thought that it would be a one-time occurrence, but two years later, bulimia had taken over my life. I was living a double life and nobody knew. It was like a game; I had to find a place to vomit without anyone finding out, I was constantly making excuses to go to the washroom or leave the room to empty the food. Shame made me secretive. I couldn't let my mom know because she had worked hard to stay sane and I didn't want to add to the problems she was already dealing with. I continued to live with the secret. I graduated from university and struck out on my own again, not knowing what was ahead of me.

My 5`10" frame caught the attention of model scouts. I've always loved being on camera and everybody kept telling me I should be a model so I decided to audition for a local agency and they took me on. I was ecstatic!! But I was still hiding the secret of my bulimia. I managed to book print campaigns with local designers, runway shows, films and commercials.

In time, I realized that I wasn't happy making excuses after meals to void my food; it was draining my energy and soul to continue with the lies. I decided to take a nutrition and wellness specialist course to learn more about eating and digestion and the human body. One day, the lecture was on eating disorders and the teacher asked if we knew anyone who had one. Nobody said a word, but I felt like I couldn't sit there silently. My heart pounding fast, I raised my hand. With the tears rolling down my cheeks, I stood up and said,

"I had one, I was bulimic." I have been on rollercoasters and have had scares in my life, but that moment was the scariest one for me. I used the past tense when I confessed because I decided I wasn't going to hurt myself anymore; it was time to love myself and help others as well.

Now, I'm 5`10" and I weigh 160 lbs. I continue to model and act and have been busy shooting commercials and films. I am a spokesperson for an eating disorder organization in Ottawa, a Nutrition and Wellness Specialist, Personal Trainer and mentor. I've decided to use my experiences to help others. I want to continue making a difference in people's lives. I continue to play the piano and use music as a form of therapy. There is still research needed for people suffering with illnesses like my mother. I have faith that she will be better. I'm not a movie star or famous, but maybe one day I will be; never limit yourself and keep dreaming!! Life is beautiful and so are you!

Kim Angeles

Time is a funny thing. It can heal and ease your pain or it can do the opposite and totally destroy you. I have experienced both the gift of time and its wrath. I had a great childhood and always thought life would run smoothly. Things didn't change all at once; the tragedy that was looming above my family's home gathered slowly.

My mom was friends with everyone in the neighbourhood and my father was a man that all looked up to. He was a successful graphic designer and a very talented artist. Both my parents were very loving and cared deeply for me and my two sisters. No one could have foreseen that things would take a wrong turn. My sisters and I were very close and believed that everything in our lives would come together as we were growing up. We were different girls with different goals. At fourteen, I was unsure about my life goals, but since I was a little girl, I've enjoyed cosmetology and dressing up. My older sister wanted to be a lawyer and my younger sister wanted to be a dentist. We were all set on achieving our goals. My first year in high school was difficult; I had trouble making new friends, so I stuck with the friends I had in middle school. As time progressed, however, my grades gradually started to slip and the friends I thought I had turned against me. This discouraged me from continuing my high school career; I was content to stay home. Instead of disciplining me, my mother condoned my decision because she didn't have the heart to see her daughter become a victim of bullying in the school system. Although my mother had good intentions, the result was that I became a high school drop out at the age of sixteen.

Almost a year-and-a-half later, my life consisted of eating, sleeping and watching television. At first, I was living a fun and carefree life. However, I started feeling as though I had no purpose and no goal to follow. A month later, I enrolled in an adult school because my previous school wouldn't accept me back. The new school was easier because it was only four hours a day and I would get six credits in four months. After two months of hard work, I began regaining confidence and was working hard to complete my required credits. Everything was going well, but things took a turn for the worse.

The family that was renting the basement of our bungalow moved out and my parents decided to move in. They got heavily involved in music and starting receiving strange visitors until the wee hours of the morning. My dad wasn't able to juggle work and partying, so he started missing work and soon he just stopped showing up for work at all, which left his boss no choice but to let him go. My sisters and I started taking care of each other. Basically, my parents had become strangers to us and we saw very little of them during the day.

Before long, the music was getting louder and the daily parties were lasting until four in the morning. My older sister was getting really irritated because she had to go to school in morning and to work at night. None of us were getting any sleep. We were becoming very suspicious and didn't quite know what to say to our parents. I mean, how were children to ask their parents to stop partying? I didn't want to approach my father because he had a really bad temper, so my little sister and I decided to confront our mother about the situation. Mom simply replied casually that everything was fine; as if she didn't take us seriously. I definitely knew something was going on. I was doing laundry downstairs one day and I came across a little baggy with white powder in it. I knew it couldn't be good, so I flushed it down the toilet and told my older sister as soon as she came in from work. She was furious and confronted my parents and their friends, but they just laughed at us and continued to play their music. My sister told me to always keep the door between floors locked and not to let them upstairs anymore.

A few weeks later, I was watching television and my older sister had just come home. As she stepped from the room, something compelled me to look out the window. I saw nine heavily armed police officers swarming out of a black minivan and two navy blue sedans. They ran up the stairs and were screaming that they were the drug squad and they had a search warrant; they just kept repeating it over and over again. I was frozen in panic; I couldn't move. I saw five men run downstairs, trying to get into the basement, but my mom had the door locked. I heard them yelling and breaking the door down. I watched them take my mom down as she tried to escape. Never in my life could I have imagined my mom trying to get away from the cops, let alone my parents being in handcuffs.

The SWAT team had us all sit in the living room while the Commanding Officer took down our information and took pictures of our faces. He explained to us that they had a search warrant for the house and an arrest warrant for my dad. My mind went blank and tears just flowed. My dad was dismayed by what his children were being put through. I looked at my older sister and was surprised at how calm she was.

I believe this was a watershed moment in my life. I had thought dropping out of school and going back was the turning point, but this incident would always stick to my heart and will make me push forward for a better life. I had never felt so accused before in my life. The cops are supposed to be there to protect you, but on that day, I was treated like a criminal, although I was clearly a victim of my parents' mistakes. It was on that day that I realized I would value my family and remain loyal to them, no matter what.

Those cops were brutal. They weren't there just to make arrests, they also wanted to find anything that would incriminate my parents. Never mind that these two people they had arrested had a family, or that their three daughters were freaked out of their minds because of what was happening with their parents. At that moment, I felt so much animosity toward those cops and their goal to bring my parents down.

When they finally left, rather than feeling any sense of relief, I worried more than ever, not knowing what to do. My sisters and I were left to spend the night alone in a house with the front door broken down. Needless to say, no one slept that night. After a long day at the courthouse, we were able to get our parents back under strict bail conditions. When we went home with our parents, we didn't question them about the incident; we just started cleaning up.

Eventually, my parents sold the bungalow, my older sister moved in with her boyfriend and my little sister and I moved into a townhouse with our parents. I was still in school and fell behind a bit, but eventually caught up. Eventually, I was forced to get a job to help out with the bills. My Grandma came to help too, because it was getting tough to make ends meet; my parents were really affected by what had happened. They weren't functioning, so I had to take care of most of the bills and my little sister. I had to drop out of school again because I needed a full-time job to cover at least half the rent. I realized that nothing had changed with my parents; they still had the same bad habits that I hoped they had left behind. I thought they had learned their lesson when they were in jail.

After a few months, the same people started coming over and playing music till the wee hours of the morning again. Whenever I got paid, I gave my mom money to pay rent and the bills. Later, I discovered that we were facing eviction because my parents owed an exorbitant amount of money to the landlord for months of rent. I was hurt because I worked hard for that money. When my parents were confronted, they got defensive and figured I was accusing them of something. Angry and frustrated, my sister and I moved out.

As a year or two passed, my sister and I were getting along great. I had very little contact with my parents. They were having difficulties maintaining their home and it was inevitable that they would have to move. When that time came, my sisters and I helped them, but it was really difficult because no one else would help; the friends that my parents had were long gone because they were only around if there was a party. The good friends that they used to have had basically given up on them and all our relatives were in the United States.

Now and then I sometimes wonder how a loving mother and a devoted father could turn their children's lives into a total nightmare. In most cases, the children are the ones that cause their parents' major headaches and problems, but in my case it has been the total reverse. Throughout it all, I cannot help but still love my parents and make sure that they're safe. All my sisters and I ever wanted was a sense of normalcy. Due to the fact that I work at a mall where families flock, I long for the sense of togetherness and happiness that I see between parents and children. Within the span of three years, the holidays that I longed for during my childhood, are the same days that I now dread. Christmas and New Year's are the worst days of the year for all of us.

While many of my friends are thinking about their future and living and partying for the present, I have to think about my parents and what might be the next step in my roller coaster life. Although I know I have serious problems regarding my family, I always feel that as long as I have the motivation and the support of my other two sisters, we will persevere. The way I figure, it could have been way worse. For example, on the day my parents were arrested, the cops could have shot my mom for panicking and we would have been left motherless. I know some people are in worse situations than my family; some children are tortured by the sight of their mother or father suffering from cancer. Some families are torn apart by constant war and violence. After all this, I think I have become more aware of the different situations that one might encounter in life.

Some people who are aware of my situation have been very sympathetic, but I know they always wonder why my sisters and I are so insistent on helping parents that we should have given up on long ago. My answer is simple. We love them and want to make sure that our family remains strong regardless of everything. People don't understand; they wonder why our mother and father can't just get jobs and work for a living, like everyone else. The reason they're not working is the bad habit that overtook their lives a few years back has since left them with an empty hole in their hearts and a complete lack of motivation. I try hard and can only hope for the best and make sure that no matter what, I will not turn my back on my family. My sisters and I have a close bond and even more we share a special understanding of making sure that my parents are protected. People may not get this, but in the end it is not something for them to get, it's our own understanding and the way we were brought up. My parents have made many bad decisions the past few years, but in a weird way, they have taught us many things. Many may believe that they must not have been good parents because of everything that they've done. In some cases, people feel superior when I tell them my story. Many of them believe that our tragedy would never befall them because they would not make bad decisions like my parents have. My comment to them is that you never really know what the future holds. Unfortunately, some situations are beyond your control and the most you can do is hold your head up high and believe that adversity will make you stronger.

Kim Schraner

The day my mother died was a beautiful Saturday in August that seemed to go on forever. We all knew she was dying, so, without anything being said, the entire family had gathered at the house to be with her; my father, brother, husband, son, twin girls and myself. We all wanted to be there that day; we took turns sitting with mother and trying to comfort her. She was in tremendous pain, so we called in the doctor to give her some relief. However, the doctor made it plain that there was nothing to be done.

At around 6:30 that evening, my mother collapsed in my father's arms and appeared to die. My father called for my brother and me to come quickly. We held her hands and cradled her head and told her we were all there with her, we loved her and we were going to miss her. All of a sudden, my mother gasped for air and came back to life to say goodbye.

She was unable to speak properly; she kept making a "puh" sound. We struggled to make out what she was trying to tell us. She was fighting to the end; we later realized she was trying to tell us that she was 'perfect'. My father turned her head to face each of us and we said our goodbyes. We realized she was breathing her last breath. It was a truly surreal moment for all of us when we realized that it had happened; she was gone. We stayed with her all night. We laughed, we told stories, and we cried and as we remembered and honoured her life. The next morning, the doctor pronounced my mother dead and the funeral home came to take her out of the house for the last time.

It was a few months before I could bring myself to enter the house without her there. My father was up north and the house was empty. As I slowly opened the door, I heard the alarm chimes and seemed to hear my mother greeting me, like she always had. I wasn't sure if I could handle being in the house where she had suffered and died. As I walked through the house, the silence was deafening. I sat in the chair she had always used; I closed my eyes and just felt her. I started to cry, looking at all the pictures on the walls. I walked through the dining room where we had so many dinners, went into the kitchen, her domain, where she cooked endlessly and taught me to cook. I made my way up the stairs, walked through what was my room, my brother's room and my parent's room, where she had passed away. The memories, good and bad, were everywhere. I stood for a minute, weeping, and said goodbye one more time.

Walking back down the stairs, I was overwhelmed by grief. I fell back onto the stairs when suddenly I heard her chimes; my mother's favourite chimes, the chimes I always heard growing up. They were ringing and I ran to the back door looking for the chimes; looking for my mother. I knew she was talking to me. I couldn't find her, but I knew she was there for me. I stood at the back door and it dawned on me, my mother was now in my heart. I smiled and held my hand to my heart, and after a few moments of my newfound discovery, I went home, more at peace than I had been since my mother's death.

When my father returned, I told him of my private goodbye and he must have been affected by my story. One Saturday morning not long afterward, I was pulling out of my driveway when something caught my eye; my mother's chimes were hanging on my house. I sat in my car and cried; I couldn't drive. It was my father's Mother's Day gift to me.

Those chimes will stay with me forever. I've had them placed outside, where I can see them from almost every window in my home. Every time I hear those chimes ring, I hear my mother talking to me. It doesn't take away the pain, but it's a constant reminder that she will always be with me.

Making It in High Heels

Kristiana Hurley

All my life I have wanted to help people, feed them, care for them and save them from the unfairness of life's circumstances. Why do I have so much and others have so little? Why am I fortunate enough to be born here in this great country? How could I do nothing to stop the hunger and suffering of many of the world's children? My journey began with two years of attempting to qualify for medical volunteer work. When volunteering in third world countries, it was naturally expected that the volunteer pay their own way and I wasn't able to do so. The alternative was to find an organization that, through a selection process, would cover my costs. As a young woman with no real medical training, the possibilities were limited. I continued to go to school and work at Sick Children's Hospital while I attempted to be deemed acceptable to a volunteer agency.

Then, in the summer of 2005, I was chosen, out of 30,000 applicants, to interview for one of nine positions available to Canadians. I had applied to go to Africa, my country of choice, to help with their medical policies and work in the hospitals. This had been my dream; I would put away my designer jeans and make a difference in the world. After a full day of interviews with six people, group work, team scenarios and psychological testing, I was starting to have doubts about my ability to qualify. I kept telling myself that it was an accomplishment to have made it that far and I shouldn't be too upset if I didn't get any further. Still, here I was ready to make the world a better place and I didn't want anybody telling me that I wasn't going to be allowed to go.

After two weeks of waiting, I finally heard back from the agency. At that moment, being told that I had been accepted for the summer program was one of the most satisfying feelings I have ever felt. I called my Mom, crying, to tell her that I was happy and scared at the same time. I was being given the opportunity to make a difference and fulfill my desire to make someone's life better. What I couldn't have imagined was how difficult would be the days to come, and how they would change my outlook forever.

I was not to be sent to Africa, but to the poorest parts of Brazil. I wasn't concerned about the fact that I didn't speak Portuguese because we were told that someone would always be available to interpret for us. This was the first of many half truths we were told.

There were eight other Canadians in the program with me, from all over the country and with varied backgrounds. Our first group session was only two days before we left. We were briefed about some of the customs of Brazilian villages, some essential phrases and the kind of work environment to expect. Some of the group was behaving as though we were going on some mini vacation and were doing more partying than helping; others were just happy to be getting away from their families or not-so-great lives. I suddenly felt that being chosen was no longer such a special thing.

We were told that we'd be meeting up with one another every Friday for educational days. We were also told that we would be living with host families who spoke and understood English and that we would always be safe. I wasn't ready for the list of things we could pack; it was a very detailed list of the basic essentials; how many pairs of socks and underwear, no jewelry, no designer sunglasses, nothing that was deemed a luxury. They didn't want us to be the subject of jealousy or theft and we had to be able to travel light and carry our own bags. My mom questioned my ability to go for months without my hair irons and perfumed creams and lotions.

The day had finally come; nine of us got on the airplane for the nine-hour flight to Sao Paulo, Brazil. I was twenty years old and ready to change the world! I couldn't wait to meet the people of Brazil, to touch their lives in a meaningful way and give them the help they were waiting for. I felt as though no other young adult was getting the great opportunity that I was being given. I was climbing so high on my self-righteous ladder that the fall was going to be painful.

Upon arriving in Brazil, I felt like I was walking through water, between hearing only Portuguese and the heat and we weren't even close to our final destination; we still had a bus ride to Porto Alegre and another three-hour bus to Rosario Du Sud, which felt like the most southerly tip of the planet. Considering the number of nights I have danced away at clubs, I was shocked by how tired I was. By eleven that night, our new village was before us. It seemed to be a small town, but it was hard to tell at night and with me half asleep.

Our new host families warmly welcomed us with a traditional ceremony. An older man and his wife were introduced and, voila, I had a new family. Although they spoke no English, they took me home. I found it weird and scary to be leaving with these strangers without phone numbers or any other contact information for the others in the group. It felt disorganized and I was very worried. None the less, I was trying to go with the flow. My mother had told me at a young age that if I said a prayer for help, God was always listening; well I have never prayed so much in my life, as I did that night.

I attempted to hide my dismay when we arrived at the house, really a shack. It was absolutely freezing. It was difficult to communicate without sharing a language, but they showed me to my room; I was exhausted. My room was very small and smelled of mothballs. I realized very quickly that I was no longer in lovely, safe Canada. That night, I almost froze; I had no heat or extra blankets and I had never felt so alone. My only solace was the knowledge that I was going to start making a difference soon; I was going to teach and bring comfort to Brazil's most vulnerable. My dream was becoming a reality and that would get me through the night, if not the next four months.

In the morning, the house was still very cold as I walked into our small, but quaint kitchen. I had a choice of bread and honey or bread and some jam- like stuff. I quickly ate some breakfast and had a cup of some interesting drink that seemed to imitate coffee. I love Brazilian coffee at Starbucks. They gave me a map showing me how to get to the municipal building, where I was to meet with the other Canadians to discuss our work plans. All I could think about was how cold it was for June. I was to learn that in southern Brazil, the temperature frequently dips below zero; good thing I brought a sweater and one fall jacket.

Upon arriving at the municipal building, I was pleased to see the now familiar faces of the other Canadian volunteers and the supervisor. We all began quickly relating our experiences; how different it was, how we didn't know a word of Portuguese and in many cases had no heat or blankets to fend off the cold weather. Many of the volunteers had tales of families not knowing they were coming; host families that only wanted the extra money they would receive or having to sleep with the families in one big room. I realized that I didn't have it that bad, although it was rough compared to the nice lifestyle I had left behind in Toronto. I knew I was giving it all up to make a difference; four months is not long to suffer compared to the suffering endured by people living in poverty.

That afternoon, I started work at a medical clinic within a fifteen-minute walk from my little village. One thing became apparent immediately; the organization didn't have enough funding for the vast quantities of gloves and bandages that were needed. The clinic was like a walk-in clinic for patients who couldn't afford private medical care; only, we would go out to the homes instead of the patients coming to us. We would walk for hours from village to village; some of them looked like the villages one would see on the news, in the aftermath of war. We would visit the villagers, checking on their health. Again, everything was made more difficult by the fact that I didn't speak Portuguese.

It's funny how expressive a person can be through their eyes when they can't communicate in the traditional ways. Watching these young woman and their children suffering, I didn't need words, I felt their pain. It was difficult knowing that we have all the medical necessities at home and these people that needed so much were never going to see them. One woman in particular stays very close to my heart. She was illiterate and had the most beautiful daughter that I have ever seen; they were both suffering from parasites in their feet. This was a common problem that affected the hands and feet of the remote villagers. The painful treatment involved cutting out the infected area with a razor blade and of course, without anesthetic. The child watched stoically as we treated her mother and vice versa; I felt so cruel to be causing them so much pain. As a child, your parents are your heroes and they are supposed to be the strongest people you know. Their pain penetrated my very soul.

It was terrifying to be halfway across the world, doing procedures never imagined. The worst heartache was in knowing that the supply of bandages would run out before the wounds were properly healed and the parasite would probably return, necessitating amputation for some unlucky patients. At that moment, I knew that everything I had gone through to get there was worth it. I was empowered by the strength of these women and children; with their ability to remain cheerful in the worst situations. I was somehow going to make things better and get all of them cured. They had huts with tin roofs and sometimes it rained all day and it was almost at the point of freezing. It was terrible to know this was going on while we have so much at home.

Without really noticing, I started to become accustomed to my new universe; where personal choice was out of the question. Freedom was no longer available; it was not what I had expected at all. The women and children seemed to be the constant victims of poverty and hardship in most of the villages. I wanted to teach the children how to write their names and to count, but this was met with great resistance; I was told that to do so would give them false hope and that we were there to tend to medical needs only. That's when I fell and hard; I had come all this way only to be told that I could only help a little and not enough to bring about real change. My dream was crumbling.

The months finally went by; I learnt enough Portuguese to get by and I forgot about the small things that used to matter. The view in front of me took hold and this new home was all that mattered. I was able to call home once every few weeks, which always produced waterworks. My mom would tell me that it was all right; that if it was too much for me, she would bring me home. Just knowing that inspired me to stay and finish what I had started, but I went from an emotionally strong girl to a world-saving, emotional wreck. I was becoming so emotionally drained every day; it was hard to live like that. There were some high points, and I encountered some great people along the way. I convinced some of the other volunteers to start a food drive and I started to teach some of the children to read and write when I wasn't exercising with the senior women of the villages.

After about two months, I started to get what looked like mosquito bites but turned out to be fleas. I had been blessed with a nice olive complexion and was proud of my smooth skin. That vanity in one's appearance is almost as bad as a parasite was something I realized as I became breakfast, lunch and dinner for a large family of fleas. There wasn't much I could do about it without hot, running water or clean clothes, so I had to cope with it. I was told it would go away once back at home since the fleas couldn't live in our climate. Looking at the big picture, I was fortunate to have a flea problem and not some life-threatening disease.

I returned to Porto Alegre for my final week in Brazil. We had survived the worst, I thought, fleas and all; I was out to have some fun. The fashions were quite different in Brazil and the clothes I brought were a far cry from **Vogue** or **InStyle**, but after experiencing the isolated, desperate life of the villagers, I was ready to appreciate everything.

With my new attitude, I was ready to go out and enjoy myself, so off I went with some friends. Around a corner, a man shot another and ran away. The Brazilians on the street just stepped over this guy and told us not to get involved or we would have monumental problems with the police. How could I not stop and help; that's why I was there, right? Sometimes, the risk is too great to take the plunge. Deeply upset, I went into an internet cafe to email my mom. There was an email waiting for me; it was dated that day and marked 'urgent.' It said, "Kristi, I am sorry to have to tell you this through an e-mail, but Natalie passed away last night in a car accident."

I sat there, reading the lines over and over. No tears were running down my face; I couldn't register what had happened. A girlfriend from college had died. At twenty, this wasn't supposed to happen. I told the people with me what I had just found out and I decided I needed to go out. It may seem wrong that I went out to party and drink at a time like that, but I had never felt so alone. I had just gone through one of the most difficult experiences of my life and I felt so lost in translation. I didn't have one person around who really knew me or the friend I had lost. I was feeling the futility of trying to make a difference only to have good people die anyway. I was twenty years old and attempting to help people when a dear friend of mine dies; now I'm miles away from my friends and miles from feeling that I was accomplishing what I had set out to do.

When the tears finally came, I thought they would never stop; I was feeling so numb and lost. Nothing seemed to matter anymore. I didn't feel that I was actually helping anyone; once we left, things would go back to the way they had been, as if we had never been there at all. I just wanted to go home, eat normal food and speak English again. I was afraid to leave, because I would have to deal with death, but I didn't want to stay, either. I had one more week to be there and I didn't know how I was going to stay motivated enough to stick it out. The poverty, the fleas and now death were all too much for me, physically and mentally. I called home, crying to my mom, telling her how awful I felt and how could such a thing happen to such a great, young girl. My mom told me to just get through the next week and all would be okay in the end. It sure did not feel that way at the time.

The day had finally come to fly back to Toronto. I was still feeling vulnerable and useless. I couldn't sleep at all during the ten-hour flight; thoughts of the past four months raced through my head. We landed around three in the afternoon. Seeing my parents waiting for me was like something out of a movie; I dropped my bags and ran so fast I could have tripped over my own feet. I hugged them like a five-year-old going to bed in the dark. I've never been really close with my father before, but all I wanted at that moment was to feel love. We all just sat there and cried. I wasn't too sure what I was crying about or what I was feeling, but I knew I needed it. I couldn't believe it when I got home; I had absolutely forgotten the feeling of taking off your shoes when entering the house. It was amazing to feel wood floors and carpeting under my feet as opposed to dirt floors. We had heaters and running water, hot and cold.

The weeks that followed were difficult ones. Coping with the loss of a close friend at a young age was a challenge, but dealing with finding my identity and trying to belong was even harder. I felt like I had abandoned the children and people of the villages of Brazil. I couldn't bring myself to use the dishwasher or hot water in the showers; it felt foreign and unnecessary to me. It's amazing what four months can do to your outlook on mankind and life as a whole.

I went on that trip with the exciting goal of 'saving one country at a time' by changing attitudes and providing a better lifestyle; or at least imparting some knowledge. I came back changed; I had become more patient, I listened, rather than waiting for the next chance to speak. I realized how easy it could be to get caught up in what's cool and worry about things that now seem so trivial.

Well, the fleas did go away, but I still have some scars that remind me never to forget the pain, poverty and passion that marked my time in Brazil. I am very glad I went; when asked if I would do it all again, I always respond with a resounding "Yes!" The whole experience made me more aware of the world around me and the limited views I had held about how to help others. My trip to Brazil has taught me to be kinder and a more understanding person. I realize now that my knowledge of life was very limited. I will be forever grateful that I had the courage to go on such an amazing journey; which has provided me with further courage for life's journey.

Making It in High Heels

Leyla Naghizada

Welcome to the story of my life. Allow me to first introduce myself; my name is Leyla Naghizada and I'm 23 years old. I would love to invite you to take a ride with me through the rollercoaster experiences of 'My Life Story'. I hope you're able to sit back and enjoy the next few pages, as I hope my story will inspire and awaken the recognition and importance of positive thinking and what it means to really take charge of your life.

I was born in the city of Baku, which is the capital of Azerbaijan, one of the fifteen countries that once belonged to the former USSR. Azerbaijan is a small but beautiful Eastern European/West Asian country located on the west coast of the Caspian Sea. I will always respect and love Azerbaijan along with its warmhearted and hospitable people, but I have to confess that as soon as I gained a conscious understanding of myself and what life is about, I knew that there was something 'off' with me; I simply couldn't consider myself average or normal by society's standards. I was never fully able to fit in or feel like I belonged in any environment. As a child, I remember many internal conversations about what it meant to be me, and what my purpose on this planet was. Like most children, I was one of those kids with a curious mind and an endless supply of questions; except most of my questioning was going on internally. To the outside world, I was just another shy child; up until my late teenage years, I would have classified myself as being timid and fearful.

Over the years, my self-image developed deep rooted insecurities that I wasn't able to identify and heal until I started on a process of self-discovery. There is no doubt that before I ventured in this direction, I was not the happy, well-balanced individual I am today, as my soul was in need of healing. Thankfully, I come from a very loving family and I was never subjected to any physical harm; most of the suffering that I'm referring to was self-inflicted.

My younger sister, Mimi, and I were quite close growing up. Back in

1996-97, around the time when Backstreet Boys were created, consider-able changes started to occur in our lives. Along with millions of women around the world, we were infatuated with BSB as a group, as well as the individual members; I was 'in love' with Brian Littrell and Mimi had a crush on Nick Carter. It was our passion for those guys that motivated us to start learning English. Our first languages are Russian and Azeri (which is very similar to Turkish). We started to learn English with the enthusiasm and eagerness that only real love can evoke. With a basic knowledge of the language, we were finally able to start translating and comprehending the songs a lot better. Our passion and love for the group also inspired an overwhelming interest in North American lifestyle and culture and within a few years, Mimi and I were convinced that we had to move to America.

We started to reject every aspect of our native culture, which at first made our parents and the rest of the family very uncomfortable. I got a negative reaction every time I made a comment about not belonging where I was born or said that I knew with absolute certainty that I was going to live in the States one day. It's painful for me to remember the countless battles Mimi and I had to endure during those years. It's a sad reality that because most people don't believe in themselves, they tend to ridicule the dreams of others. Luckily, our parents realized that with or without their help, we had made up our minds; we were leaving Azerbaijan forever and moving to North America in hopes of forming a new home full of vast possibilities, boundless dreams and unlimited opportunities, which we knew could never be attained if we stayed in Azerbaijan.

Our original dream was to move to America, but with tough new immi-gration laws in the US, it was decided amongst the family that we would immigrate to Canada instead; the laws were more forgiving and our odds of passing all the stages of the immigration process were much higher back then. Since I'd rather spare the talk about all the excruciating details of this process, I'll say one thing: I never want to go through that experi-ence again. The process of immigration, from start to finish, took about three long and painful years. We were kept in suspense the entire time; not knowing what each new day would bring. My family endured a lot of anxiety through every step of the process; from applying to the Canadian Embassy in Poland (because there isn't one in Baku), to filling out miles of paperwork and flying to Warsaw and back for the interviews and the never ending waiting, it's hardly surprising that the stress developed into unfortu-nate health issues for my parents.

Needless to say, leaving everything and everyone behind and moving to a foreign country is definitely one of the experiences that alters and defines the character of any human being. The experience tested our patience to the fullest, both as a family and individually. I couldn't possibly express in words the tremendous sense of relief and happiness we all felt the day we finally received the package with our visas; that was a day I'll never forget.

Because I grew up in a war torn country and have also survived an earthquake and a serious car accident, I realize that near-death experiences will act as defining moments in one's life. I believe that if I didn't have to live through these extremely challenging and demanding circumstances, I wouldn't have the wisdom and courage that is crucial to one's mental and internal growth as a human being.

After a year or so, we were settling in and getting used to life in Toronto; the time had come for me to find a suitable career for myself, one that would bring happiness and satisfaction to my soul. I found the process to be extremely complicated. Growing up, whether or not I had money was never important to me, although today, living a luxurious lifestyle is definitely part of my vision. Creativity and appreciation of art flows through my genes and a large portion of my life has been devoted to studying art. After a careful examination of possible paths, I chose Interior Design; it combined both creativity and business and I felt that I could potentially be successful in that field.

The three years of my life that I devoted to the study of this line of work has been without a doubt, the most challenging and demanding period of my life. Being an overachiever and perfectionist by nature proved to be a weakness during my college studies, as I would drive myself insane by striving for flawlessness and excellence on every little detail of every project. This extreme dedication produced an awful imbalance in all aspects of my life; everything suffered, from my personal life to my mental health.

It was disappointing to discover, after graduating with honours, that although I had the potential to succeed in the industry, I would not find contentment and fulfillment by working as a designer. Once again, characteristically for me, I found myself wanting more out of life. Unfortunately, I found myself in debt, with student loans, something that doesn't allow me to relax and enjoy life to the fullest. My goal at the moment remains obtaining financial freedom and comfort.

Although my current sales job within the building/design and architecture industry offers a great deal of opportunity for long term financial gain, I find myself facing another dilemma: I know I'm not content and I need to make a decision to turn my life around, but how do I get myself from where I am today to where I want to be tomorrow? I haven't come up with the answer just yet, but I know it is brewing inside and the only way to bring it to the surface is to allow for some much needed time of relaxation and reflection. I sense the resolution is near and I know I need to practice patience in order to allow for that realization to arrive. Although I sometimes sense a lack of support from my family, friends and surrounding environment, I continue to believe in my personal power. I am certain that having an extremely competitive and proactive nature actually helps me to sculpt this process into a fun experience.

After some careful reflection on my past experiences and life in general, I realize that I have no regrets about my life. As unbelievable as it may seem, I am grateful for the past and present hardships and challenges that life has thrown my way. I'm positive that if I hadn't experienced it all, I couldn't have grown into the strong-willed, determined and independent woman that I am today. I'm positive that this attitude assists me every day in creating the life that I desire.

Life is truly a journey and not a destination and I put my wholehearted effort into every moment. It takes hard work to keep a positive attitude going despite all the negativity that is present in the world today. However, I am a firm believer that negative thinking creates a mental block to achieving success. Continuously learning from the surrounding environment has the potential to bring unlimited success to all aspects of life. The more I learn, the more I realize that we shouldn't limit the amount of knowledge that is possible to us; the sky is truly the limit and our extraordinary universe is undeniably infinite.

Maria Panopalis

You can ask me anything about acne; I'm an expert. I'm not a dermatologist, or an aesthetician, but I am a self-taught, self-trained aficionado of all things complexion related. I can tell you how and why acne forms; it's not chocolate, by the way. I know about all the remedies and treatments; effective ones are few and far between. I especially know about the lasting scars; both physical and emotional. Back then, my greatest strength was the cover-up. I was a concealment guru; I could hide a zit like nobody's business. But no matter how great a cover I achieved, I always worried that someone would see beyond the mask. When you have crazy acne; the kind that hurts both physically and psychologically, you're **never** without a breakout.

I was a cute kid; people would stop my mother on the street to admire me. Early in junior high school, I remember sitting in the schoolyard with some girlfriends, many of whom had already experienced their first zits. As if to curse me, one of my friends said, "Maria has the clearest skin." It was true; my skin was smooth, even and flawless. That was likely the last time anyone had anything nice to say about my complexion for many years. By the end of that school year, my raging hormones and overactive oil glands had turned my face into an acne battlefield.

Eventually, the condition of my skin became an aesthetics emergency. I was, in my mind, my ugliest self; and it hurt! Acne vulgaris is the medical term; vulgaris, as in vulgar, it adds insult to injury, doesn't it? It was painful enough to confront my inadequacies in the mirror; it was even more painful to hear my mother and Aunt Helen lament: "What are we going to do about your face?!" As if I was afflicted with some debilitating disease; as if I had scurvy or a severe drug addiction.

I remember a schoolmate who had beautiful, smooth skin. In a misguided attempt to be helpful, she would offer acne solutions to a group of us who hung out together. Granted, some of the other girls had a few pimples, but I had full-blown acne. In my paranoid teenage mind, I believed she was speaking directly to me. I can still hear her saying, "I had a zit this morning and put toothpaste on it; it's gone now!" or, "I change my pillowcase, like, every night and don't get breakouts." I'm sure she meant no harm, but if she knew that I washed my face about a million times a day, had tried the toothpaste remedy long before she suggested it, and wouldn't even touch my face with my own hands, let alone a used pillowcase, she might have used a bit more tact and sensitivity.

When someone with porcelain skin would point out a whitehead they were battling, as if it were the worst thing that had ever happened to them, I would instantly conclude that they thought I was hideous. I can't stand it when people fuss over a lone pimple. It's like a skinny person complaining that they need to lose some weight; it's not chronic, so zip it. Or at least, do us all a favour and keep it to yourselves. You don't know who's listening, and how they might interpret what you've said. Keep that in mind.

A lot of people I grew up with had no idea my complexion bothered me so much. I didn't talk about it and certainly never drew attention to it; it's natural to want to be noticed for positive accomplishments – not embarrassing things, especially in high school. Every time I heard, "You're going to be so pretty once the acne clears." The words registered in my mind as, "You would be so pretty if you weren't so ugly."

My greatest ally in disguising my pocked skin was makeup. I couldn't fully hide my blemishes, but it made me feel better. Makeup became my security blanket and I would spare no expense. I would start with concealer, apply a liquid or cream foundation and finish with powder. And still, with all those products plastered on my face, unsightly bumps and grooves would still be visible. Cover Girl and Christian Dior couldn't solve my misfortune; and Dior just took a bigger chunk out of my wallet. Anywhere that people could potentially see me without makeup gave me anxiety. The beach, rainy days, sporting events, sleepovers; what would people think if they saw how bad my skin really was? And it was bad; red, irritated, pus-filled bumps and cysts covered my face. From the ages of fourteen to 25, I was never without a cluster of acne somewhere on my face. I didn't want people to look at me. I wore my hair down for maximum coverage of my face; turtlenecks and high collars were good disguises too.

Hiding my skin condition became the easy part; getting rid of it was near impossible. I started with drugstore remedies; creams, soaps, serums, astringents and exfoliants. You name it, I tried it; and it didn't work. Then came the home remedies; scrubs, herbs and spices, ice cubes, peroxide, olive oil. I mixed and sampled various ingredients trying to concoct my personal cure; but to no avail. I even smeared egg on my face; first the whites, then the yolks. Don't bother; you really just end up with egg on your face. I graduated to spa treatments; facials, microdermabrasion, peels. All very expensive, and again, I wasn't getting the results I was hoping for.

There were various edible items I ingested in hopes of a clearer day. I remember watching a TV sitcom that featured a teenager who had some event to attend and an unsightly blemish was about to ruin his life. He became obsessed with vitamin E to cure it; I took this idea and ran with it. I'm sure I overdosed on vitamin E; I was slathering myself with creams and popping pills like candy. Eventually, I decided that vitamin E was not what I needed; I needed vitamin A, then Vitamin C, then apple cider vinegar, fish oil, the list goes on. I stopped eating tomatoes, my favourite thing in the world, because someone said the acidity in them causes breakouts. I would put pepper on everything because a friend of a friend said, in passing, that it helps combat acne. I would try anything.

When the constant pain of the acne was too much, I went to see my doctor. He prescribed pills that did absolutely nothing. Then I was sent to a dermatologist who placed a huge magnifying light and glass over my face and confirmed that my skin was definitely in turmoil; as if it had been a mere theory to that point. He got out the big guns; the most potent acne medication there is, Accutane. I couldn't even begin taking the medication unless I agreed to submit to regular blood tests, to make sure that my kidneys were functioning normally. Accutane is a powerful drug, but I was willing to take the risk; that's how desperate I was to be rid of the misery of this plague.

After a few months, I did see a difference in my skin. The Accutane didn't stop the breakouts altogether though. I still got zits; I can't remember ever being without one in my late teens or early twenties. In fact, in my early twenties I had another flare up; it seemed the poison was back. I went back to the dermatologist and endured another round of Accutane; this time it worked and the chronic, painful acne finally stopped. Still, even at 30, I occasionally get a reminder of my past.

While the battles raged, in my heart and on my face, I made a decision. I would be noticed for things beyond my appearance. I concentrated on school and became a better student. I got involved in sports and became a better athlete. I focused on being a good friend and making people laugh. Soon, I got better at being comfortable in my own skin. It may be harsh, but I was convinced that people weren't going to like me for my looks; I didn't even like the way I looked. It sounds grim, but it may have been a blessing in disguise. I had more to offer than just looks. I didn't believe that I was a pretty face, so I had to be more than that. It was a lesson in human nature too. I empathized with people who were dealing with "social afflictions"; overweight, too tall, too short, glasses, braces. I knew how it felt to stand out for something 'shameful'. In a way, one of the best things that ever happened, was the worst skin a person could ask for. Easy to say now that the acne's all gone, perhaps.

I've grown into a decent complexion; it turns out oily skin can be a blessing once the overactive glandular years have passed. Perhaps naturally, there are remnants of my troubled past that affect me today. I'm still pretty hesitant to be seen without makeup. The pimples are gone, but I'll probably always be self-conscious about my skin; it's a hard habit to break. With every year that passes, I become more confident about my appearance; which is ironic because I'm aging now; wrinkles, cellulite, new fat and gray hair are all waiting in the wings to make an appearance. Although I would love for the hands of time to stop specifically for me, I've come to realize that looks are tangible and finite. You can't have a conversation with soft, supple skin or a well shaped nose. You can however, learn from the heartaches you've endured and you can show others through your example that they'll get through it too.

What's your best feature? Or your worst? Of the two, which do you put more focus on? For me, it's finally my better features. I like my eyes and my smile. Interestingly enough, they're both on my face. For so long, I put the spotlight on my skin.

Funnily enough, I've chosen a profession where appearance is important. Television morning show hosts don't have to be gorgeous, but being presentable is absolutely necessary. Thankfully, an abundant supply of makeup with the right application helps many flaws fade away. No one has their looks more closely examined than a television on-air personality. Turns out, all those years of living under a microscope in my troubled mind were just training for the 'real' world. Viewers have many opinions about how I look on television and when they meet me in person, they're only to happy to tell me, "You're taller, shorted, thinner, fatter, prettier, uglier, blonder, than I thought!" Do their opinions matter? Sure they do; otherwise I wouldn't still blush when someone tells me I'm pretty. But when an unflattering comment comes my way, I take it in stride, become insulted and move on. Would I have become who I am without my struggle with acne? Perhaps. Would I relive those years as a 'pretty' girl, given the chance? No way! I like how I turned out just fine.

Meagan White

My professional success has been in the fitness industry so I've made it in running shoes, in spite of my love for high heels. Most of my life has been characterized by a burning desire to succeed, but my definition of success has evolved over time, so too have the challenges I've encountered. We have all faced many challenges in life and I would like to share some of my experiences. I have come to know myself through identifying my greatest fears and overcoming some of the many obstacles life has thrown my way.

As an only child growing up in the country, I had to find ways to entertain myself and I made the most of my imagination. I spent much of my childhood mucking around in the river, dirt biking and capturing local critters like crickets, mice and frogs to add to my bedroom pet collection. Although my childhood was an active one, I also enjoyed reading and writing and had a special talent for dancing, music and the arts.

My parents were very liberal and I was encouraged to think for myself and express my thoughts openly. Since I was surrounded by adults, I matured quickly and developed an independent nature. I was competitive, stubborn and assertive, but also emotional, and a dreamer. Aside from the usual arguments that parents have with their kids, we had an honest and relaxed relationship until I realized that our tight knit family might be the black sheep of the county.

My parents had once lived in the city and small town ways may not have appealed to them; they were reluctant to conform to local pressures and standards. As a teenager however, my main goal was to fit in and be like everybody else; our relationship became strained for a time.

My parents taught me valuable life skills that have influenced many of the decisions I've made throughout my life. Encouraging me to reach for my dreams, but more importantly, actually believing in me, has helped me to develop the confidence I have needed to achieve my goals. At an early age, I developed high expectations for my future and was committed to following through with the goals I had set. When I recognized that my efforts could be rewarded materially, I developed a positive relationship with success. Once I started to be rewarded with trophies or ribbons, I really strived to reach my goals and was disappointed if I wasn't able to do so. Success at this point meant being recognized for my achievements and without that recognition I felt deflated; as if I'd failed.

I reached puberty at only 9 years of age. I was already well-developed and taller than my classmates; I felt like an outcast and had no self-confidence. I was overly conscious and critical of my image. My body language changed; I started to slouch, walk, talk and smile differently. I spent hours in front of the mirror trying to figure out who it was staring back at me.

With puberty I developed a desire to blend in and look and act like other girls. I would try on different personalities and images to see which fit. The bittersweet realities of puberty and the associated raging hormones had set in; the pressures to conform were real. Once I noticed and wanted to be noticed by boys, I came to the conclusion that it wasn't desirable to be smart, so I dumbed myself down for a significant period of my youth.

In my teens, I tore my ACL in my left knee during running long jump. I consequently had to undergo surgery which put me out of commission for several months. Losing the opportunity to dance, compete and play sports really deflated my ego and challenged my relationship with success, because I had largely tied my identity to my athletic ability. I lost some confidence and knew I needed to find a new focus

Like many teenagers, I was highly-charged, rebellious, defensive and confused about my position and direction in life. The desire to fit in, compounded with the pressures to balance school with a part-time job and trying to figure out what I wanted to do with the rest of my life were very real and success at this stage was largely measured through grades and popularity.

I started dating in grade eight and I had many acquaintances through-out high school, but mainly hung out with a few close friends. As I grew older and became more independent, I became more withdrawn around my parents and although we maintained a good relationship, I became secretive about my whereabouts and selective with what I told them. I spent the majority of my spare time with my boyfriend and friends. I started drinking and smoking early, which seemed to be part of the small town cultural norm. After re-injuring my knee and undergoing two more surgeries, I was forced to develop other interests and outlets besides athletics and so became a peer mentor, the head of the sexual assault committee and joined the school band.

Like most teenagers, I was conscious of my appearance and got caught up in trying to live up to the unrealistic images society has developed for females. Going to modeling school further exacerbated my sense of self esteem and instead of increasing my confidence, left me feeling more confused. Being advised to lose weight when I was already petite warped my reality, but luckily, the effects were temporary and I later came to realize that it wasn't so much my appearance I struggled with; I was still feeling lost in an artificial persona, confused about who I was and who I was meant to be. The drive I had to succeed still existed and I wanted to be perfect in everything I did.

My greatest struggle however was trying to find the balance between making adult decisions while still being under the direct supervision of authority figures.

I've learned that the choices you make in your adolescence set the stage for future growth and opportunities and I developed good time management skills and a strong work ethic.

After high school, I took a year off and moved to London, Ontario to figure out which direction I wanted to take before investing in my post secondary education. I worked in hair salons and restaurants and spent a lot of late nights out and early mornings in bed. Family and friends encouraged me to go to university, but I chose instead to spend some time in pre-health sciences and then opted to pursue a Diploma in Fitness and Health.

It wasn't long before the lifestyle I kept, drinking, smoking and eating whatever I wanted collided with the world of fitness and health. I was soon seen as an outcast by fellow classmates and teachers. I struggled with challenges similar to the ones I faced in high school, as I still had to balance school with a part time job to pay the bills and I still wanted to keep up with the social scene.

I developed a passion for fitness and health however, and since graduating, I have pursued work along my anticipated career path at a local fitness club to make a name for myself in the industry. I have gained considerable experience through the positions I have held; I have worked as a receptionist, a dance instructor, a personal trainer and for the majority of my time there, as the Personal Training Director for several club locations. During that time, I also had the opportunity to co-host a fitness TV series on Roger's Cable Television for four seasons, including the *PVL Finally Fit Challenge (1 & 2), Interactive Fitness 911 and Living Well with PVL*. I also wrote various fitness articles and columns for the London Free Press.

Not everyone was excited about my advancement into management though; some of the guys didn't take well to having a female boss of a

similar age. I struggled to find a balance between managing these relationships and eventually developed a thicker skin; I realized that I couldn't
always control what others thought of me, no matter what my intentions
were.

While I tried to build the department from ground up, I lived for work
and my drive to succeed within the company outweighed most other
aspects in my life. The pace of my life was quick and I was very career
driven and focused during this period. I was fully committed to getting the
job done, but it came at the cost of an unbalanced life and emotional state.

I partied as hard as I worked to blow off steam; the majority of relationships and friendships I developed were with co-workers. The memories
from this period are blurred by the influence of alcohol and late nights, so
it is not surprising that not all of these relationships stuck. My existing relationships were challenged the more career driven I became.

Intuitively, I knew that success was more than a label and that if I
could just gain the courage to step outside my comfort zone, the skills I
had developed over the years would be transferable to other career paths.
Before making the decision to step down and into personal training again,
I developed a business plan to start my own training studio; although it
didn't come to fruition, doing so gave me the confidence I needed to redis-
cover and pursue my passions.

Naturally, some people were confused and shocked by my decision.
They questioned what I intended to do with my future, but I resisted the
urge to answer, knowing that end of the day, I was accountable to myself.

Stripping myself of a label and the associated expectations left me
feeling a little lost and detached in the beginning, but it was also liberating. Breaking free from routine and going back to the basics, financially
and intellectually, helped me to face my greatest fears and challenged my
perception of success. At first, I worried about how I would be accepted
by the same trainers I once supervised, as well as how I would respond to
being managed by the person stepping into my previous role. Surprisingly,
I adapted quite quickly; the necessity of doing so forced me to check my
ego. I also learned to enjoy my own independence.

I forced myself to do some serious soul searching and although I didn't
like all that I uncovered, digging a little deeper triggered a domino effect;
I started to re-evaluate all of my relationships and the role I played in my
life. It's not easy to look honestly at yourself, but if you're brave enough,
you'll uncover the answers you need to move forward. To keep my sanity,
I spent the majority of my time reading, writing and researching and also
became actively involved in yoga, meditation and environmental causes.
By pursuing other passions, I discovered a whole new way of living and

although modest, my new lifestyle helped me to gain a new appreciation and insight into my life and my future.

A year later, I was offered my old position back, but, with all the bells and whistles. I accepted, feeling that I could come back with a renewed sense of self and a clearer vision of the future. Looking back, I think I tricked myself into believing that because future opportunities hadn't knocked in the year I took off, my options were limited and I should take what I could get. I liked the role, but internal politics quickly took their toll and it wasn't long before I realized once again that I wasn't a good fit. But, my time off had given me the tools and communication skills necessary to transform myself from a mere manager into a leader and I earned a new level of respect from my peers.

I celebrated my 30th birthday after I accepted my old position back. Turning thirty meant a new list of goals and expectations, one of which was to complete a mini-triathlon. I achieved that goal with some friends this past summer. Considering that I was never a runner, biker or swimmer, this was a huge feat for me. My greatest challenge and accomplishment yet was moving to Toronto on a whim after accepting a job offer. I guess I was ready for opportunity to knock.

I have come to realize that I've learned most from the mistakes I've made; the challenges and obstacles I've overcome. For better or worse, my life's experiences have shaped who I am and have enabled me to live with a greater sense of independence and fulfillment, knowing that I can own my choices.

A healthy dose of traveling has given me an appreciation for my place in this world. Traveling has also helped me to realize that I'm not so different from others all over the world; we all share similar pleasures and pains and are motivated by the same basic human needs and emotions. Knowing that I'm not alone in my struggles has helped to soften my views of others and connect me to the bigger picture. We're all on the same team, but the ways we respond to life's ups and downs are what make us unique.

Many of the philosophies I've embraced have come from a continued effort to challenge my belief systems. Being less rigid and fixed in my way of thinking has enabled me to explore many new opportunities. Putting it all into perspective is humbling and I have come to approach life with a greater sense of gratitude, knowing that I am lucky to have all that I have. Possessions mean less to me now; building memories seem more important. Releasing the chokehold I had on life has helped me to learn to live with uncertainty; instead of running from reality, I try to ride the tides as they come and go. Facing reality, whether pleasant or unpleasant has allowed me to live with a greater sense of joy, wonder and clarity.

One of the most important and challenging lessons I've learned is that strength shouldn't be defined by one's ability to mask emotions, but instead should be based on one's willingness to be vulnerable. I have worked hard to tear down the walls I've spent a large part of my life building up. I rarely turned to others for help or advice and depended mainly on myself for the answers so I could control the outcome and avoid disappointments. But, not trusting anyone was a lonely plight and I realized that I could be missing out on some incredible relationships if I chose not to have faith in others. I have come to accept people as they are and not for who or what I would like them to be. Dropping false expectations has allowed me to enjoy these relationships even more and I've found it liberating to let go and to trust others with my emotions. Acquaintances will come and go in life, but certain people come along for a reason; if you're lucky enough to meet a mentor along your path, embrace them and let them push you to your limits.

I'm still in the process of understanding that what others think of me is not as important as what I think of myself. Some people may have seen my desire to succeed and the choices I've made as selfish, but I'm confident that by pursuing my dreams, I am a better person; able to give back even more to others and to the world. The desire to impress and be fully understood by others has always been important to me, but I've learned that expecting everyone to relate to my personal goals and aspirations is unrealistic. I've resigned myself to accepting that not everyone in my life will stand behind me, want me to succeed or wish me well with my future endeavours; knowing this gives me a whole new appreciation for the people in my life that do stand behind me. What matters most is knowing that nothing in life is out of reach and sometimes making decisions are as simple as following through with the courage of your convictions.

Everyone wants to find their place in this world and I'm no exception. I don't presume to have it all figured out, but I do know that you get out of life what you put into it and you will be well rewarded for your efforts. The path of least resistance won't offer many opportunities for growth and while it's true that some successes may be the result of being in the right place at the right time, most of life amounts to the summary of one's choices.

These days, my definition of success is one without labels; I believe the key to success is the ability to move forward in life with a sense of purpose and integrity without having to sacrifice identity or moral values. I feel successful now because all of the decisions I've made have helped me to find a secure place in the world and enabled me to live a life without regrets. I haven't compromised my drive or focus to arrive at this point;

instead I have come to realize that although I may not have control of my future or destination, I can choose how I relate to the challenges and obstacles that are part of life.

My choices will always be affected by a variety of tenets that I believe will foster success: facing fears; accepting new challenges; maintaining a positive frame of mind; remaining tolerant to change; pursuing passions; accepting responsibility for all actions; giving back to society and to the environment; practicing patience; finding balance between planning and spontaneity; being humble; holding strong, but not fixed to one's sense of self; and staying true to one's values and morals.

At thirty, I have much yet to learn and look forward to, knowing that my story has yet to be written and my future is still in the making.

Miriam Cohen

I was in an on-again, off-again relationship for three years with someone I thought was the most charming guy in the world. I loved him, my friends loved him, my colleagues loved him and no one could say a bad thing about him. When I was with him, I felt like I was the only person in the world; I never doubted myself when we were together because he showered me with attention and praises. The downside was that he wasn't around often enough to keep those good feelings alive. Sometimes two weeks would go by between dates. It was confusing and frustrating. How could someone care about me so much when we were together and then forget all about me when we were apart? I always tried to keep myself busy; I didn't want to be that 'clingy girlfriend' that we've all heard about; the one who calls her boyfriend seven times a day. I would wait over a week sometimes before I finally gave in and called him. My first words to him would usually be, "whoa… you're alive?" No matter how frustrated I was that he didn't think about me when I wasn't directly in front of him, he would always sweet talk his way back into my heart and I would welcome him with open arms.

It was December 30th and we had made plans for New Years Eve. I was looking forward to finally having a New Years' kiss and was thinking about all the amazing things we could experience together in the New Year. I called him to confirm our plans. The conversation began with me telling him about my new job and as usual, he encouraged me and praised me for being so successful at such a young age. I assumed everything was great. But, when I asked if I could pick him up for New Years, he became aloof and mentioned that he wanted to go to his friend's cottage instead. That was probably the only time I ever got angry with him in a conversation. Before this, I would always vent my frustrations by talking to my friends. Out of the blue, he told me he had slept with another girl! I felt fire burn through my body. I went dizzy. I couldn't see, breathe or talk. I was nauseous; I thought I was going to throw up. I hung up the phone; what else could I do? It was like a bad dream. How could this happen; how could I have let this happen? How could he do this to me?

He called back. I was crying and could say nothing but, "All I did was care for you and treat you well." He began describing his infidelity in detail! Now I had pictures in my head; I wanted to die! I have never felt so bad in my life, *ever*! I felt dirty, unattractive and so stupid and naive. I yelled, "Have fun with your girls," and hung up. What else can you say when someone tells you he cheated on you? Thank you for being honest? I had been doormat enough in our relationship. He texted me that he was really sorry, but it didn't matter; I had learned my lesson. Never again!

The first thing I did was jump into the shower; I felt so dirty. We had been physical after he cheated on me. How could he care so little about my health? Now I would need an STD test. I think I went through three bars of soap before I felt clean.

I called my best friend and she invited me over to watch a funny movie. The movie temporarily distracted me; I was laughing and trying very hard to get those terrible pictures out of my head. Every so often, I would give my friend more details about the break up. She just listened and didn't judge. She kept telling me that I could do so much better than him and that he would regret his actions in the future. Whether he really will regret it or not isn't the point. It was something I had to believe to get over it.

On December 31st, I woke up feeling ill. I had promised a friend that I would take her step class in the morning. I know myself and I know that the quickest way to cheer myself up is by working out. I tried to eat break-fast, but could barely touch my cereal. Every time I thought of eating, I would feel sick, but I knew I had to have something; especially since I was heading to the gym. As I drove, I kept trying to push the images of him cheating out of my head. I reminded myself that I was able to get over my first love; and the first cut is the deepest, so I knew that one day I would look back on this and laugh at myself for being so naïve.

I'm a Regional Manager at a fitness club, so I didn't want to show how upset I was. I plastered a big grin on my face as I walked in, but I guess I've always been bad at hiding my emotions. I'm usually such an ener-getic, upbeat person that the second I'm not bouncing off the walls, people know something is wrong. As soon as I walked into the club and said, "Hi" everyone crowded around and asked what was wrong. I didn't want the world to know, so I said, "Nothing, don't worry about it." Every time someone asked about me, it would bring me closer to tears. My friend, the step instructor and her boyfriend walked in. She, of course, asked why I was not my usual, happy self. I had to tell her; especially now that I had no New Year's Eve plans. She consoled me and told me he was crazy. She told me she would teach my favourite step class.

She must be magic, because for most of the class I was smiling. Other times, I would be concentrating on working out as hard as possible. There is one move called the 'nutcracker' that I used some visualization with.

After class, my friend invited me to go for all-you-can-eat sushi. But, I hit the weights instead; I figured that if I couldn't control my relationship I can at least control myself. I pushed myself harder than ever and achieved a personal goal for chin-ups. That mini-success helped restore some of my self-confidence.

I had some offers from friends to go out that night, but I wasn't in the mood to dress up, get drunk and meet guys. I don't usually drink and I would never want a one night stand; especially not on the rebound. What would a one night stand accomplish? I'm pretty sure I'd feel much worse about myself if I went with someone to 'get back at him.' Why compromise my well-being because of the pain I was feeling? Drinking or sleeping around might temporarily take away the pain, but know I would feel a million times worse the next day. Haven't I been through enough?

Instead, I went to my friend's house to play board games. They were fun and it was nice to be surrounded by sober people who truly cared about me. My friend suggested that we write down our goals for 2008. I wanted to learn some new fitness disciplines, take Samba lessons, spend more time with my family and friends and do more things that make me happy. I also told myself that I didn't want to cry over a guy again. This goal was exceptionally hard to keep because I had just been cheated on the day before, giving me only a day-and-a-half to cry!

On the other hand, I was lucky that he told me on December 30th. I was able to compartmentalize the event as something that happened in 2007 and start fresh in 2008. I vowed that 2007 would be the last year that I would spend in a lopsided relationship. From now on, I was going to demand equal time and effort. Whenever I started thinking about his actions, I would distract myself with my promise to myself.

I have a theory that helps me get through tough situations. I figure that if I only live once, I shouldn't spend too much time feeling badly. I allow myself to react naturally to the bad situation by crying or screaming into my pillow and talking it out with my friends. Then I try to think of positive reasons why the event happened and move on.

I told myself that his cheating may have been the best thing that ever happened. He hadn't been a good boyfriend and getting him out of my life has made room for me to meet a more suitable guy. Maybe recovering from infidelity will help me become stronger; maybe it will make me a better, more understanding person. Maybe it will allow me to grow on a personal level.

My advice for anyone going through this situation is to remember it's not you; it's him! No matter how beautiful, smart, kind or talented you are, he will cheat if it's in his system. Just be strong, reach out to your friends and family for help and do something good for yourself. In the end, the only person who can make you happy is you. Happiness is a choice. Choose to be happy and good things will happen. Maybe not immediately, but down the road- they will.

How am I doing now? I am still healing. I still feel betrayed; I don't feel as though I could trust another guy at the moment, but I know I'll be ready one day. I'm in no rush to find someone, but dating and meeting new people really helps me believe that there are other fish in the sea.

As for my goals… I did learn two other fitness disciplines; I took Samba lessons; I've gone out salsa dancing as often as possible and had the time of my life! I spent ample quality time with my family and friends and took more trips to visit my friends out of town. Believe it or not, I haven't cried over a guy once in 2008! I got very close while writing this, especially the first half, but I didn't shed a tear. He isn't worth a tear. He isn't even worth the words I said to him that night. The only worth I am concentrating on now is my self-worth and no matter what anyone does to me, they cannot take that away.

Monica Starr

Wednesday, July 11, 2007 started off like any normal day. Brady and I woke up at 5:30 that morning and headed to the gym to work out. We usually worked out for about an hour, but today we stayed a bit longer. We were hitting the weights hard, and we were really 'in the zone'. We lost track of time as we sweated our way through the grueling workout.

Finally, Brady said that he was running behind; he had to be in Nebraska at 9:00 a.m. to fix a bank's computer system. Back home, he showered quickly. After gobbling down a light breakfast, we bid our good-byes for the day. It was 8:45 and he had a 30 minute drive ahead of him. He was going to be late.

Brady said, "My baby loves me." I replied, "Yes, I do love you." We always said "My baby loves me" when one of us was leaving; it was our reminder to each other to buckle up, drive safe, and come home to each other. Our biggest fear was losing one another in a car accident. At the end of each day, we wanted to be back in each other's arms, safe and sound.

Brady and I met in the summer of 2004 at a race track. Brady raced stock cars. My brother, Colby, and I raced Cruiser cars. I noticed Brady as soon as Colby and I arrived at the track that Saturday. His pit crew was next to ours. How convenient! I could watch this handsome man all evening! I was feeling a little giddy as I tried to make eye contact with him. I'd catch him glancing at me from time to time; each time I caught him looking at me, my heart raced with joy.

As Brady went onto the track to race that evening, Colby and I climbed on top of a trailer for a better view of the race. While I was watching Brady race around the track in his 25KO Stock Car, an older man approached me. After the man got my attention, he immediately began peppering me with question after question:

"How old are you? Do you believe in God? Do you drink? Do you do drugs? What do you do for work? Where do you live? Are you single?"

Caught totally off guard by the stream of questions, I replied automatically,

"Twenty-five. Yes. Sometimes. No. Farming and personal training. Oberlin. Yes."

Laughing, with a twinkle in his eye, the man then said, "I'd like you to meet my son."

I was thinking to myself, "Oh Great! His son must be a real doozie if his dad has to meet girls for him!"

But I said that I would be glad to meet him; I didn't want to be rude.

After the stock cars were done racing, the man led me over to his son. He said, "Brady, I'd like you to meet Monica."

As his son turned around, my heart jumped. His son turned out to be the cute guy I had been keeping my eye on since Colby and I showed up at the track!

We talked briefly, but I could sense that he was busy getting his car ready for the next race. I said goodbye and walked away. Before the races ended, Brady and I exchanged phone numbers. Over the next few days, we chatted on MSN and spent countless hours on the phone each night. I was amazed at how perfect this man was turning out to be, and I told him so on our first date.

Our first date was spent at the races. Brady had to race that Saturday, and he took it very seriously. Racing his car was his greatest passion in life; during the summer, every weekend was spent at the track. After the races, we talked for awhile. I told him that "he'd better be careful, because I was falling in love with him." I was so nervous when I said that because I was terrified that I had scared him away. To my surprise, he smiled. The look he gave me was unforgettable as he said that the feeling was mutual.

At the time, Brady lived in Nebraska and I lived in Kansas. We soon found ourselves spending every weekend together. He would come to Kansas every Friday and he would leave early Monday morning so he could get back to Nebraska for his job. The weekdays were long and lonely without him. We hated the distance between us, and the 2 ½ hour road trips each weekend were growing tiresome. Soon after we met, we started looking at engagement rings. Although it all seemed so sudden, we knew in our hearts that we were made for one another. It just felt right. I loved his family, he loved mine, and we loved each other.

To close the distance between us, Brady decided to move to Kansas. He wanted to open up his own business and then we could start a life together. He said we should take care of each other; he and I wanted to spend forever together. So that's what we started working toward.

In 2005, we moved in together. I admit, getting used to sharing a home together was a bit of a trial; but we adjusted quickly. While Brady was getting his new business going, he worked on my family's farm and ranch. I don't think he liked farming all that much, but he had fun because he had become close to my brothers, Carl and Colby. They all spent a lot of time together. My Dad, who had never approved of any man dating his daughter, absolutely loved Brady. Everything was perfect.

After much thought and a lot of money spent, we found the perfect office and opened a business in town. Brady was the backbone of the business, and I was his faithful assistant. It was just the two of us, and we loved every minute of it. We fixed computers; built websites; made business cards and flyers; and did vinyl decal work for store windows, billboards, racecars, semi trucks, and just about anything anyone wanted a decal for. We had a blast. Brady took so much pride in owning his own business and I was proud of him. We were busy and happy.

Brady and I had become inseparable. We worked out together; we worked together; we rode horses together; he even did photo shoots with me, which was an amazing experience. I model for fitness magazines and doing photo shoots is one of my favorite things to do. Brady took an interest in modeling as well and we soon had several shoots set up together. He supported my dreams, my goals and my goofy ideas; I supported his, as well. We complemented each other completely.

In March of 2006, I had a photo shoot booked in Las Vegas. We decided to spend a few extra days there and make it a much needed vacation. Brady and I had a blast sightseeing and shopping.

One night, we got dressed up and went to a Vegas show. Afterward, we spent hours walking around the Strip. Our journey back to the hotel found us watching the water fountain show at the Bellagio. The music, lights and sprays of water were all so romantic! Like a fairytale, Brady got down on one knee in front of the crowd of people. He said, "Will you be my wife?" We had the attention of the entire crowd; I could hear the ooh's and aah's of our appreciative audience. Much to the surprise of the on-lookers, I said that I didn't think it was the right time. We had just got the business going full speed ahead, we were looking at buying a home, and we had a lot going on at the time; I just didn't think we should tackle one more thing. Our trip ended the next day, but our relationship was growing stronger and stronger.

That Christmas, Brady popped the question again. This time, with Brady on one knee and a ring in his hand, I said, "Yes." We decided to wait for the right time to tell our families; we were afraid they would think it was all happening too fast. Nevertheless, we started to make plans for the wedding. We wanted everything to be perfect. The planning was a lot of fun for both of us. I was anxious to tell everyone, but we wanted the timing to be perfect. Our life together was like a fairy tale. Brady was my knight in shining armor and nothing could stop us. Together, we were on top of the world.

I was out at my Dad's ranch that afternoon on July 11, 2007. We were fixing the fence surrounding the horse corral. My phone rang at 2:10 pm. It was Brady, saying, "Hey baby, I'm almost home. I'm nine miles out; meet me at the office. I'll see you soon and I love you, Baby."

I left the farm and headed home. Although I had just seen Brady this morning, I missed him and couldn't wait to see him. At 2:30 p.m., he still hadn't showed up. I tried calling his cell phone; he didn't answer. I tried texting him and still had no luck getting through. I figured he had just stopped to talk to someone, but I was starting to worry.

At 3:00 p.m., my phone rang. It was a cop from town; he told me that there had been a bad accident and that I needed to get to the hospital right away. I rushed out of the house and drove like hell. Outside the hospital, a crowd had gathered. I ran up to see what was going on. Then I saw the helicopter; EMT's were rushing to put someone in the Flight For Life helicopter. My heart stopped. Everything around me stood still.

I ran forward trying to get close to that helicopter. I was screaming Brady's name over and over. A cop grabbed me to stop me from going any closer; I was about 50 yards away from my sweet baby and the helicopter. The officer said, "Monica, you have to pray. This doesn't look good; he's beat up pretty bad. All you can do is pray." I fell to the ground, praying and crying.

Brady had called me at 2:10 that day to tell me he was almost home. Less than five minutes later, a truck crossed the center line. They collided head-on in a mess of metal and glass. Our worst fear had come true: One of us was in a car accident, and there was nothing either of us could do. I prayed over and over for God to let him be okay.

To my horror, Brady passed away on the helicopter flight to Nebraska; the collision had caused major internal damages that were far too great for him to fight.

That night, I could only lay on the floor with my dog. I cried and screamed and begged Brady to come back to me. I just kept thinking that it was all a bad dream; I just knew I was going to wake up, but when?

On Thursday, my house began to fill up with family and friends. Flowers filled my living room and kitchen; people brought food and gifts. I was grateful for their concern, but it was all very overwhelming. All I could do was sit on the floor and cry.

Brady's mother called to say that she needed a suit for Brady to wear at the funeral. I knew it couldn't be put off, but the thought of picking out the last outfit he would ever wear seemed too hard to bear. With my mom's help I pulled myself together and found a suit that I liked. After Brady's mother picked up the suit, I went into our bedroom and shut the door. I opened up our closet and grabbed Brady's clothes and breathed in his familiar scent; it was comforting.

A few days later, I went to the funeral home for the visitation. My first step toward his casket was the toughest step of my life so far. I couldn't bear to see him so lifeless. It seemed so surreal. His mother took my hand and we walked up to see him together. I immediately lost it. I went home and again cried. It seemed that crying was my only solace.

The day of the funeral came and went as if in a dream. I know I listened to the people who talked during the funeral, but I don't remember any of it. The people crying, Brady's casket, the flowers, the music, the pictures were all too much to bear; I hated life. I began to sink into a deep depression.

The days following the funeral are a blur. People stopped by to see me, but I couldn't speak to them; I just sat around listlessly. I couldn't sleep; I didn't eat anything for two weeks and lost twenty-five pounds. I was soon topping the scales at a sickly 100 pounds. I didn't shower for days. I'm sure I was quite a sight, but I didn't care. I just wanted to curl up and die.

My mom, sisters, and brothers stayed with me for several days. They were so worried about me; they thought I was suicidal. I think I was at the time. They watched me waste away into depression and become skin and bones. Nothing they said or did helped me.

One evening, not long after the funeral, an old friend from school stopped by to visit. My mom opened the door to let Tom in. I just stared at the wall. He walked right in and sat down; he didn't try to talk, he just hugged me. Everyone cried. Tom stayed for awhile, and he and my family filled the room with idle chitchat.

Tom and I had known each other in high school. He is two years older, and we had gone on a couple of dates, but gone our separate ways after graduation; I went to college and Tom got married.

I didn't think anything of Tom's visit that night, but Tom kept stopping by. He would show up periodically with coffee, donuts, and other foods that immediately got thrown in the garbage as soon as he had gone; I couldn't bring myself to even look at food.

Eventually, the time came when my family had to get back to their jobs and their lives. Without my knowing it, my mom and dad asked Tom to keep checking on me. They told him to make sure I was alive. They asked him to try to get me to eat something. He agreed to watch over me.

One night in late July, I was sitting home alone. Memories of Brady filled my head, and I was lost in my thoughts; I was miserable without him. How would I ever find happiness again? A knock on the door brought me back to reality. It was Tom. He greeted me with a smile and I managed to say hello, then plopped myself back down on the couch. He sat down at the other end and we started talking. He told me about what he had been up to since high school. He told me about his recent divorce and I could tell he was very hurt about it. I knew that he had married, and I had seen him and his wife around town; they had always looked happy together. I guess you can't judge a book by its cover.

Tom and I talked until about midnight, when he said he should get home so I could get some sleep. I just burst into tears and cried, "Just hold me for a minute." I fell into his arms, sobbing and kept asking why Brady was taken from me. He didn't say a word; he just held me.

The next morning, I awoke to find myself in bed. My eyes were swollen and red. Tears stained my cheeks. Tom was gone. I had fallen asleep and he had carried me to my room and tucked me in. That night was the first time I slept since the accident. I would nod off from time to time, but that night, I really slept soundly.

As the weeks wore on, Tom and I developed a strong friendship; the friendship we had both known in high school. He would listen to me talk about the things Brady and I used to do and I would listen to him talk about his marriage and divorce. We would spend countless hours driving around, listening to music and just rambling on and on about life. I started eating again and I was sleeping at night.

In August, Tom and I went out to see my Dad. Tom and my Dad are very good friends and they have been for years. My Dad pulled me aside and said,

"I can see that you're getting better. I know that you miss Brady, but I can tell that you're happier these days."

Tom told my Dad that he had never been this happy and he wanted to know what my Dad thought of the two of us growing so close. My Dad told him that he was happy for the both of us and our closeness was just what each of us needed.

I'm not sure exactly when it happened, but I fell in love again. I never thought it was possible; here was this man that I went to school with, a high school sweetheart and he was back in my life. I was plagued with worry that it was happening too soon. I talked to my friends and family about Tom. Every single person said that our relationship was the best thing that could have happened to either one of us. They all felt that we needed each other.

As our relationship grows, Tom and I are amazed at how much we have in common, and how well we understand each other. Tom never tries to push memories of Brady out of my mind; he lovingly listens to my stories. He understands how important Brady was to me, and that he will always have a special place in my heart. Tom and I give each other strength and happiness.

Not long after the accident, I approached the site of the crash on my way to Nebraska. I jumped out of my truck and looked at all the broken glass and bits of plastic from Brady's car that was scattered over the road and ditch. Frantically, I started gathering up every piece that I could get my hands on. I guess I lost my mind momentarily because when I finally realized how silly I was being, I had filled the entire passenger side floor of my pickup with little pieces of his car.

I think of Brady nearly every day; I can close my eyes and see his smiling face and his beautiful brown eyes as if he was right here with me. I know I will never forget him, but time is easing my pain. I still have nightmares about the accident; the image of the mangled '99 Black Firebird is embedded in my mind forever. When I saw that car, all I could think about was what Brady must have been thinking at the moment of impact; for a long time, I couldn't stop thinking about that. I still shudder every time I pass the wooden cross on the highway that bears Brady's name.

The time that I spent with Brady was a great gift that I will always cherish. He taught me so much about life, love and laughter. Brady was a kind, strong person who is greatly missed by many. He touched so many lives, and anyone who had the opportunity to meet him knows what a wonderful, caring man he was.

I have so many things to be thankful for in my life, and so many wonderful people that helped me through this hard time. A big heart felt thank you goes out to Mom, Dad, Allen, Karen, Carl, Marissa, Colby, Miranda, and Tom. I love you all, and thank you for all of your love and support; I couldn't have made it through this without you. Thank you "Tomica" for helping me learn how to live and smile again. I love you! I thank God too, for love, lessons, and life.

Nita Marquez

A t the tender age of sixteen, she held onto her baby while physically fighting her own father to maintain custody. She shoved the paperwork away and screamed at her dad, her only child's grandfather.

"I'm not giving up my baby!" There were counselors and agents standing about when the nurses rushed into the room to calm her and lay her back into her hospital bed. Among all the uninvited company in her hospital room, her father stood with papers in hand, demanding that she sign away her newborn little girl to a family that could "take better care of her." She fought, and at sixteen, Sandra won.

There was no way that anyone could have taken me from her. She was determined to keep me. Sometimes, I think about that episode with gratitude and other times, I'm disgusted with her selfishness. My childhood is strewn with occasions where I was reminded by my mother of how I 'took her childhood away.' I never quite measured up to my mother's expectations. I always felt like an obstacle or an obligation to my mom, as if I was in the way. I grew up without realizing that there was nothing I could have done or said any differently to have been a better daughter. When someone is unhappy, they just are and the truth is that it has nothing to do with what's outside of them. A person's state of mind has more to do with what is inside the soul rather than what's in the environment. I had a hard time understanding that for many years. Because of my lack of understanding, I related everything to my past. That past has impacted every choice I've ever made. I personalized so many of my mother's choices for my childhood and thus, I have been the cause of my own suffering. My mom fought to keep me, but she assuredly reminded me that I owed her for that.

It's true what they say about time healing all wounds, but in 34 years, I have also learned that only you have the power to heal your wounds.

Momma was only sixteen, but she was feisty and very hard working. She did everything she could to make ends meet. There were compromising choices that reflected her diligence. Sometimes, when I was little, I remember her working two or three jobs at a time. I always looked up to her in spite of all the misgivings. There she was, this amazing and beautiful woman and wherever she went, people just stared at her because she was so radiant. No one knew how weak she was because she had such a boundless energy.

Also, she was a fabulous dancer. When she danced, there was life just spewing out of her! She always won dance contests all around the city. Sometimes she would take me with her to dance and I would dance like there was no tomorrow. Dance floors and stages were my childhood safe houses. When I was dancing or singing onstage, I felt like nothing could harm me, like I was invincible! When I performed, I felt like my mom loved me and was proud of me. Dancing with Momma was like a dream when we did it together. I really enjoyed this as a child and that was where my love for dancing and performing began.

As a little girl, I viewed my mother as a queen and I prayed that God would help her stop being so mean to me. In spite of our dance-a-thons, she was really ruthless at times. In spite of all her insulting rants and physical abuse, there was a very tender and infinitely loving side of Momma. There were spontaneous nights where she would let me lay next to her in bed to go to sleep. She would whisper to me so sweetly that she loved me and I say even now that these were some of the most remarkable moments in my childhood. I remember these times vividly; this was when I felt my safest. When you're a little girl, it's so easy to wish to be a princess and daydream all the time, but when you are constantly belittled, you wonder if you will ever amount to much of anything, let alone a princess. When my mom would snuggle with me in bed on those nights, I felt like royalty. I felt rescued. All the hurt would disappear. I remember having growing pains, too and how she would soothe them. She would massage my legs with lotion when I was aching; Momma had the most velvet touch. When she loved on me, it was soft with the most pure and warm energy imaginable. Sometimes, I would cry and pretend I was having growing pains in my legs or say I was afraid just so she would hold me and caress the pain away; her love felt so good. Back then, I would do anything for it. As those moments became fewer and farther between, I began looking for that loving elsewhere.

Summers were often spent with my family members, who were close. I learned to look for a loving haven's likeness elsewhere. My grandpa, who had tried to have me signed away, spoiled me rotten. My mom's sister was the same. I loved it when they took me for summer holidays or school breaks. More than once, they took me in for the entire school year. No beatings, no insults, just constant love. They were always taking me shopping and letting me enjoy life and they talked to me a lot. I was treated like a person who mattered when I was with them. I still acted out with them, though. I think I knew that they would never hit me the way my mother did, or call me 'stupid-ass' or tell me what a dumb fucking kid I was. I guess I just acted out because I was testing their love and patience. When I was with them, I would push the envelope, but their love never relented. As a result, I was always happy to go with them and I felt much loved by my aunt and my grandpa.

One time, my mom told me that I had a choice, "You can either go with your aunt, or I will end up beating the shit out of you this summer." These times became more and more frequent, overshadowing the good times with Momma. These were the times I began to resenting her for keeping me. I felt like there was no point in keeping me if she was just going to hate me. She wasn't really thinking about how much she valued me when she was throwing shoes at me, slamming my head against the wall, slapping me in the face in public or cursing my name. I cried at night all the time about how little she showed me love.

Reflecting back on the nights when she snuggled me though, it really was the most remarkable joy. Our snuggle-sessions washed over all the insults and beatings. I could crawl into the warmth of every quiet moment she gave me like that. Each time she held me like that and told me she loved me, my childish mind secretly contemplated that she was ready to love me for good. My hope was always that she wasn't going to call me stupid anymore and she would snuggle with me every day. When she met Daniel, my seeking would continue.

When my mom met Daniel, she told me that she was in love for the first time. All I knew was that love made you feel safe, so I understood and began to love him, too. I thought he would be able to provide a safe life for us. His presence seemed strong and he was very affectionate. Within a few months, Daniel would be living with us and he took very good care of my sister and I while my mom worked. He did a lot of things with us recreationally. Daniel started watching us full-time. Sometimes he was a construction worker and other times, he sold cocaine or stole cars. I remember my mom marrying him and then we went to see our 'Daddy' in jail. My dreams were for him to be home with us because I missed having him take care of us. I thought that if he was with us, everything would be better and maybe my mom would be happy. When he came home, we were a family. That was the first time I remember ever feeling a family structure. Momma, Daddy and the kids; I was in a family for once. It was a solid feeling; I was happy with it and I thought that everything we had going on was normal.

Right about that time, I remember meeting my real father, who was a musician. Everyone seemed to get along just fine, so I got to go and spend the night with my real dad. That was interesting. I remember going out dancing with my dad and his girlfriend. I was happy that I got to be with my father and I got to perform for him at the dance contest he took me to. I was only six years-old and I won the dance competition! I couldn't believe it! I danced for his family too, when I got to meet his mom and his brothers. It was a fascinating feeling. I had all this family, plus I had a grandpa and aunts and uncles and now I had *two* dads, all on top of having Momma. I really did start to feel like a princess.

Eventually, Momma and Daniel moved to Texas and I was sent to live with my Grandpa and his family for a year. When the school year ended, I got to continue my summer with my grandpa, but then I was returned to my mom. We were with Daniel's family in Texas and everyone seemed content.

When my fourth grade year began, the physical abuse Daniel ensued on my mother worsened and he did more and more to bruise me as well. He used two-by-fours to spank me and if he was unhappy with me in a fit of rage, he would just grab whatever was closest to him. He once tore the molding off a door and beat me with that because he caught me kissing a boy. If there was nothing to hit me with, he just kicked me. I didn't understand why everyone was so angry all the time. Either he was beating Momma or me, or Momma was screaming at him or she was calling me names and belittling me. I was always frightened to go home. Even in the middle of the night, Daniel would wake us up, saying that someone was watching us from outside the apartment and make me get out of bed and hide. He was always on drugs. I was always sneaking around, looking through their things and finding the drugs they were both doing. He and my mom would fight over the cocaine or get high with it or he would sell it and this was life.

I started wondering if some of it wasn't normal. To vent, I started writing at about age eleven and it became more regular by twelve and thirteen. Writing gave me some peace when I completed a work that resulted from the abnormalities of our home. As I became more comfortable with my work, I also became more open to the idea of sharing my poetry and short stories. What did I do when people asked what it was about? I lied. People would compliment me for my imagination. I would never have wanted anyone to know that it was based on my own experiences.

At some point however, I finally responded with a truthful answer to that question. When I shared the work with a peer, she started tearing up in her eyes. She asked what I was talking about in one of my poems. I told her all my secrets about my home life and instead of keeping it in confidence, she used it as a gossip topic. She told everyone about my stepdad beating me and molesting me. I had told her of the molestations that had been going on for years. They had begun even before Momma and Daniel moved in together. I was always afraid to tell anyone because Daniel told me that my mom would hate me if anyone found out. He knew how desperately I sought my mother's love. He knew how to frighten me into silence with the idea of her hating me. The only person I told was this girlfriend at school and in turn, it became known to everyone else we hung out with. It was so embarrassing. Not one person went to a teacher about any of the abuses I suffered. They just made fun of me for it. As if it couldn't get any worse, Daniel ended up in the newspaper because he robbed a convenience store while he was high on cocaine.

As it all came crashing down, the stakes played on her child-rearing life were running short. There was a force behind my mother's crippling ability to bring people into our life who were no good. Her choices were always abiding in her lusts and immediate gratifications without consideration to her motherhood. While the consequences of her actions took time, the impact of those choices was heavily affecting my judgment and character development.

I was getting into her drug stash and doing lines with my friends while she was at work. By the age of thirteen, I had lost my virginity. All the while, my mother was working, drugging to work more, so she could make more money to keep us afloat and then spending time with her new boyfriend. She didn't know what I was up to half the time and when she was around, she was usually slapping me around and telling me how stupid I was. I vaguely remembered the tender times, but by that point, her tender ways toward me had grown nonexistent. I hated her.

Eventually, I lost my mother completely to her addiction and I moved in with a friend. Momma got more strung out after her divorce from Daniel and even lost her boyfriend. By then, I was nowhere in her mix. I went to California to live with her sister. That didn't work out, so I ended up going to Michigan to live with Grandpa. His alcoholism was killing him, so that move landed me in the state's system. After being in a state home for teens who were delinquents, a foster family came through for me. It was a single-mother household and she was a teacher. Honeymom (that was my name for her) was truly a delight and a determined one at that. I was shy when I first got to her home, but after being there for a few weeks, I started having outbursts of crying and screaming at her. Hatred for my new and unfamiliar life became overwhelming. The peace in her house was literally unbearable and I didn't know how to deal with it. There had to be some kind of fighting, screaming or battle going on, or I just didn't feel comfortable. Honeymom still loved on me. She would hug me with those embraces that make you feel locked in securely and she would not let me go, while I cried and cried. Yelling curses at my mother, but wanting her back, I was so confused all the time. While I cried and kicked and screamed for so many days and nights, Honeymom put up with my fits and encouraged me constantly to see myself through all the anger. She was always pushing me to see something more in myself than what I had been learning all my life.

Then, my mother resurfaced one day and tried to get me back, but the state revoked her parental rights. I then endured one counseling session after another. I was angry and bitter with my mother, but I also wanted to be with her to help her. Counselors would try to explain to me that she wasn't supposed to have my help; that it was she as the parent who needed to be helping me and she simply wasn't able to do that. I didn't know what to do, so I buried myself further in schoolwork, dancing and writing.

Honeymom still softened my emotional discord's blows with her encouragement. She didn't tolerate my disrespect, but she would not tolerate my self-destructive commentary either. Verbiage of what I was destined for as a dancer, as a writer was constantly being put into my thoughts by Honeymom. Some of my family members went to the state to petition custody of me and in time, they won. Honeymom cried as she helped me pack my things to leave her, but she has never forgotten me; nor I her. Throughout my life, I have had family members like my aunts and uncles, who have undyingly loved and believed in me. I have had a rebellious many years that made life difficult for all of them at some point. I went on to college with the encouragement of everyone in my family and through the words of wisdom that were shared with me by the mentors who have picked me up along the way. I did quite a few questionable and compromising things in the process of learning about my own destiny and I will still make mistakes and learn and grow. I accept that. However, I now believe that my past is only as powerful as I let it be. I let my past be the cause of hundreds of poor choices that have held me back so much. I went on to college at the University of Arizona and then I did nothing with my college education. I spent a lot of years learning, accepting myself and finally learning how to own myself rather than letting my pain own me. Now I am an educated and successful mother of three. My children feel loved and safe and I am honored to have the privilege to provide them with that. I can say life has become something of an adventure for me.

In recent years and during motherhood, I have come to learn for myself that mothers and all women are just doing the best we know. I finally grew up and realized that my mother just didn't know any better and maybe she never will. That doesn't invalidate the love she had for me in the times she snuggled me and danced with me. What my mother put me through had to do with her. It was never about me. When I finally understood that, I didn't have to live with her choices anymore; I used my power to create the woman I am today. We have the power to heal our own wounds through time. So I had to finally let go of my mother's impacts and wounds and I learned to allow my mother's wounds to be hers. My time is used to heal my wounds, live a proactive life one day at a time and protect my own children.

Life has blessed me with many opportunities to know better than what I was

taught as a child. I live by the faith I have in myself. The most genuine guidance came to me through people who cared enough to speak truth into me. I choose to make victimization into victory. I wrote and wrote and danced and danced. As a performer, I am ranked one of the country's top-three competitors in fitness, a venue where I am allowed a chance to do what I love across the country. I have been acting for three years and I have co-executive produced two independent films. I am currently in the process of developing my third production. My children are actors, dancers and gymnasts and I am working with all of them at various times in their training; which is a blast. My children and I have dance sessions just like my mom and I did when I was small. I'm giving my children the life I wanted when I was a child.

Roanna Sabeh-Azar

I was four years old when I was brought here from Lebanon. The truth is that I was actually born in Toronto while my mother was visiting. We lived in Lebanon for the following four years, but the relationship between my mom and dad wasn't a good one; to the point where her parents had to protect her from him. Fortunately, because I had been born in Toronto, my father didn't have custody of me. My mom's parents managed to get us out of the country; thanks to all of their airport official friends.

This was a traumatic moment for me, watching my mom and family packing their luggage and wondering where we were going. But there was a lot of love in my home and everyone was in it together and we were going on an adventure back to Toronto!

The five of us lived at Don Mills and Shepherd: my grandmother and grandfather; my mom and her sister, Eileen, and me. I remember being teased a lot my first couple of years, in kindergarten and grade one; I'm not sure why. But I also remember going home for a lunch of my grandfather's favourite melted cheese sandwiches! I miss those sandwiches and I miss my grandfather. He passed when I was sixteen. He was like a father to me and my grandmother, who passed when I was 32, was like my mom. My mom was more like my sister; young, hip and funky.

My family home was pretty normal; I was well equipped on the role model side of things. In my neighbourhood, there was a lot of shrubbery for caterpillars and snakes to live in; that was my playground. At school we did a lot of fun adventure things that included frogs and tadpoles and butterflies. I was a tomboy, but I think that was because mom would always keep my hair so short, and, of course, something about climbing trees and fences just attracted me.

When I was nine, mom and I moved into our own place at York Mills and Don Mills. I was at the bud of my socialization. There were a lot of kids around and we all became friends. We always played games like 'Spin the Bottle' and 'Truth or Dare' and other fun games and I wondered if all kids were as lucky. I was definitely sexually aware and I definitely did experiment, more with the boys than the girls, but it was innocent curiosity and I actually turned out to be a bit of a prude. I was just a normal curious kid who wanted to know everything about everything.

I attended a small elementary French school by the name of Ecole Georges-Etienne-Cartier. I made friends easily, but I also fought occasionally with other kids from my class. They were always rather innocent squabbles; we were all acquiring social skills, learning and growing. The other students were all French Canadian and I was an ethnic girl who didn't own a pair of jeans until my second year there; I guess that seemed odd to them since here I remember I still really got teased a lot! But I was a very good student with excellent marks. That probably bugged them too.

Otherwise, my life was great and mom gave me everything that I needed. She took me to horseback riding lessons every Saturday, sent me to camp every summer for a couple of weeks. I loved every minute of camp in spite of being homesick in the beginning. I also loved to hang out at the theatre with my mom when she would rehearse the plays that she starred in.

My mom was a Translator-Interpreter by trade, but by the time I was fourteen, she was also heavily involved in the theatre. She was such a wonderful actress! She mastered British comedy and so developed an accent that she never dropped. It was very cool being around such artistic people and I decided that I too wanted to act. My first role was the lead in a play called 'My Three Angels' and I was very good apparently.

I attended church regularly with my grandmother and got involved quite intensely in their social group, the Syrian Orthodox Youth Organization; SOYO. There I made some great friends and was able to express my creativity through fundraising and fashion shows. I also learned more about my culture, myself and how to socialize with others in a respectable fashion. I participated in a few writing competitions through my school and through SOYO; thanks to my mom, the editor in chief, I pulled off some pretty good stuff and actually won a few of them! Of course that meant that I had to recite the winning piece in front of a large audience of strangers. The benefit of all these experiences was the oral speaking skills I picked up and the grace, poise and confidence with which I learned to carry myself.

At fourteen, I graduated to my high school years and was sent to Ecole Secondaire Etienne Brule, another French school where I was maybe the only ethnic girl once again; but this time it was okay, people were older and more tolerant. I suppose that's what happens to people; we develop social skills and become much more tolerant of differences; and I was different. I had a lot of spunk; I always did. I was creative and loved schoolwork and projects. I loved to ask questions. I was also a bit of a trouble-maker.

By the time I was in grade eleven, I was totally sick of my classmates; I had to get out and move forward, right into grade thirteen! I took some extra night school classes, which I did typically anyway and managed to skip a year. That was the year that I learned how to play Euchre, dated the cutest guy in school, was voted Prom Queen and met the two of my class-mates who would become great friends; Ronnie and Sue remain close to this day. I graduated with honours.

I thought I had figured out what I wanted to do with my life; I wanted to be a veterinarian, but I realized in high school that although I won first prize in a science competition, and had my project on cloning frogs displayed at the Ontario Science Centre (one of my favourite places grow-ing up), I just couldn't get the mathematics. So I applied to four universities for Journalism or Psychology and I was accepted at all of them. Though, I also wanted to be a truck driver, a professional horseback rider or a police officer.

I chose to attend Western University, where I was accepted in the Psychology program. I was psyched about moving to London, Ontario! I checked into the Saugeen-Maitland dorm, met my roommate and graced my walls with Madonna posters!

It was an interesting year. Not only was I kicked out, but I officially 'came out' that year. I always wondered why my boyfriends were 'just friends' and why I was so drawn to certain girls in my life and one day, I decided to give it a try. University and London, Ontario provided me with a playground away from my family to begin my search. Although I totally enjoyed being in university, studying and participating in extracurricular activities, I was failing my statistics course and the first set of exams were coming up and I wasn't sure what I was going to do and I had so many other things on my mind that I never received any math tutoring, nor did I seek it. Instead, at exam time, I asked one of my friends to write the exam for me and she accepted; nice, helpful girl that she was. Of course, every prof that asked her for ID knew that it wasn't me and I was 'asked to leave' the university; which was actually okay since I kept dreaming about the beaches in Greece, though I had never been there, all I knew was that I was dreading the thought of the following nine years in London. So off I went, back to Toronto. Surprisingly, my mom didn't freak out at all. She had never put a lot of pressure on me or raised me as an overachiever; that just came naturally. I guess I was just better at some things than others. C'est la Vie!

Okay now more about my newfound sexuality. I remember when I first had those funny feelings for a girl; I was going on eighteen and I met her at Le Chateau in Fairview Mall. She started talking to me and somehow I ended up with her number. I did call her after a short while and our friendship began. She never told me that she was a lesbian and I didn't really need to know. The first time we met outside the mall, we went to grab a burger and it was such a fun evening of chit chat and slight flirtations. We left in separate vehicles and I was following her along RosedaleValley Drive when she stopped her car suddenly. She got out and ran over to my window and just simply laid it on me; the most beautiful kiss I had ever had! I had dated enough guys to know that this was different. This kiss was off the planet and I had found my new home! From that night on, I knew!

At first, it wasn't easy for my mom to accept. Please add: Poor mom, I was really letting her have it that year! I was actually surprised about that, considering that she's so open-minded; but maybe not when it comes to her own daughter. I think she felt guilty, as if it were her fault that I was 'different'; in a way it was, because if she wasn't so open-minded and cool, I wouldn't have had such an easy time accepting myself. She even sent me to a psychologist to help me 'change'. But the reality is that you can't and won't change unless you want to and didn't want to. I wanted to be me; a gay woman. She actually did me a big favour by trying to change me because it made me realize that who I was I liked and no matter the obstacles ahead I was very comfortable and happy in my own skin and that's all that matters. Years later, she has somewhat accepted my difference, loves my friends and only wants to see me happy. Those who love you will always stick by you and those who don't, who needs them, right?

So, there I was, nineteen, gay and out of school; what now? I got a job at a funky downtown shoe store where I outsold everyone and was invited to become store manager. But that was just not possible. My first official girlfriend, Deborah and I decided that we would enroll in the Hotel Management Program at George Brown's School of Hospitality. But I passed the entrance exam and Deborah didn't. I was doing it alone; it felt right.

By the age of 24, I had a Hotel and Food & Beverage diploma, had held several different sales and restaurant jobs; joined a gym; went through my first relationship of three-and-a-half years; backpacked throughout Europe for four months and landed a great job upon my return at the Hilton Hotel. It was now time to move out of my mother's house. I was finding my identity and moving out was imperative. Luckily for me, my mom, investor woman that she was, purchased a two storey penthouse condo which she allowed me to move into and she subsidized my rent. Suzie from grade thirteen was my first roommate. It was a penthouse with a view of the lake and I loved living there!

At that time I started my first business. I went to Puerto Vallarta with my mother and it turned out to be quite an interesting and mystical trip. I met a horse rider who was nice enough to take me to his stables where I was able to hire a horse and rider for a tour on the beach. YES! Horseback riding is my dream activity and here I was on a four day vacation of riding. On the third day there, I wasn't interested in spending anymore time on the beach, so I meandered into town. At the fourth store I visited, I came across a bag full of beige leather ponchos, folded and just waiting for a tourist to release it into a world of fashion and that's exactly what I intended to do! They were the coolest looking, Clint Eastwood-girl style things I had ever seen, so I bought both designs available and brought them home!

I started wearing one at a time around Toronto and people started commenting on how cool they were. After this happened about twenty times, I decided that I was going to import these capes into Toronto; the way to start was to show the samples that I had with me to all the leather stores in town and see how many orders I could accumulate. So, I got on the phone and appointments were made and one by one I visited all of the leather stores and the orders came in; I was in business. Now, all I had to do was get the stuff from Mexico. So, back to the phone and by the grace of God, I discovered that a trade show of Mexican decorative wares manufacturers would soon be taking place and the designers of the capes were going to be there.

This was a turning point in my life. I had to call up all my strength and courage and just do it; that's exactly what I did. I packed my bags and off I went to Mexico alone, but never lonely because I always felt that God was by my side and that I was protected; to this day, ten years later, I still feel the same way!

Wow! It all flowed as though there was nothing else I was supposed to be doing! I had a ball and everyone I met was so nice! And oh the tequila!!!

During the same trip, I discovered many other products that I ended up importing into Canada; restaurant-safe dishware and great looking housewares and decorative items from all over Mexico.

My relationship with Mexico lasted ten years. I started out selling from my penthouse to the trade and two years later I was offered a retail space on Bellair Street in Yorkville, the glam and hot, European looking area of Toronto. I called it Barroco, short for the 'Clay Company'. I had big dreams for my new company; I envisioned a sort of Pottery Barn concept, selling wholesale/retail and really making it big!

With everything going on, I started feeling as though I was missing something, like a dog. I looked everywhere for the right one but no luck for months. It was on a buying trip after the opening of my store that I found him.

I had met a lovely young Mexican gentleman by the name of Cesar and one night, while walking downtown in Mexico city, I looked down and in front of my feet was a box full of puppies and lo and behold, there he was; the cutest white dog with one black and white ear and a heart shaped design on his nose and big black eyes staring at me saying 'Hey it's me, take me home'! And so I did, I was now the happy owner of an Old English sheepdog. I named him Mex, short for Mexico, I mean that seemed pretty appropriate! That was one of the happiest days of my life! Fifteen years later, Mex is still with me and I love him as much as the first day he entered my life.

My store on Bellair lasted a year-and-a-half, working seven days a week, late nights and weekends, since Yorkville is a tourist hotspot. It was all going perfectly well; until I got a little bored. I missed the restaurant business and all of the excitement it offered. Since so many friends would come by and hang out with me, I thought why not serve them coffee or something? It wasn't long after that that I found an available location right on Yorkville Avenue and the new Barroco, Restaurant and Retail shop was born. In fact, it was the first retail and food location of its kind. Sam the Record Man did the same thing a year later, as did another shop up the street. I was proud to have such popular concepts and yet upset because I wanted to be a one-of-a-kind place.

For three-and-a-half years, I cooked, tended bar, went to the market and worked on my best behaviour everyday. That's how long it took for me to start getting fed up with all the stress and feeling trapped in my own creation. I couldn't handle it anymore; I felt trapped. Owning a restaurant must be the hardest thing anyone can do and my subsequent days in therapy made me realize that I just wasn't cut out for it.

Neo-Paws! At eight months-old, Mex started running with me. After our runs, I would see little blood patches where he walked; his paws would be bleeding! 'Now, why don't they have running shoes for dogs?' I thought. The shock absorption factor alone is huge. That was the start of the Idea that continued to grow into what is known today as 'the Leader in Safety Pet Apparel'!

I turned the restaurant/shop to my mom and her husband and off I went into the world of pets.

Success was immediate. I got samples from China and then I educated pet owners and convinced them that these were the best dog shoes around and they had to acquire them. After all, we were the leaders in the dog shoe industry and there really was no competition at all.

This was the beginning of new worlds for me. New lingo, for example I coined the term 'dog-pair' which means four shoes; new territories, our company sells worldwide, via the internet, distributors and retailers and a whole new education. I educated the public through tons of advertising; I could have been living in the Ritz Carlton for what I spent monthly and selling to veterinarians helped market the shoes as well. I had uncovered a whole new industry to which few were privy and which I now dominated!

Owning your ownbusiness, means 100% dedication; it's the only way to make it happen! It's your baby, it's a love affair! As with my previous company, I continued doing trade shows. I would drive across the country just to get myself and my business there. I was driven and Neo-Paws consumed my life. I owed it to the company; it needed time to grow. Eventually, more and more people were coming out with their own versions of dog shoes and apparel. I just ignored them and kept perfecting my creations. Today we are known as 'Nike to the dog world'!

At this time, relationships came secondary to me. As important as relationships are, they can take away from your end goal. An equal amount of energy has to be placed in a relationship and this can be distracting in many ways. It has to be the right one, otherwise it can be counter-productive, although necessary too, for it is in relationships that we grow emotionally.

Ten years later my company has become a success story all the way! Everyday, I know what I want and need to take it to the next level; though I am enjoying the journey. I do my company's sales, design work, ads, catalogs, customer service, product creation and perfection and a whole bunch of other things on a daily basis. I guess that's the reason I'm never bored. Though more than anything, it's the gratification I get knowing that we are helping millions of canine friends and their owners to lead more healthy, active lifestyles.

Along the way, one day out of the blue, I received a phone call from a director friend of mine who knew about my restaurant and dealings with Mexico for the many years. He told me that a casting agent, friend of his was looking for someone to host a television show called: 'Entrada, 'Journeys in Latin American Culture and Cuisine' and would I be interested in traveling around Latin America for a year? 'Of course I want to, I yelled into the phone'! So for the next year after that I toured around Latin America taping cooking shows. We filmed 26 episodes in 26 cities, in seven Latin American countries. My job was to assist in cooking with top chefs from the regions we visited. I would translate what they were saying into

English and speak to them in Spanish and it was fabulous. The series is still playing on many channels worldwide and a recipe book was published to support the show! This has been a proud accomplishment!

I returned to Neo-Paws from South America and it was nice knowing that I was going home to something I equally loved doing. But I miss TV work as much as I missed Neo-Paws when I was there. I hope to return to the screen and I pray it will come to me just as it did the first time and if not, at least now I know how to do it and I definitely have the determination to go out and get it!

In the meantime, I am working on my next project; opening a Neo-Paws branch office in Brazil, a place I fell in love with while taping. I discovered that Brazil is the third largest pet market worldwide and this would be the portal for all of South America: Brazil, Argentina, Chile and Uruguay, to name just a few. I am excited about this because the North American market is saturated with competitors; South America is a virgin market that's there for the taking and I'm taking it!

Though it is hasn't been an easy process; I need a Brazilian partner and, of course, it has to be someone I can trust and that can be tricky to find and the country's importing laws are very taxing. I am close to achieving this for I have networked myself into a group of people who may very well be what I need to move forward.

I'm also working on many other things. I'm developing a new pet related TV show, I'm doing event planning, throwing parties, horse-back riding painting and dancing. I love my friends, go to the gym regularly and love living; even when it gets shitty and I lose all hope (usually when PMSing). Every minute of Life is worth it and one day, I may even get married!

If I have to be on this planet, shared by billions, I might as well make it worthwhile. Believe me, no one makes it for you; some may help, but it's all about you and your attitude!!! So whatever that it is that's broken, fix it; that's the bottom line, truly. Most importantly, be honest with yourself and don't be afraid to be exactly who you are. Love what you do !!! Be proactive, be real and be smart; whatever you do, look for every opportunity the Universe throws at you! There are plenty, everyday! Don't let any pass you by, trust your intuition and don't confuse intuition and fear. Life is meant to be lived to the fullest and I'm doing it. Are you?!!!

Making It in High Heels

Sapna Jain

P eople always tell me I have a lot of friends.

"Sapna, holy crap, you know tons of people!"

"Sap, you have way too many friends!"

"Sapna, people love you!"

If I think about it, I guess I would have to agree. I DO know tons of people. I DO have a lot of friends (I wouldn't say too many because I don't think you can ever have too many friends). And yes, many of them DO love me, as I do them. But I've worked hard to cultivate my friendships; I give more than I take, and as a result I can say that I am blessed to have many people in my life who care about me and who are there for me when I need them.

But it wasn't always that way. I can remember a time when I didn't have a single friend. It was one of the most difficult periods of my life. It was a long time ago, but whenever I think about it, the pain is so vivid it's like I've been transported back in time to grade nine, at the tender age of 14.

Before high school, I was a middle of the road student. Not academically, but socially; I was never the most popular girl, never one of the cool crowd, nor was I a geek or the kid people picked on. I was somewhere in the middle; and that was fine with me. But then came high school, and my social life took an eighteen-month detour off the road of comfortable mediocrity into a dark alley of rejection and isolation.

I started grade nine with friends; girls I had known for a number of years. Amy, Rina, Yoko and I had all grown up in the same neighbourhood. We had always walked to and from school together, hung out at each others' houses and at the mall together. We shared everything together; we were a clan. At first, things seemed okay; we were caught up in the anxiety and excitement of high school. There was so much to talk about and explore; new classes and teachers, new boys and new friends . One of the new friends was a girl named Chantal, who had moved into our neighbourhood from New York that summer. She didn't know anyone and was struggling to fit in. She asked if she could walk with us to and from school.

"But she dresses weird." Rina made a face.

"She won't fit in with the rest of us." Yoko crossed her arms across her chest.

"She's a loser," said Amy with a defiant glare.

"But she's new, guys. She doesn't know anyone. Let's at least give her a chance." I convinced them. I felt bad for Chantal; I remembered what it was like to be the 'new girl' myself four years ago. Plus, I was always a bit of a soft touch; I still am.

So, Chantal eased her way into our routine and eventually, into our group. It wasn't long before I began to feel that I was being edged out. I found it increasingly difficult to relate to the group like I used to; it felt like we didn't have much in common anymore. I was in the Enhanced Program at school, which meant that while the other girls flitted from class to class with different kids, I stayed with the same small bunch of kids all day; I didn't get to meet any new people. To top it off, most of the kids in the Enhanced Program were considered nerds and geeks. As Amy, Rina, Yoko, and now Chantal, compared stories about boys and new friends, I found myself at a loss for words; uncomfortable and increasingly insecure with my supposed best friends. I felt left out and inadequate.

At first I tried to ignore the way I was feeling, telling myself that it was all in my head and that my friends were my friends, no matter what. Surely they would introduce me to their new friends, the cool kids. If the situation were reversed I would do the same, so of course it didn't matter that I was in the Enhanced Program. These were my girls; we were a group. I hid my insecurities and tried harder to make conversation, to be cheerful, to be part of the gang.

The harder I worked to fit in with these girls I had never had to try with before, the more I felt like an outcast. It was then that I realized they didn't care. They were slowly fazing me out. I became Increasingly uneasy and started asking Amy what was wrong:

"Nothing, Sap. Why?"

"I don't know. I just feel like things aren't right. Is there something wrong?"

"No, there's nothing wrong."

"Are you sure?"

"Yeah, I'm sure. You're being paranoid."

So the conversation went. Every time we had 'the conversation', I got the same answers. But they were empty words, because it was clear things were not right. The other girls started doing things without me; walking ahead of me, not saving me a seat in the cafeteria, excluding me in their conversations. I tried to ignore it; I pretended as best I could that things were okay. I prayed that things would sort themselves out. But it only got worse. Then one day after school, they gave me a note :

"Sapna, we are writing you this note so you will stop asking us what is wrong. Instead, we will tell you. We hate the way you always ask us what is wrong. We hate the way you always save us seats in the cafeteria and how you have to buy a cookie everyday. We hate the way you brush your hair. We hate a lot of the things you do. You've been annoying us a lot lately."

They stood around me as I read those awful words that rainy afternoon in the park. They all watched as my hands started to shake and my eyes welled up with tears.

"I'm sorry guys," I sobbed, "I didn't realize I was doing so many things to annoy you. I will change. Please give me another chance; I'll change."

"I don't know..." Chantal hummed and hawed. They gathered in a circle and whispered. "Fine, we'll give you another chance. But you'd better change." Chantal ordered. I nodded.

For a couple of weeks, everything was fine. We hung out after school, went to the mall; we were friends again. But, just as fast as things had gone back to normal, they went bad. They started ignoring me again, whispering and making plans that didn't include me. Then one day, as we stood in the park after school, the situation got worse. As I turned to go home, I saw Rina give me the finger. I pretended not to notice as I walked away. They started to yell after me:

"Bitch!"

"We hate you, don't you get it?"

"You're a loser!"

"We don't want you hanging around with us anymore, okay?"

I walked faster. My heart was racing. I tried to hold back the tears. I thought we had just sorted things out; this must be a joke.

As soon as I walked into the house, the phone rang. I grabbed the receiver.

"Hello?"

"Hi Bitch." Chantal's voice seared through the telephone line. "Did you hear what we said? We don't want you to hang out with us anymore. You're a loser."

"But..."

"No buts. We can't stand you. We wanted to get rid of you for a while, but you're like a persistent burr."

"But I did what you wanted me to. I changed. Please don't do this."

"Don't tell me what to do! It's a group decision. Here's Amy."

"Hi, Sapna. Listen, it's over okay? You don't fit in with us anymore. We hate you."

"Amy, how can you do this to me?"

"Because, we hate you. If you ever come near me again, we'll kidnap your little brother." She hissed. Hot tears ran down my face. I couldn't believe my best friend was doing this to me. I cried and begged as each girl came on the phone to tell me why she hated me and to warn me to stay away from them. I wanted to hang up, but I couldn't. I was numb with grief. I cried and cried. A part of me hoped that maybe it was all a joke and the next day they would tell me it was a just a prank; a horrible prank.

But things weren't better at school the next day, or for the next year and a half after that; I became even more of an outcast. Not only had my best friends, my girls, kicked me out of their group, but they made sure I wasn't accepted anywhere. They spread rumours and told people to stay away from me; that I was a loser. People believed them. No one wanted to be my friend; not even the geeks and nerds in the Enhanced Program. I walked the hallways at school with my eyes down. I went home for lunch everyday because it was better than sitting in the cafeteria alone. I walked home from school taking a longer route so I wouldn't run into the girls. I started eating junk food and watching TV after school instead of socializing or going to the mall. I begged my parents to let me change schools, but they refused. Every night I cried for hours; it got so bad I contemplated suicide many times. If it hadn't been for my baby brother, who I cared for everyday after school, I think I may have attempted it. He kept me going. Somehow, I managed to continue at school. I got used to loneliness and being ignored. I went through my daily routine on autopilot.

One day, early in grade ten, my depression reached a breaking point. I started channeling all my energy into exercise and diet and began to lose the weight I had gained in the past year. For awhile, I became obsessed, eating only 800 calories and exercising for 2 ½ hours each day. Eventually, I moderated my exercise and diet so that I could stick to it. I got a part-time job at a local grocery store and began socializing with a few kids from different schools that I met through friends of my parents. Then, miraculously, I started making a few random friends at school, too. It's possible that because I felt more confident, people started talking to me; then, slowly, they started becoming my friends. They said things like,

"You're a really nice person."

"You're so different from what I heard."

"What I heard about you is not true."

From there it snowballed. My social circle and confidence grew in tandem. By the time I finished high school, I was more popular than any of the four girls who had made me an outcast to begin with. It was a strange paradox.

I have never looked back since then. As horrible as it was, I learned a lot from that experience. I learned the difference between being a bad friend and a good friend; that it's important to have confidence in yourself. I learned that I must never let people disrespect me, or put me down; that negative thought attracts negative action and positive thought attracts positive action. It is important never to compromise who you are for other people. Life can be challenging, but you must learn to deal with those challenges. No matter how bad the situation is, it will get better.

They say that the more a butterfly struggles to break out of its cocoon, the stronger its wings become; enabling it to soar higher and farther. Remember that; embrace your struggles. Tackle them head on. When you can grow and learn from the obstacles that life throws before you, there are no limits to how high you can fly. You are a butterfly.

Sara Bouvier

M ost people remember high school as a really great time or a really bad time. For me, high school was the best time of my life. I had a lot of friends and was highly motivated to finish school and escape small town life. In my last year of school, I discovered I was pregnant. I finished my last year, giving birth to Zachary in March, but I was unable to graduate, being short one required credit. I was totally bummed, but I soon had my son, Zachary, to cheer me up. When my parents split up two months later, Zachary and I moved in with my father, Jerome.

In October, 2004, I found out I was pregnant again! WOW! 19-years-old and pregnant for the second time. I was terrified. Without telling my family I was pregnant again, I moved to Winnipeg with Zachary and his father, Bradley. It was a month before I could bring myself to tell everyone the news. They took it better then I expected.

My mother, Noreen, and sister, Victoria, came with me to my ultrasound appointment when I thought I was seven months pregnant. Twins! I was having fraternal twin girls. If that wasn't shocking enough, it turned out I was only five months pregnant, not seven. I went in that day thinking I only had two months left, and discovered I was only halfway through my pregnancy.

In February of 2005, I had Amy and Hailey. For the first six weeks of their lives, I breastfed both babies. It was very difficult, but completely worth the effort; until my milk stopped producing as quickly as the twins were consuming. Once the twins started on formula, life got a little easier as Daddy was able to help out at feeding time. The kids and I lived with Bradley in Winnipeg until July, 2005. At that point, Bradley and I decided our relationship wasn't working and it was affecting the children. The children being our main concern, we packed up our things and moved back in with my father.

By that summer, we were settled in and I had the kids into daycare down the street. In September, I made another attempt to finish high school.

YAY! I was done in April and started looking for a house in Winnipeg. By June of 2006, I was back in Winnipeg and I had finally graduated from high school. I enrolled at Red River College a month later. I had always dreamt of being a lawyer, but knew that would take years of dedicated hard work and study. I wasn't willing to put my kids through that, so I did what I thought was the next best thing; I took a Legal Administrative Assistant program. By December of that year, I realized this course was not what I wanted, and it was becoming really hard to succeed without the passion needed to motivate me. I tried to go on, but it was too much; the effort was affecting my beautiful children. The end of 2006 saw the end of my school career as well.

A year has passed and I have done nothing! For the last year I have been feeling sorry for myself. Why? I thought that as a single mom trying to raise three kids on welfare, I had the hardest life out there. But I look at my life and realize I am blessed. I look around at my world... how many people want kids and can't have any; how many people have kids and can't feed them? So why should I feel sorry for myself? I have three gorgeous, healthy children and a future with so many options.

So before you waste a year, like I did, just remember that someone out there will always have it harder than you! You can change things.

Making It in High Heels

Sasha Fine-Rose

I've always known what I wanted to do with my future; I was one of those kids who was always focused. I was what you would call a life planner; I knew what I wanted and where I wanted to be at every stage of my life. I sought out a mentor wherever I was and used their skills and knowledge to my advantage. My family would joke that everything I touched turned to gold. I guess you could say I was lucky. I had more friends than I knew what to do with; I spent my summers at sleepover camp, which I would count down the days to; I always had a boyfriend; I was a competitive figure skater; I had a great family, even though my parents were divorced and a younger sister to fight with. I struggled in math but excelled in the arts. I attended an Arts High School in which I studied dance for five years and loved it. I was surrounded by creative minds and an endless amount of opportunities. I was a driven and determined teenager who didn't have time to waste. Relaxing was hard for me; I thought life had too much to offer. Why would I want to relax when I could keep going? But, little did I know what my future had in store for me. I was about to be hit with a tornado of uncontrollable emotions, a constant surrounding of death, a personal struggle to grow up in the blink of an eye and tragedies that will stick with me to the day I die. No matter how determined I was in life and how planned out I had everything, nothing could prepare me for what I was about to face.

I truly wish that the first time I got my heart broken would have been the worst thing possible growing up, because to my friends, it was. But I was faced with problems much bigger; problems young children don't ever think they'll have to face until much later on. Our parents aren't supposed to leave us. They're supposed to be there to raise us and support us, watch us get married and have children of our own. That wasn't the way my life turned out, though. I was about to face seven very difficult years; years that taught me to grow up in a matter of seconds; showed me what's important in life and how to deal with the unexpected.

Dealing with the death of a parent isn't easy. That thought never crossed my mind until one of my friends lost her father at sixteen. I still remember the day we got the call with the horrible news. Four of my friends, including myself, went over to pay our respects. I remember vividly saying I couldn't even imagine what she was going through; I could never imagine it happening to me. Little did I know that two months later, I would be in the same situation and that I would skip my teenage years of going out, drinking and doing drugs.

It was in late May of 2000 when my mother answered the phone and it was my stepmother explaining that my father had a massive heart attack and was in a diabetic coma; it was doubtful that he would live through the night. There was no time to waste. A call was made to my aunt and grandmother and next thing I knew, I had a suitcase in front of me and I was literally throwing everything in sight into it. My sister and I had no idea what to expect, nor did we know how long we would be in Florida. Two hours later, we were on the red eye.

We arrived in the middle of the night. My fourteen-year-old sister and I headed to my father's house to fall asleep for the night. The next morning, we all headed to the hospital. I will never forget what I saw there; it's an image that has stuck with me ever since. I was literally clutching my sister's hand as we walked into the hospital room. My father was swollen and black-and-blue, he was paralyzed and in a coma; on life support. He had no way of talking to us or even any idea that we were there. This was the image of a very sick man; a man who was dying. The next few days were spent at the hospital; he stayed alive longer than they predicted. My sister and I would each go in and talk to him about everything and anything. He didn't respond, of course, just stared at the ceiling. He wasn't getting better, but he wasn't getting any worse, either; it was starting to take an emotional toll on my sister and I. We both decided we had seen enough and wanted to go back to Toronto. We said our goodbyes, not knowing if that would be the last time we saw him.

We flew back on a Friday and Monday, June 5, 2000, the phone rang at 6:45am. My mother woke us up to the news that our father has passed away. At first it didn't sink in. But as the hour progressed, it slowly hit me. I convinced myself somehow that he was better in heaven; he was too sick to live and if he had, he wouldn't have had a good life.

I didn't know what to do with myself, but I did convince myself that life goes on and so I must go on. Most people think it was wrong for me to go to school that day, but I figured I had two choices: I could sit at home and feel the pain or go to school and dance and be with my friends. I chose the latter. Do I regret it? No, this is how I dealt with my pain and everyone is different.

A few days later, he was buried. I will never forget the night before my father's funeral. My sister knocked on my door, late at night and we both just started to cry. It was the first time we both realized that we were different; we have been given a path in life that wasn't going to be easy. The next day was by far one of the hardest days of my life. We arrived at the funeral home along with everyone else. My sister and I both eulogized our father. For some reason, it felt like the words were coming out of my mouth with me not even being aware, I felt strong and didn't cry until I said, "I love you, daddy." As I watched the pallbearers take the casket, I lost control and finally broke down. The tears were flowing non-stop as he was laid to rest in the earth. Shiva followed, which is the Jewish mourning period of a full week; as much as I tried to understand what had happened, it was very hard. I couldn't quite grasp the idea and wasn't sure how to mourn.

Imagine at sixteen knowing you will never see one of your parents again. You will never be able to ask them another question, hear their voice and tell them stories. They will never see you grow up and you will not watch them grow old.

A few months after my father passed away, my sister and I got the news that a lump had been found in my mother's breast. I couldn't quite understand what all of this meant; I couldn't stop asking the question, why? My mother wasn't allowed to leave her two children behind; then we would have no one. I couldn't understand what was happening; my sister and I had just lost one parent and hadn't even begun the healing process when the other one was diagnosed with breast cancer.

We grew up instantly. We were now faced with many issues that most sixteen and fourteen year-olds don't have to think about. What if our mother doesn't live? What if our mother's cancer comes back? Would someone want to adopt us? Do we know all the bank accounts? The life insurance? My sixteen year-old mind was now transformed into an that of an adult. All of a sudden, I had to grow up and was faced with adult questions and decisions. What would I do with my sister? How can I go away to university and leave her? What will I do with the house? Questions, questions and more questions; none of them had easy answers. Everything happened so fast from the day my father was buried to the day I found out my mom had breast cancer to the day she had her surgery. That was when we would find out how severe the cancer was.

I had to get my driver's license before my mother went in for surgery; I would need it to buy groceries, run errands, get to the hospital and pick up my sister. Early one morning my mom and I got into the car and I drove her to the hospital. I couldn't leave her side; I knew I had to be strong, stronger than her. I was her shoulder to lean on; our roles were reversed. Usually, she's my support.

As she was getting prepped for surgery, we said our goodbyes. I was assured by her that she would come out alive and well. You can imagine the fear I had, knowing that I might lose my mother only a few months after losing my father. She joked with the doctor as I stood nearby, waiting for her surgery time. The next thing I knew, she was being rolled off, tears in both our eyes. I was alone in the hospital, waiting for the news.

A few hours passed; by that time, the rest of the family was there to join me. She was alive. They removed her lump and she got to keep her breast and would hopefully make a full recovery with chemotherapy and radiation.

I thought once the lump was removed, chemo and radiation would be simple. I was wrong. My mother's challenge and the challenge my sister and I again had to face were just beginning. I watched my mother, an extremely strong and independent woman, be beaten alive. But, I've always admired my mother's strength, I still do; she held on. Chemotherapy was so hard on her that she was in and out of the hospital with blood transfusions because her body couldn't take much more.

It was actually a few months into her chemotherapy that we got the news that my grandfather had fallen and had been taken to the hospital. My mother wasn't allowed to visit due to her low immune system and during Grandpa's time in the hospital, she was in the hospital across the street. I remember picking my sister up from school and then getting my grandmother, driving downtown to visit my grandfather and walking across the street to see my mother.

The times when my mother was home were very hard. Sometimes the simplest task, such as getting out of bed, was difficult. Fourteen days after she started chemotherapy, her hair started to fall out. I remember that day so well. I got home from school and phoned my mother. She was crying, telling me that her hair was coming out in clumps. It was the same fear in her voice as the day she called home to tell us the results were positive.

My mother changed a lot. She lost a lot of weight, went completely bald and her energy level was very low. Going to the mall didn't happen anymore, in case someone was to knock into her and tear out the pick line. She wore a wig or a hat on her head whenever she appeared in public. Life changed and it wasn't easy. No one knew what was going to happen. But, we all stuck together and my mom fought for her life. She would keep telling us she wasn't ready to leave.

Eventually, chemotherapy was over and radiation was about to start. At this point, my sister and I really learned how do to things on our own and we knew that this disease inside my mother was going to be beaten. When my mother finished her last radiation treatment about eight months later, we celebrated. A few days later, my grandfather passed away as if he was waiting to make sure my mom would be okay. All I could think was, "Another funeral; when is life going to get easy?"

Over the next few years, my mom continued her battle with cancer; it takes five years in remission before she can declare herself cancer free. We were always worried. I continued to grow up during these five years; continuing to do things for others, because if I didn't do an errand, I would feel guilty. I found it very hard to go out and very hard to be in a relationship, because opening up wasn't what I wanted to do. What I focused on most was getting my career in gear. All of a sudden, material stuff didn't matter; my future did. I did everything to keep myself busy and to keep adding to my resume. I realize now that I did it so I wouldn't have to face reality. I never wanted to stop, so I kept going and the busier I was, the less time I had to think; I liked it that way. But I knew I would have to face the truth sometime.

I was in my third year of university and was presented with the opportunity to go on an exchange. I thought, "Why not, this would hopefully be the experience of a lifetime."

No one knew the real reason I wanted to go so far away. I was constantly asked why, of all the countries, I chose the farthest. I would simply reply with a, "Why not"? Deep down, I knew that I had to escape. I had to take my past and somehow heal from it. Toronto had become a grey area in my life and I always see things in black and white; the grey meant pain that had to heal. I had questions that needed answers: Who am I? What do I want in life? Why did this happen to me? How am I going to grow from it? Most importantly I had to relearn how to be twenty-one. The first steps were booking the plane ticket, saying my goodbyes.

Suddenly, I was in Hong Kong; a city that never sleeps. It is a city that makes it easy to forget reality and the past. It's a city that lets you get caught up in the bright lights, endless noise, exquisite smells and vast amount of people, friends and conversation. To me, it's a golden city which I fell in love with. This was the first time in my life that I only had myself to worry about.

I was there to study International Journalism and I also secured a job working for a magazine. Work was all I knew; going out was something I would have to learn all over again.

From the moment I landed in Hong Kong, I knew I was going to love it. I was surrounded by international people. I was taking new courses with a whole different outlook and I made friends that will last forever. I had a job working with a magazine I loved. But most of all, I loved the city. Every day was filled with excitement and so much to do. Whether it was Thailand with a group of people one week or the Philippines another, I was free; I had time to think and to have fun. I had no one else to worry about. I loved it. I was living life. I went out, had conversations about silly stuff and serious issues. I was finally feeling what a twenty one year old would feel. Most importantly, I was away from my life in Toronto. I didn't have to hear about death, sickness or worries.

After my year in Hong Kong, I was ready to come home. I had a new outlook on life. I faced what was happening to me by talking to others and realizing that there are others who might have had it worse. I saw what it was like to live in poverty while traveling; I saw how happy people could be with so little. I saw the potential I have and I grew up. I matured, I was becoming an adult with more experience in life. If it wasn't for Hong Kong, I couldn't have started the healing process.

I ask myself everyday how much stronger I'm supposed to be. To the outside world, I'm seen as a strong, independent and determined young woman. People have even told me they find me intimidating. Other people see me as someone with no emotion, very cold hearted because it takes a lot for me to cry. But, they're wrong. Yes, I have a hard edge about me, but I also have a very soft side that does take a little work to bring out. Inside, I'm your typical emotional girl. I cry, but when no one's around; unless it's a sappy chick flick. I even cry in the car when a song comes on that reminds me of my father.

A few months ago, my grandmother, with whom my mom, sister and I were extremely close, passed away; shocking us all. I have learned to face the curve balls life is always throwing; it has all made me stronger. I'm not sure I'm ever going to say I have overcome what has happened. Not a day goes by that I don't think about all the people I have lost. But, I have accepted it. If it hadn't happened, I would have turned out differently. Maybe life would have been easier. Maybe I wouldn't feel alone and struggle to let people in. Maybe I would have an easier time trusting people, but maybe I wouldn't be independent and determined. No one knows what the future holds for us. I just know that whatever life is going to throw at me I have no choice but to accept it, deal with it and learn from it.

Shannon Leroux

I have always believed that rules are like bad-tasting medicine, you know it's good for you, but you hate to take it. I had never taken a liking to rules in my early years, I believed they didn't apply to me. Of course, rules are essential for maintaining some control in society. Believing otherwise has provided me with more than my share of complicated life experiences.

I was never a middle-of-the-road individual; the mountains and valleys were far more appealing than the monotony of consistency. Living on the edge was my reality and the closer to the edge the better. I was always reaching for what many viewed as impossible; I was convinced that more benefits were tied to riskier routes than the predictable ones. However, in the earlier years of my evolution, I came to terms with my own version of the rules and how they could keep me from falling off the edge. When I created the rules, holding myself accountable to them wasn't such a challenge. I began to see the benefits of holding myself to a value system.

Today, I have no regrets. I'm personally responsible for writing the script of my life and I wouldn't change one thing. An accumulation of great and not-so-great choices have landed me where I am today.

As an only child, born into a tumultuous household of alcoholism, I learned at an early age to be self-sufficient. I also learned that adapting my personal style to fit the needs of others was the easiest way to gain approval. I became the resident expert on how to best read what people wanted from me and then deliver. If I thought that funny was the necessary antidote for the day, then funny was what I delivered.

Trying to please all of the people all of the time, is an effort that's doomed to failure. As a six-foot tall twelve-year-old, I was expected to be as capable and emotionally equipped as most young adults. As impossible as it was, I insisted on trying to live up to those expectations.

I don't recall a time in my childhood or adolescence when I felt accomplished or worthy. Growing up was a painful process and my private thoughts were clouded with self-doubt. Without positive reinforcement, my sub-conscious thoughts began to run wild, and I began to wonder why I had been given a shot at life. What we speak is what we are; the more I tuned into this voice, the more I struggled with my own importance.

Discovery can be part of the healing process, however. As degrading as my self-loathing was, that vicious cycle of defeat and searching for answers caused me to swim upstream and find a better way. My insatiable curiosity is likely responsible for persevering and developing into the woman I've become today.

As a young teen I had a strong desire to be a model. I was convinced that the Ford Modeling Agency would assist me in bringing this dream to life. My dream was met with great resistance from friends and family, however. Growing up in a small town provided many community ideals, but a lack of strong individual thought. I was told frequently that modeling agencies were out to get young girls. Furthermore, I was suffering from 'ugly duckling syndrome', and had to fight hard to resist listening to my voice of self-destruction. My negative interpretation was always too ready to twist the reality in my thoughts; I wasn't smart enough, pretty enough, or deserving of any opportunity. Nothing can beat you down faster than your own mind. Today, in my portfolio of professional achievements is a composite card embossed with the Ford logo. I'm not their star supermodel, but that doesn't matter; I wanted a spot on The Ford Modeling agency roster, and I got one. I could check that dream off my list and move on. If you can dream it, you can indeed achieve it.

I had almost become preconditioned to discredit my achievements. When I became the valedictorian of my grade eight class, I downplayed my success by convincing myself that I was the required choice.

High school wasn't exactly loaded with highlights, either. I wasn't particularly good at athletics; I wasn't an academic superstar and I certainly wasn't cool enough. My six-foot height made me feel like a circus attraction. I observed members of the 'A' list crowd and began making notes about what it might take to join this group. My family circumstances didn't provide for designer jeans and polo shirts. I remember being especially curious about why some were the 'haves' and others were the 'have nots'. I discovered in those painful experiences that I was unsettled and seeking a better way.

Trying out for the high school drama team proved to be a turning point for me. Although my self-doubt prevailed, I dedicated time to perfecting my presentation. Hoping to overturn years of mental torment, I marched onto the stage and recited my first monologue. The stage became an outlet from which to escape my negativity. Performing gave me the chance to rid myself of self doubt and allowed me the freedom to be Shannon. I took ownership of this opportunity and the voice of negativity became diminished. In the moments that I was onstage, I was captivating, strong, beautiful, and capable. I walked onstage in a state of euphoria and my appetite for more freedom increased.

I began to enjoy life without the tune of negativity running through my head. It was breathtaking; I couldn't get enough. I was awarded a lead role and I quickly grew to love the process of theatre; rehearsals, blocking, and wardrobe. We all have a need to belong and for the first time I felt like I fit somewhere. It was a powerful feeling to entertain and it was big step in the right direction for me. It became a very comfortable place and a place of reckoning. I could leave my negative voice at the theatre doors. The healing process was not complete, but my love for the stage had provided temporary relief.

Professional acting is a career path that few take seriously, so it was no surprise that my friends and family were not supportive of my newfound love. My need to be unique helped me to hold onto my dream. I believed there was something greater in store for me and I remained committed.

At some point I learned to be thankful; recognizing the good fortune in one's life and counting one's blessings is a habit that takes time to master. I have learned to make a conscious choice to be one of the lucky people; rather than listening to the voice in my head that said I couldn't, I have chosen to hear a voice that says I can. I have had many interesting and positive experiences; other than landing a spot on the Ford roster, I have traveled to Dubai for a weekly television series, won Professional Fitness competitions and met some of the most interesting and powerful people in the entertainment industry. All of this has been as a result of changing my thought process and never giving up.

Today, in the maelstrom that is my life, between shooting schedules, wardrobe fittings, fitness competitions, covers shoots, industry networking, contract negotiations, PTA meetings and being Mom 24/7, remaining true to my dream is sometimes more challenging than at other times. When driving one 'Child A' to activity 'xyz' and 'Child B' is yelling that she forgot her spelling homework for the next morning's quiz and both children are hollering that they're starving and the washing machine repairman is calling on his cell phone from your driveway, it really can be a challenge to maintain one's personal vision of success. Keeping a constant reminder of the desired outcome is an important step toward winning. 'Whatcha think about, ya bring about', are such powerful words, as I keep discovering; we are truly in charge of our handling of the challenges and obstacles in our lives. It is up to us to ensure that our goals always remain bigger vision than any of the challenges.

Shelley Porritt

When I reflect on my early years, I remember mainly the fun I had growing up. My memories of my childhood were storybook, everything was great and I had no worries or stress. But when I allow myself to really look into my past, I realize how different was the reality. There was a time when I was bullied by an older girl in my neighbourhood. I never would have thought it possible to forget such a horrifying time, but if every cloud has a silver lining, mine is the strong, confident person that the incident helped shape me into.

When I was young, I didn't have a care in the world. I was involved in sports, had lots of friends and a happy home life. Then I began to get teased by an older girl who lived in the area. At first, I thought it was something I could handle, although I never understood why she picked on me. Perhaps she bullied me because I was younger and smaller, or because she was jealous in some way. I'll never know the reason why. In hindsight, I realize now that my reaction to the situation only caused her to become more aggressive towards me. As time went on, I became frightened, and instead of getting help I tried to hide my fear. I wanted to ignore the problem, so I didn't do anything, hoping that eventually it would just all go away. As time went on, the bullying progressed to a whole new level.

Naturally, the bully sensed my fear, pushing her to greater acts of torment. To her, my apprehension meant weakness. Bullies prey on the weak and insecure to compensate for their own weaknesses and insecurities; no bully wants a fair fight. I only wish I had learned this much earlier in life!

I don't know how long this continued, but it seemed that it would never end. My friends were afraid of my tormentor too, so none of us took any action against her. In the beginning, her own friends encouraged her, perhaps in an attempt to make sure she didn't turn on them; or maybe they thought it was tough and cool to be a bully. But soon, the pushing and shoving worsened and even her friends became uncomfortable with

167

her behaviour. As the situation got worse, they told her to relax and calm down, but she never listened.

She had free rein, with nobody to stop her. I wouldn't stand up for myself; my friends were afraid to help me lest they become her new target, and even her own friends could not persuade her to leave me alone. I could have stopped it immediately, by standing up for myself or by telling an adult about the situation. But instead, the bullying escalated.

To this day, I ask myself why she treated me that way. She may have had her own issues to deal with; maybe problems at home made her want to lash out. Maybe she was being treated that way by someone else, and needed to feel in control by treating a weaker person just as cruelly. Sometimes people just don't know how to handle stress; as a result, they act badly. I'm not making excuses for her, believe me, but it remains a mystery to me why she behaved in such a way.

I never gave myself enough credit. I never let myself be confident, until one evening when I decided enough was enough! I stood up to that bully because I just couldn't take it anymore. Things changed instantly! That night, when she tried to bully me, I challenged her to a fight. That was the first time I dared, and I would not back down. She was shocked, and although I was scared, I felt that if I was going to get a beating, I might as well go down fighting. I was ready. I was angry and the adrenaline was pumping through my veins, from fright, from rage and from courage.

I was actually standing up to this bully, and the feeling was incredible. I was empowered, and the more empowered I became, the more she recoiled. My confidence was growing inside me with every second and I felt larger than life. It was the most amazing feeling to see her back down. She didn't want to fight after all; she didn't have the confidence or the courage to take me on. I could see it in her eyes, and it was at that moment that I realized the power of my own confidence over her lack of confidence.

I don't condone fighting, and fortunately, in this case it wasn't necessary. But the confidence that empowered me to be ready for a fight can mean the difference between having a happy life or an unhappy one. As an adult, I draw upon my self-confidence daily and it has helped me face many challenging situations, such as meetings with high-powered clients, dating and standing up for my opinions. Confident people will gain the respect of those around them, and will achieve greatness. Bullies are afraid of confident people and will avoid them at all costs.

Once I stood up to my bully she realized that I wasn't weak and vulnerable and she never bothered me again. Her friends respected and admired me; they wanted to befriend me, instead of her. She was on a slippery slope downward.

That was my first lesson on bullying. Had I trusted my instincts and listened to my inner voice, I would have asserted myself with the bully sooner, or I may have looked to some adults for help. I should not have tolerated her behaviour; I should have dealt with the situation much sooner. My story has a happy ending, but it could have been worse.

We can't avoid bullies in our lives, but learning how to deal with them will make us unattractive targets for them. Having confidence gives us strength, which in turn gives us power; it is that power which will guide us through the hardships in life and encourage us to take calculated risks in the future.

Confident people project strength which is necessary for a leadership role. That day changed my life. Now I know that I have the strength I need to make myself a leader and a success. That self confidence comes to play in both my personal and business life; I'm not afraid to take chances and I never question my decisions after I have thought them out completely. I listen to my inner self, or instincts, and I do not back down from issues or causes that I believe in just because they are unpopular. I am very passion- ate about my work and the charities I support.

Tap into your strength and power by becoming more confident, and doors will open for you. People want to be around strong confident people, and look to them to lead. You can accomplish great things if you believe you can. Make this your reality.

Shobha

Picture a brown girl in an essentially all white school; she has one eyebrow because the two have conjoined, the silhouette of a moustache above her plumper-than-average lips and a funny accent. Her thick hair, cut straight across to an unflattering length by her well-meaning father, smells of coconut oil with the slightest hint of curry. Her teeth aren't perfect, nor would she ever get braces to fix them. After all, she is the seventh child in a low income family. She lives in an unsafe neighborhood where she experiences minor racism and violence and is subject to the influence of the area's older, belligerent teens. She plays among future drug addicts, convicts and prostitutes. What's keeping her from the same fate? She and her older brother are the only kids on the block who attend private school. Her parents sacrifice everything and work like dogs to send them there, believing education to be pivotal in assuring a better life for their children. At school, she denounces her immigrant ways and tries to adopt that of her peers; right down to their jargon, clothes and food. When she arrives home from school, she makes a beeline for the front door so the other kids won't see her hideous navy blue and white uniform.

If you haven't already figured it out, the girl is me. I'm not looking for pity; merely trying to paint a picture of what it was like growing up, first generation Canadian in an immigrant family. It was hard to feel like I belonged, either in school or on a block so unaccustomed to the likes of me. It was even harder to establish an identity, let alone hold onto it. In a way, I believe I lost it and am finding it only now. Certainly, being the brunt of many jokes for being different only made me want to be the same as everyone else. For this reason, I fought with my parents daily to either send me to public school or move to the suburbs so I would fit in with the school kids. I also shunned my South Asian background for a long time. This, of course, was fruitless; as was trying to fit in with anyone who had a completely different belief system than the one I was raised with.

In high school, I decided it was time to overcome or be overcome. I wanted to be somebody and do great things. I concentrated on the things I was good at and embraced the things I loved: sports, video games and anything competitive. This competitive spirit spilled over into academics and fine arts and that's when I found music. There was nothing I loved more. I had to work at it, though. I was no child prodigy, but there was definitely something magical that happened when I opened my mouth to sing or put my pen to paper to write. I felt an exhilarating rush and finally, a sense of belonging.

I live and breathe to make a difference in the lives around me through the best way I know how, writing music. When I'm going through trying times, there's nothing better than to have someone who can say, '*hey, I totally understand*,' somebody who can empathize. My goal is to be able to do that on a large scale. What an honor it is to have a platform to say not only do I understand, but here's what I've learned and here's what helped me.

I began songwriting for many reasons: to express myself creatively; to entertain; to share my experiences and personal revelations; to give my opinion and probably most importantly, to encourage others. I love it when people relate to a song I've written. I don't care if it's cliché, but when someone says, "that song is so me," I feel as though it's worth all the grueling hours spent practicing and the endless work in the studio. The thousands of dollars invested; the long drives to play shows for 11 people; the blood, sweat and tears are all worth it when my music touches someone.

Like every writer, I have experienced my share of writer's block. Looking back, I can almost always pin that writer's block on a lack of being challenged in life. In other words, going through hardships can be the best inspiration. This is not to say that I want to go through struggles, but rather that good can come of them if you're willing to see it. I began writing a song about the pain that comes with struggling called *A Special Kind of Misery*.

Lessons are priceless
Coming always at a cost to the one who's in the process of learning
The path that's less beaten
Is persevered by the feet of those whose suffering has shown them meaning

It's a special kind of misery
The kind that makes it better for me
A special kind of misery

No pain, no pleasure
No work, no play
No grief, no sweet relief
No rain, no ripening
No cross, no crown
No death, no debt paid
No wrath, no redemption
No sacrifice, no salvation

It isn't finished yet. However, the words speak to me all the time. We learn and grow from hard times. Challenges are rewarding.

After completing my education at Dalhousie University in Halifax, I took some serious steps to further my musical career. I packed my bags and moved to Toronto, one of Canada's most bustling music centers. I'm a small town girl at heart, but I knew I would have to make some sacrifices if I was going to be serious about music. I spent a long time trying to press my first album. I had to work my tail off to see it into fruition. I was exasperated by the long process and overwhelmed by two full-time careers. I know one thing; I wouldn't have appreciated it as much had I not worked so hard for it.

Challenges can come in many forms; failure is surely one of the biggest. One of the hardest things for me in the music business is feeling like a failure. What do you do with a poor performance, a bad interview or a blown opportunity? Either you let them destroy you, or you learn from them and use them as *Fuel*.

Broken bubbles have left you standing
In an ocean sized puddle on the ground
I'm glad to see that you're still treading
The other option is to drown
Is it that you want more from life?
Or is it that you get what you don't like?
Here's what you do
With things that never go your way
Save them for use
Like pennies for a rainy day
Like fuel
That little something extra
To make you do better
Like Fuel
Let it spur you on

It's better to burn it off
Like fuel
    —*An excerpt from* Fuel *by Shobha*

I'm not here to belittle your problems and tell you to suck it up; I'm just talking about gaining some perspective. We all have to go through the motions of grief. It's normal and healthy but when you're done, reflect on how much you've learned and more importantly, how much you can teach. Maybe you don't write songs, but you write poetry or fiction. Maybe you don't write at all, but you paint or enjoy public speaking. Maybe you can just pass on your newfound wisdom to the people around you. On whatever scale it is, your hardships make you a stronger person; a stronger person who can go on to strengthen others.

I once wrote a song for someone very dear to me, a young girl, who had gone through an unfathomable amount of hardships in the form of eating disorders, sexual abuse and the loss of close family members; all at a tender age. As expected, these things took an enormous toll on her health and happiness. In high school, this girl had a nickname; she was known as *Little Tank*. She was 5"7' and all of 100 pounds, but boy, could she play football and plow through her opponents. I knew right away this would become the title of a song written for her, and girls like her whose trials were great, but the power to overcome these trials even greater.

When I grew up I'm glad I had you
Somebody to be a big sister to
Everything I did was times'd by two
I ran through the garden and you came too
We stomped on the ground, on everything that grew
It was probably my idea, but you took the heat too

I know you're too old to wanna do what I do
But if I could impart a little of what I know to you
Remember your smile lights up the room
That you're delivered you're not doomed
Remember these years are hard, I should know
          I stumbled through them before you

Plow through it
Between two points it's the shortest distance
Plow through it
It falls on the just and the unjust

The rain from the storm, good thing you're not alone
Cause you will be afflicted even more
Hand in hand we can oppose them
Run into the waves though they crash down on us
It wouldn't be the first time, we'd just get back up

The power in me, is the power in you
I made it and there's a way unique to you
So plow through it
    —*An excerpt from* Little Tank *by Shobha*

Keep in mind, much of *Little Tank* is specific to me and this special girl. She really did copy everything I did; we really did stomp through her mother's garden and get the scolding of a lifetime. Growing up near the ocean, we really did hold hands and try to run against the waves; when they knocked us over, we really did get back up. I thought, 'what a powerful metaphor.' It really resonated with her. *It wouldn't be the first time we'd just get back up.* How about the part where the rain falls on the just and the unjust? This is always a tough pill to swallow. The question of fairness and why bad things happen to good people is eternally frustrating. We will never face anything in life beyond what we can handle. That doesn't mean we have to handle it alone. For me personally, the power I talk about, the strength I found is God given. I believe it with my whole heart. One of the most well-known passages in the Bible teaches us we don't have to handle anything alone, *As I walk through the Valley of Death I will fear no evil, for thou are with me. Thy rod and staff comfort me (Psalm 23:4).* Whatever you believe, just know that you were never meant to go it alone. Nor are you alone.

When I talk about how I overcame many adversities that could have otherwise held me captive, I don't want to sound haughty. It was a much lengthier process than I am alluding to and I am nowhere near the end of my struggles. I am a *Work in Progress*, which means there is hope for my imperfect self. I was carefully and wonderfully made and so were you. I have a purpose and a set of skills that nobody else can bring to the table and so do you. We all make bad decisions, have our weaknesses and yet possess unbelievable potential.

Why can't I be addicted to
The things that I'm supposed to do
Why don't I want to choose

Good circles good habits good food
Why do they sit inside my head
Words that go left unsaid
Things like 'I'm sorry I was wrong,
You were right all along'

Oh, if you give up on me now
There is a chance you will miss out
I wish I could show you more somehow
Oh, I don't let it get me down
Cause there's no getting around it
A change is gonna come soon but for now

I'm a work in progress
Nobody starts at a hundred
Still takes a couple takes to hit
Those notes I always miss
I'm a work in progress
Nobody starts at a hundred
Coated in paint and still wet
But I'm not finished yet

I'm well aware of all my flaws
I've got a million of them, all
Just like my fingerprints
They are what make me different
One day I'll change before your eyes
Just like a butterfly
One phase at a time I know
How the cycle is supposed to go

Don't close your case on me
Don't go there's more to see
Don't worry I'm not complete
I'm not yet who I'm meant to be
Don't know how long I'll need
Don't grow over night so please
Don't show up expectantly
I am a started masterpiece
    —*An excerpt from* Work in Progress *by Shobha*

As women, we have a unique burden to bear. I would say most women face interferences on their road to success that many men will never have to. Women in the professional world can be placed in uncomfortable situations, be put on display and get ahead based on their looks. Women are generally seen differently than men. While they can be just as successful as men, being a woman can either be an advantage or an obstacle, when it shouldn't be an issue at all. Our capabilities should be the deciding factor.

Being relatively new to the music industry, I have more than once let my naivety get the best of me. Many wolves in sheep's clothing have approached me with wonderful offers claiming to love my sound, but with an agenda to love much more than that, if you know what I mean. I have learned that as a woman in a business where image matters, being different is a plus and being exotic is sexy; I have to weigh the benefit of getting ahead against the difficulty of maintaining my dignity at times. I've since accepted the way of the music industry because I understand how image does play a role whether you are male or female, but in reaching my goal I would like to know it's because I'm good at what I do, not good at how I look.

Regardless of your identity—woman, immigrant or musician—challenges will always confront you. You will always have choices to mitigate these challenges, and there will always be an easy way out. The easiest, and usually wrong, choice often entails giving up and letting all sorts of negativity in. In my experience, letting myself be swallowed by adversity is not only a shame, but an injustice to the survivors who have gone before; a slap in the face to everyone who loves and believes in me. Next time you have an overwhelming urge to give up, please don't even entertain the thought. Dismiss it and get far away from it. Think of watching a scary movie; when something frightening is about to happen, I close my eyes, plug my ears and bury my face in the shoulder of the one next to me. In a sense, this is the flight response. But, when the temptation to give up rears its ugly head, you should look, or better yet, run the other way.

Can anyone relate to me, standing up but just barely?
Is anybody hardly breathing, cause you're so tired and weary?
Nobody said it was easy
Easy? No one said it was easy to be ready to flee
Always on your feet

Here's a promise
You will only get what you can bear
And you will stand up under it
   —An excerpt from Always on Your Feet by Shobha
Rest assured that whatever burden you bear, you can stand up under it.

Making It in High Heels

Susan Persaud

I wake up in the morning and the first thing I see is a $50 bill stuck to my mirror. Today my goal is to triple the zeroes on that bill.

Fifteen years ago, my goal was to break free of authority and anything that resembled conformity. Twelve years ago, my goal was to be as much like the pretty girls as possible. Ten years ago, my goal was to make someone, anyone, proud of me. Five years ago, my goal was to disregard whether anyone was proud of me and just make myself happy. Two years ago, my goal was to finally reach one of my goals.

After high school, I wanted to get as far away from home as I could, as quickly as possible. I'm not sure if attending university was my plan, but with no real excuse not to, I left home with a goal to enrich my world in ways that had nothing to do with school.

After changing undergraduate majors three times, two jobs and $60,000 in student loans co-signed by my discontented parents, I decided I needed a break from the restrictions of undergraduate study and moved back to my hometown in Long Island. I brought with me extreme debt, an affinity for underground culture and many memories of New England dorm life.

I found a job at a collection agency, making $8.00 an hour. The agency was located in a one-storey important looking building, in the center of a huge parking lot. The area was mostly industrial so the closest deli was about six long blocks from the building. There was a huge open area where six rows of desks and computers all faced each other and were interconnected to an automatic dialer system. Most of the desks not connected to the dialer system were set up in groups of six, where three people would face the other three people. The most disappointing feature about working there was that all the lighting, though bright, was artificial.

There were always beautiful, shiny new cars outside the entrance to the building and a very conspicuous Harley-Davidson parked inside the front atrium. I learned that most of the nicer cars belonged to the owner's sister and his favoured employees; the Harley belonged to the owner.

177

Since the agency served the entire country, the hours of operation were 8am to midnight, seven days a week. The shortest shift a 'collector' could work was four hours before having a break to go outside and see whether it was still light out. I worked there with about thirty people who were either college or high school drop-outs; part-time or full-time students who needed to work or per diem employees. We competed against each other for permission to stay on as long as possible.

I was a fixture on public transportation, which in Long Island consists of only thirty to fifty passenger buses. I traveled to work and then back to my part time job at a frozen yogurt store. My travel time on buses rivaled the hours I actually spent earning and ironically the sole rationale in having the part-time job was to fund the cost of bus transportation to the collection agency. I inevitably became caught in a paycheck to paycheck lifestyle where each day mirrored the next. I continued my routine for about a year before I realized that most of the collectors who had started training with me had been appointed coveted Junior Manager, Manager or Supervisor positions. Along with those titles came uncompromising confidence and superiority on the collection floor, a minuscule raise to $10.00 an hour and most importantly, a desk where one could take time off the automatic dialer system. The idea of having a desk where I could manually dial the telephone was so enticing that I quit my job at the frozen yogurt store and dedicated my efforts to working 16 hour shifts.

After six months, I couldn't understand why I hadn't been recognized for my changed work ethic; my absolute dedication was either being overlooked by my superiors or they just didn't like me. Efforts to gain a higher position in the agency were at best ignored and although I started to receive praise on a monthly basis for meeting my collection quota, I was never considered for a raise or a desk. I finally mustered enough courage to approach a Supervisor who I thought was my friend and I asked her why I hadn't been promoted yet. I explained that I had been working more hours than anyone else, I had learned all the manager protocols for handling problem debtors and I had been helping to train new employees. She laughed at me; that was pretty much the extent of the conversation. Then she told me to sit down at the automatic dialer or punch out for the day.

I became acquainted with a feeling I had never felt before. This feeling is best described as discontentment with my life, my accomplishments and my path. For the first time in my life, I was unhappy about where I was and what I was doing. I was angered that some 'higher' person was in control of my happiness. This feeling was the first thing I encountered every morning and the lingering cloud over my bed every night. After that day, I blamed bad weather on this feeling, when I tripped on the bus I blamed it on this feeling and I blamed failed relationships on this feeling. As I look back, this feeling was the beginning of thoughts of inadequacy, discouragement, low self-esteem and self-doubt. This time, the feeling wasn't about shunning authority, this time it was about winning.

I waited for three days before I saw an opening. The owner had come into the office by himself; I watched him as he walked with purpose into his office. I got up from my seat at the automatic dialer and I walked directly into his office before anyone could stop me. I closed the door and said,

"I need to speak with you."

I asked Mr. Harley-Davidson why I hadn't been promoted and why I hadn't had a yearly review and raise. His surprising reply was,

"I've seen you here, working a lot of hours. I heard that you aren't in school. Why not?"

That question embarrassed me. How could I explain to my employer that while I was asking for more responsibility and a better position in his company, I couldn't handle the simple responsibilities of student life? The argument that I needed time to 'find myself' didn't seem as appropriate in the office as it did when I said it to my family. Mr. Harley-Davidson seemed to know what he wanted to say to me. In very few words, he suggested that I find a means to get back to school and turn myself into someone that could be of some worth to his company. I will never forget Mr. Harley-Davidson explaining to me that if I didn't go back to school it wouldn't matter where I worked, there would be no reason to promote me or give me a raise, because I wouldn't be of value to anyone. In his experience, there were plenty of people who didn't go to school who would work more hours for less than he was paying me. After all, I wasn't a brain surgeon or an expert in actuarial sciences. Before this conversation I truly believed I was an asset to any employer and that the agency was lucky to have me. I thought I was irreplaceable.

I enrolled in a university about two blocks from the collection agency within three months. Mr. Harley-Davidson allowed me to work before classes and between and after classes to maintain at least forty hours per week. I usually got to work around 8am, after a one hour bus ride, walked to class to get there by 10:10am and was back by 11:30am. That remained my routine every day of the week, until I completed my undergraduate degree. As promised I was eventually named Junior Manager, Manager, Trainer and held various other job titles at the collection agency.

After graduation, I was given a generous salary and a desk at the front of the office, facing all the collectors so that I could bask in my superiority.

More miraculous than all these perks and never on my list of goals, was that I graduated from college with a Bachelors of Business Administration degree in Accounting. On the day of graduation, I felt my entire body afloat with pride. I cried when I moved my tassel from left to right and I felt once again content with my life and my path. I visited the collection agency immediately after the graduation ceremony so that my co-workers could share in my accomplishment. I also went there to make sure that the feeling was gone.

Two years later, on a sunny morning in March, I was laid off along with about 60 other employees. It didn't feel as though I had only lost my source of income; rather it was like finding out that my entire family had moved out of the country without saying goodbye and that my house as I remembered it had never existed. There were no hugs and no promises to keep in touch. I belonged nowhere. I had inadvertently made my primary home base the office; it was where my friends were always waiting and where I felt on top of the world. Around the same time, my long-term relationship ended due to an indiscretion. Slowly, but surely that feeling began to emerge again; this time it was accompanied by a new component: failure. I became enveloped in inadequacy, discouragement, low self-esteem, self-doubt and now failure because I didn't keep my partner happy.

Often when you lose a boyfriend/husband/ partner, you also lose most of your friends. You become a social pariah because no one wants to take sides and no one wants to hear about your broken heart during dinner or dancing. Loneliness can be the darkest of times for you or you can choose to make loneliness a blessing. I made a choice every morning during those following years to turn loneliness into peace and I made time for selfish, small joys. I went to coffee shops like Starbucks or Barnes & Noble in Manhattan with a book or a newspaper and read alone for hours. I took bubbly baths and moisturized and cared for my skin and hair for hours on a Saturday night and now I look ten years younger than I am. I giggled every time I left my cellphone at home and didn't freak about missing a call because I didn't have to explain where I was. I breathed in forgiveness and exhaled out anger on the Long Beach boardwalk every morning. I realized that I loved sushi because I started to date and tried new foods, new places and new things. I joined a gym just for the sauna. I bought myself a leather jacket and didn't feel guilty. I went to Six Flags Great Adventure to ride every single roller coaster that I had missed while in a relationship with someone who was afraid of heights.

My goal after losing my job and my love was to renew my unemployment insurance for as long as possible. As long as I had an income, there was a façade that I was earning during the week. The check was in the mail every week and I spent my days sleeping and working out and show-ing up at various Manhattan events on Monday or Tuesday nights, similar to a mini-celebrity. The words résumé and interview scared me. I could not imagine what a resume looked like or who I would send it to if I had one. I pondered writing that my long term objective was to retire as soon as possible; or that my greatest skill would be to provide a well-rounded office personality. Various conversations with friends and people I met in Starbucks or on the beach led me to the conclusion that accounting and auditing weren't things I would enjoy.

After several months, my lifestyle was beginning to get on my nerves; not to mention my parents', with whom I was living, free of charge. I have been known to make bold statements to my family that I was going to "climb Mount Everest," or "move to Bermuda," or "be a vegetarian forever" with a focus to entertain and prevent people around me from thinking I didn't have any plans or ambitions. In reality, I didn't have the ambition to do much.

I half-heartedly began job searching. I had a weak resume that stated my objective was to work "with a team in an entry level accounting posi-tion" and I hadn't much interest in writing thank-you notes after interviews. I learned during those few months that tan suits, designer high heels and a stylish handbag does not help you get a job when your interviewer is a woman.

I was home on the couch so much that I developed a love for daytime talk shows and a hatred of the soap operas. As I lounged one day, I said to my father that I knew exactly what I was doing; I was going to law school that September. He looked at me in silence and as I recall, he didn't respond in any significant way. It's possible that images of me in a pale yellow suit like Marcia Clark, prosecuting a man twice my size, while my reputation and family were torn to shreds in the media, danced in his head; I suddenly had a vision of me in a black robe, like Judge Judy, bang-ing a gavel on my bench every time I heard that an 18-year-old girl 'gave' all her money and her car to her boyfriend and now he won't give it back. The idea of being in one of these powerful suits grew on me so I enrolled in a class to practice for the LSATs. I attended that class about three times simply because I had made two friends in the class who made me feel like I was doing something important.

I applied to two law schools I had heard of in the New York area. I didn't have the necessary funds to apply to more, so I put my destiny in the hands of those two applications. I accepted the first invitation I received to attend a smaller school in a remote area of Long Island. I later learned that the law school campus was one component of a larger educational institution with campuses specializing in everything from physical therapy to theater and the arts.

I moved into the basement of a residential home near the school and I had no windows. In the evenings, after a three hour constitutional law or contracts class, after I had daydreamed through the last half, I descended the 32 cement steps into the basement, accessible only in the rear of the home, past prickly brush and with my trusty flashlight to ward off raccoons and possums. Once inside, I never knew when daytime was approaching or whether an entire day had passed. It could have been snowing in July or an atomic bomb could have wiped out everything above ground and I would have continued to sit at my kitchen table, studying the intricacies of obscene speech under the First Amendment. During that year, the cold gloom of dark wood paneled walls enveloped me for what seemed hours and often I would emerge expecting to find that a few days had been lost. I started to remember stories my mother told me about how our family lived in a basement apartment in Brooklyn when I was born and how the gloominess made me a depressed child. She said I loved to be outside and it was almost as though my innate ambitions and my outgoing personality could have been thwarted by the lack of sunshine and air that windows allow. Ever since our family moved from that apartment, I remember living in homes with multiple windows, bright sunny rooms to play in and back-yards where I could always be outside. Returning to the darkness of a basement apartment did not suit me well and I frequently made the two hour trip to my parents' home.

Many of my family and friends would often applaud my status as a law student, when the truth is that I never expected to take the bar exam or even practice law. My sole interest in law school was learning something new everyday or meeting a new person or simply to convey the impression that I was doing something important.

During my first year of law school I had a female professor who I secretly worshipped for her intelligence and her no-nonsense attitude. She maintained a family, a law practice in the area of Intellectual Property and a teaching position. She was small in stature, like me, but she spoke in a commanding tone which kept me memorizing endless court decisions before her class, in case I was asked to stand and recite the newest ruling on zoning regulations.

I never spoke to her directly, though I lingered while she had discussions with other students so that I might steal her powerful secret. As the year ended, a competition to be appointed a member of the Law Review, the highest honorary organization in law school, was approaching. I heard the professor encouraging her favorite students to enter the competition;

which was structured so that the two weeks following final exams, when we were all at our lowest points both mentally and physically, would require constant researching, reading and writing an answer to a legal question. If you didn't attain a certain grade point average, your answer wouldn't be read. So, in addition to many sleepless nights, we had to enter the competition without knowing if we would qualify to be considered. I listened to her discuss the honors and recognition that accompanied such an acceptance and knew that her recognition and respect would be earned as well.

Competitions and rivalries to prove my intelligence were not part of my agenda. I saw no real gratification in joining a club of people who would sit around and talk about how much smarter they were than everyone else. When the professor realized I was listening, she made a point of addressing me and saying that only exceptional students would be considered and not to get my hopes up. Recalling that moment, she infused in me that same desire to win that I felt years before.

I was accepted that summer into the Law Review, a.k.a. 'smart people club.' I saw that same professor the next semester and she made no effort to disguise her shock. I advanced to become a Law Review Board member the following year and maintained charisma and kindness in my social life and humility in my academic life. It was in the course of my last year, when I embraced my comprehension of accounting and I began to actively apply my interest in tax to the law I was learning.

After graduating, I made a decision that has changed the last year of my life. I was offered a position at a small firm for a salary less than I made working at the collection agency. I was also offered a different position at an international firm in Manhattan which promised to pay off $180,000 in student loans in exchange for two years of assembly line legal practice where I was expected to draft documents blindly and without recognition and never be seen in court. I weighed the options of buying a new car or keeping my 1998 Toyota Corolla, which had no radio and no heat. I fantasized about buying a beautiful home in which I would only sleep because I would be expected to work tirelessly to pay for that home. I imagined spending Christmases, Mother's Days and birthdays alone, at my desk, wearing a $2000 suit.

I chose to accept the position in the smaller firm, practicing tax law and asset preservation techniques under the guidance of an adjunct professor from my school. Over two years, in addition to learning how to practice law, I have become skilled at secretarial and clerical responsibilities, paralegal duties and every facet of the office structure from process serving to dropping off the Federal Express packages after work. My car broke down twice on the way to court, costing over $1500 in repairs. My shoes were scuffed from being worn everyday. I owned two suits and at any given moment, one was too tight and the other too big. I ate frozen yogurt for lunch because I couldn't afford to spend $5 a day on lunch. In the end, the most valuable tool I was left with was the insight into running a law practice as a business.

I had watched my boss drive off into the sunset on his Harley after only ten years of working for himself because he knew how to respect people. I met his children, who went to hockey camp each summer and lived on the beach because they knew how to take advantage of opportunity. I watched the partners at my firm pull into the parking lot in Ferraris after only twenty years in private practice, because they knew how to invest. I visited their homes, secluded by private beaches and met their children who drove Lexuses and BMWs at the age of seventeen and chose theater or journalism as careers, because they knew how to live.

In the past year, I have built my own law practice and I have remained human from all the mistakes I've made and the obstacles I have prevailed over, but I don't know what comes next. I lease office space in a prominent area of New York where there is only 30 minute parking, so I walk the few blocks to my office. I share the second floor of a building where my office is the size of the bathroom in a luxury home, but I have windows. I invite my clients and friends for coffee or green tea in a conference room where there are pictures of the devil playing chess with an angel and winning. During these consultations over coffee or tea, single mothers fight for child support, retired millionaires plan to minimize estate and income taxes and college students fearfully recount an arrest for drinking and driving; all with the same undertones of loneliness and struggle. Eventually most people adopt me as a friend and then an attorney because I'm open about my past and therefore trusted to approach difficult situations with practicality and sensitivity. I treat each legal situation as though I was in that position. I have maintained friendships with people from all stages of my life and that is a success in itself. My personality is that I will always embrace the eccentricities of the world and I love to wear a mini and go dancing with people half my age who have no idea that I'm an attorney.

At 30 years old, I am still in various transitional states of maturity and idealism and once in a while that feeling creeps up behind me. The missteps I have made in my lifetime stem from comparing myself to those around me or measuring myself up to what others thought I ought to be; whether aspiring to be different, aspiring to conformity, aspiring to make someone proud, aspiring to be better than her or aspiring to behave worse than a tramp. In fact, the key to setting goals is to do everything your own way, just because you want to and because it feels right.

In the meantime, while I continue toward goals that may never be reached, my first triumph is that I have accepted that some goals will never be reached. I've called everyone on their birthdays. I've managed to forgive anything in a matter of precious moments, but not forget. I've survived true love and true heartbreak. I treat myself to a manicure and pedicure at least twice a month. I've paid for my own BMW. I realistically look at homes for sale with private beaches and multiple rooms which I hope to fill with a family someday. I always wear a pretty piece of clothing, jewelry or lip gloss that makes me feel happy. I remind myself daily how truly extraordinary I am.

Suzana da Camara

At the age of five, I knew I wanted to be a singer. There was no convincing me otherwise and my mother found this strength of conviction at such a young age surprising. Everyday, I would place my dolls, stuffed animals, transformers and my brothers' G.I. Joes in neat rows on top of my dresser. Before I started singing, I would introduce myself to all my 'kids', as I called my audience. I would always start my song softly, then once the flow was going strong, I would clench my fists and my face would appear to almost weep and I would rip into a thunder of long notes and end with a curtsey. My songs would always be about my curiosity: how could roses always have the same perfume, even if they were different colours? All I knew was that singing was my favorite company; with it I never felt alone.

By the time I was six, I was going to the doctor's office a lot more than usual. 'Big Joe' was my doctor's name. To me, he seemed like a giant with a Tom Selleck hairdo, hence 'Big Joe'. He would poke this strange looking glowing device into my ear while kind of murmuring to himself, then just tell me to keep my ears dry. Curiously, I would touch all of his ear devices, and ask him tons of questions. He would patiently answer all my questions with a gentle smile.

I didn't think much of these visits; they started to feel normal for me. But by seven, I noticed a shift in my mothers concern. I remember being told I had to stay in the hospital because I had something in my ear that wasn't suppose to be there, which I thought was like having your bellybutton where your nose should be. As I grew older I learned that there was a tumor in my right ear and it was connected to my three ear bones; staple **malleus and incus.** It was a risky tumor and an operation was necessary to remove it.

I awoke to find my mother next to my bed. I was thirsty, hungry, confused and nauseated. I could do little but sleep and when I was awake, I was bored. I would get out of bed to go to the washroom and I would be looking at the bathroom door, but my legs would be heading for the exit; my balance was completely off. I learned that balance is controlled through the vestibular system which shares the temporal bone space with the cochlea , the main auditory nerve. My cochlea was removed during surgery. I had to relearn how to walk and run without falling.

My youthful activities became a whole new adventure. Every little sound agitated me like nails on a chalk board in stereo. Going to school with friends and cutting them off walking was a topic of conversation. A family member would call my name and I would look in a completely different direction. So instead of looking like I was clueless, I started to pretend I couldn't hear at all. My voice sounded foreign to me. It felt like I was hearing myself on an old cassette tape in an echo chamber. I would get so drained from trying to listen to people talk. Conversations sounded like Snoopy dialogue.

My ears became an obsession, not just for me, but for my mother and just about *everyone* who knew my mother, as well. I would keep cotton balls in both ears because I felt like it evened out the one-sided sound and the cotton ball in the deaf ear was simply comforting.

When it was time for me to go the Azores in the summertime, my mom packed my suitcase with my rubber cap and my new summer staple; earplugs. I remember her incessantly lecturing us to **always** wear earplugs! To avoid infection, she would often insert eardrops into my ear. My best friend's brother used to tease me by whispering my name, *su—za—naaa,* about five hundred times. I confess, I heard him way before the five hundredth *su—za – naaa,* but I would pretend I couldn't hear him because I thought it was kind of neat to have a teenage boy teasing me. Sometimes I would weep in frustration, at other times I simply closed my eyes and concentrated on hearing what was around me. That actually became interesting and I eventually became pretty good at it.

In grades four and five, I felt isolated because I could not hear what anybody was saying unless they were right next to me. I felt odd enough as it was; I had a boyish face with big hair, long fingers and the skinniest ankles in the world. I learned to play by myself; when I couldn't hear a conversation, I would simply go off and do my own thing. I sat in front row so I could hear the teacher and that made me the goody-goody. It was fine; as long as they didn't know my secret, they could call me whatever they wanted. Due to this, I started to listen with my eyes and I became observant and developed a keen sense of awareness that has since allowed me to read people through their body language. To this day, I can determine how many years a couple have been sharing kisses by the way they interact with each other.

It was awhile before I sang again; I was afraid of my voice. I felt very insecure about singing because it seemed that my world of sound and hearing were in harmonic battle. But quite naturally, like a seed growing through attention and care, I started to sing again. I would practice listening to soft sounds and try to decipher the words. But, I learned to embrace my new voice as I heard it because there was no other choice; to sing was to live.

I kept my love for singing a secret from most of my friends. But, one day, my love came knocking at the door. Sarah, a classmate, was very open with her own love for singing; she had performed in front of the school a few times with her angelic voice and I remember thinking she was lucky to have so much confidence. Our upcoming talent night was two weeks away and Sarah needed someone to take her place for talent night. A surge of emotion flared inside me like I've never felt before.

She asked again, "Would anybody like to take my spot and sing?"

I remember looking around in desperation as if I was dying of thirst. I passionately wanted to renew my desire to perform. My mind screamed, "ME..please pick me!" But nothing came out. I clenched my hands together and looked over at my best friend; she was the only one who knew how I felt, and she suddenly said,

"Suzana does!" while pointing at me.

Sarah looked at me and said,

"Do you want to do it?" Everyone looked over at me; looking down and painfully lying, I shook my head, *no*. Carelessly, Sarah proceeded to ask if anyone else could do it. I panicked and became mad at Sarah for not recognizing my lie. Then someone started to raise their hand and my arms jumped up as I blurted out,

"Okay, I'll do it." I tried to keep as cool as possible, but for the rest of the class I was so exhilarated that I could hardly contain myself. My first public appearance! This time not in front of dolls and family but all my teachers and peers! What was I thinking?!   I met Sarah at recess. For the first five minutes, she was singing the song I was to sing; I couldn't hear a thing because I was completely deaf in fear.

The big day came. My heart was palpitating and I went pee several times before I started. I stared into the audience wearing a face full of fear. It was dark and nobody made a sound. I felt like the audience could only see my trembling calves and the tiniest ankles in the world encased in fluorescent white stockings as my black dress blended perfectly into the darkness. I looked over at Ross, my guitar player, in desperation.

I whispered, "Wait," but he started anyway. I felt bits of explosions go off; five seconds of humiliation because I was going to sing off key due to being almost deaf in one ear and five more seconds of all my insecurities stampeding through my brain. By the time I came back to reality, my hand gripping the microphone, Ross had gone through the intro four times; this was *not* how I'd planned my premier performance. Finally, I began to sing 'Tears in Heaven', by Eric Clapton. I lost my breath and my voice was shaky at first but eventually it smoothed over. I remember thinking how odd this was for me to be in front of all these people, singing?! I felt relieved when it was over but bittersweet because I was just getting comfortable. I didn't really want it to end, and it wouldn't have ended so quickly if I had not skipped a whole verse of the song.

However, my accompanist, Ross, followed through without any trouble and nobody noticed a glitch. That felt like the hardest thing in the world to me and, in that moment, it was.

I am now 28 years old and I have made 3 albums with my co-writer, Mike Dell. I have been singing professionally for eight years. We have traveled Western Canada and Europe performing all original material along with some cover songs. We have worked with legendary producer Jack Richardson, who has produced "The Guess Who". An original piece of our music, "Searching Deep Down", has been released on a compilation album featuring Norah Jones, Ella Fitzgerald, Holly Cole and Michel Buble. A remix version of our song, 'Let's Spend the Night Together' was released by Koch Records as part of an album featuring artists such as Django Reindhart, St. Germain and many other recognized musicians. We have distribution in Canada and Asia and are currently working on a fourth album to be released in 2008. I hope to release many more albums of all different tastes from around the world.

I still have insecurities to overcome, but I work on them as they appear; often. As I expose myself in this short story, I know I am not alone on this journey. My heart leads me along this path; will I do it perfectly? Not very likely. I will do the best I can; I will always try to move forward, even if I feel like being invisible.

I still struggle when I have to appear on stage, even after eight years of performing. I obsess about how my monitors sound and worry that the venue will get too noisy to hear myself sing. I still feel like looking over and asking my guitar player to *'wait'* a few more seconds and I still have to pee before every performance. My ambition is strong, but at times my heart is weak. When I was eight, I would sing without inhibition; now I am 28 year-old singer who ritually performs, not with high heels, but with my naked feet planted on the ground while singing scintillating melodies of broken hearts, lost desires and the simple beauty of life; which is pretty darn lovely to me. My plan is simply to sing as long as my heart desires. I believe that there's no such thing as impossible. When I do what I love, I believe I exude love. Seeking truth and overcoming our fears is a journey I hope we all embark on.

Tee-Lynn

It never ends. Just last night, as I tried to enjoy a night out with my friends, I encountered one of life's 'special individuals' whose passion in life is to ruin the harmony of others. As I pushed my way through the crowded dance floor, inching toward the group of friends I'd spent half the night looking for, I collided with a big foot; I tripped and fell. I looked up at the guy who belonged to the big foot; he stood there, appearing to be amused by my stumble.

"Excuse me." I said, shooting him a look of discontent. I mean, who would be 'Little Miss Sunshine' after taking such a tumble?

"This isn't a race-track." Spit shot from his mouth, and his breath reeked of beer.

"Yes, I realize it's not a race-track; I wasn't running." Now my patience was being tested, "It is a walkway, though, and you shouldn't have your feet stuck out in the middle of it for people to trip over."

He smiled nastily. With his face inches from mine, he said, "Shut up you stupid gorilla."

I couldn't believe what I'd heard. I hadn't been confronted with racism in a long time. In this day and age, I would often sense it, but nobody (at least not lately) had been ignorant or bold enough to look me in the eye and just say it. But this guy was, both bold enough and ignorant enough. Suddenly, things made sense; the foot in the aisle wasn't an accident. He was calling me a gorilla because I was black.

My eyes started to well up; I was angry and mortified. My friend, Candace, saw the tears in my eyes; I saw the look in hers. I thought she was ready to kill him; I gripped her hard, but I couldn't stop her from going over there. Thankfully, the Neanderthal hadn't rubbed off on all of his friends; one of them stepped in front of her before she could reach the moron.

"I'm really sorry about my friend," he said. "Please just ignore him."

It was at this moment that I realized it wasn't worth it. The creep wasn't worth ruining my night over. Allowing myself to be upset by this ignorant human being, who had obviously been misinformed somewhere along the way, just wasn't worth it. I was so much stronger than that. I had been through too much in my 24 years to let a minor event like that bring me down. And suddenly, I felt stronger than ever.

August 19, 1983 should have been the most important day in my parent's life. It was actually sort of a hindrance; I was born. I don't know very much about that day, but I do know that I was born to two teenagers; they weren't ready for the responsibilities that came with parenthood. My father was of Jamaican descent and my mother was British; both were raised in Canada. Luckily for me, I had wonderful grandparents; while my mother was off with her 'friends', hopped up on cocaine and drunk and my father was busy committing armed robbery and dealing drugs, I was at home with my mom's parents.

It was a loving environment. My grandparents loved me to pieces, and why not? I was so cute. I often went to visit my dad's parents as well. I well remember the fragrant aroma of rice and peas and stewed beef coming from the kitchen at Grandma and Grandpa W's. Ketchup chips and Snickers bars were my favorite snacks when I visited. We would stop off at the same convenience store every Sunday to get treats. I have so many great memories from my childhood; I try not to let the bad memories overshadow them.

Both sets of Grandparents sure loved me; but they didn't love each other. What seemed to be extreme love for their granddaughter turned into a harsh custody battle, driven by stubbornness and selfishness on both sides. For years, both sets of grandparents fought over me and who I should live with. As young as I was, I remember the conversations, the arguments over the phone, the death threats from my dad, the threats to 'take me away' and the racial comments.

"She should be with her roots," my Grandpa W used to say. "She needs her black family". I don't know if those quotes were coming from him or from my extremely controlling and manipulative father. I'll call him D; I'd rather not refer to him as my father, because I never thought of him that way. My Grandpa W never seemed controlling or mean; not to me, anyway. I remember all of the fun times I'd sit on his lap and watch all the Bugs Bunny videos; I loved Elmer Fudd the best. Grandpa W and I could recite the words from memory; we watched it that much. I never understood why my mother's parents blamed Grandpa W; because I'm sure a lot of his actions were motivated by D and his manipulative ways. I will call my mother's parents my Grandma and Grandpa J.

Every time my Grandpa W came to pick me up for a visit, my Grandma and Grandpa J would worry that I might not come home. I think they were more comfortable while D was in jail, because they didn't fear my Grandpa W as much as they feared D. My Grandma J would hold me tight, showering me with hugs and kisses before I left for another Sunday with my Grandpa and Grandpa W.

I was the best kid ever; or so I've been told, and I like to believe it. I was exuberant and full of the joy of life. I loved the spotlight and craved attention. I would talk to anybody who would listen. For as long as I can remember, I've wanted to be a journalist. I loved to read and write. I loved dancing, singing and magic; and for some reason, I loved putting my Grandpa J's hair in rollers. Most of all, I loved to laugh. Although I was a happy little girl, I was not oblivious to the goings on around me; I was also an incredibly smart girl. It didn't take me long to figure things out. I knew very quickly that my life wasn't typical.

By the time I was five, it got harder for my Grandma J to convince me to go for 'visitation'. As the custody battle continued, my Grandma J would resentfully allow me to visit D and my mother at their townhouse across the city. That was whenever D was out of jail. It was never a great experience for me. I never wanted to go and kicked up a huge fuss every time. I would beg and cry and plead with Grandma J, "Please, please, please," I would say, "don't make me go." Her gentle voice always convinced me to go, to avoid a confrontation with D. "It's only for a day," she would say. "I'll see you tomorrow". Grandma J and I even formulated a special handshake, and we would always squeeze hands tightly before I entered the townhouse.

I hated that townhouse. I was often left alone for hours at a time. When my parents were there, the door was always open, with different men always coming and going. They were weird people; I didn't like them very much. I wonder now what they thought about the bright-eyed five-year-old staring up at them as they intruded on her visit with her parents. "Get in the living room," D would yell at me. "Get in there, NOW!" I hated the living room, filled with snakes and spiders. After hearing about his pet store robbery escapades, I'm almost positive they were all stolen. Pythons and other creepy, crawling creatures stared back at me from their cages; I was petrified. D would emerge from the basement with a big black box; I had to know what was in that box. One day I tiptoed quietly into the hallway that led to the kitchen. There they sat, all the weird men at the kitchen table. D opened the box and lifted out some sort of shiny device with a flat panel; it looked like the thing my Grandma J would stick fruit on in the grocery store. D poured white powder onto it; I didn't know what it was at the time, but I sure do now.

The worst day was the day that I didn't have to stay. My Grandma J pulled up in front of the townhouse and we were nearly blinded by flashing, red lights; police cars and emergency vehicles surrounded the property. Blood streamed from the front door of the house and was all over the steps. Yellow tape cordoned off the entrance to the house and part of the yard. My heart raced and I started to cry. "Stay here," said my Grandma J. She got out of the car and headed towards the police officers standing around the front of the house.

My mind flashed back to the time I had seen Mommy bleeding. My mom had picked up the phone to call somebody, but D wouldn't have it; he grabbed the phone out of her hand and smashed her in the face with it, over and over again. She was bleeding and crying. My little legs pounded the floor as I ran on the spot, screaming for my Mommy, "Daddy, stop! Daddy, stop!" I was hysterical. Blood poured from her nose and from a gash in her head. She was on the floor in the kitchen; blood was everywhere. He raised his fist higher into the air, and she yelled out a horrible cry—

"Tonya," my thoughts were interrupted by Grandma J getting back into the car. I was crying even harder now. "Don't cry sweetheart," she said. "What happened? Is Mommy okay?" I asked. "Yes dear, your mother is fine."

I don't know how long D went away for that time; I'm not sure of the timeline, but he was in and out of jail very often. At some point, when I was around five, before he went to jail for the longest time, he was out long enough to impregnate my mother again. My little brother lived between my mother's apartment, and my Grandpa and Grandma W's house. My Grandma W took very good care of him.

I would often receive letters and cards; almost every Sunday at Grandpa W's house, D would call collect. I liked talking to him; I think it filled a void for me. But I felt safer when he was 'away'. After the incident at the townhouse, when he almost killed someone, he went away for quite awhile. I remember talking to him on the phone from different jails. There are pictures of me as a baby, talking on the big red phone at Grandma and Grandpa W's house, to D. By the time I was seven, my Grandma and Grandpa J gained full custody of me and became my legal guardians.

Through most of my childhood, I was happy. My Grandma J enrolled me in modeling classes to boost my self confidence. I took piano lessons and participated in pageants to stay busy and out of trouble. My Grandma J didn't really have the money for all those things, but she did them anyway. She did it to keep my mind off other things, to keep me thriving. My Grandma J and I have always had an exceptional bond. She is everything to me; I couldn't imagine my life without her. My mother's sister was also a big part of my life. She lived with my Grandma and Grandpa J for a fair part of her adulthood. My favorite trips were to the African Lion Safari; almost every weekend, Aunt T would take me. I would bring a big pillow for the fifteen-minute drive. It seemed so long to me then. Now that I look back, she treated me a like a daughter.

I enjoyed school. I was very smart, but my behavior was less than ideal. I was always lashing out; I didn't know how to deal with my emotions or understand what I was feeling half the time. I remember hiding in closets and pulling out my hair or pinching and hitting the other kids; intentionally not following directions from my teachers. The very extreme behavior usually followed some sort of upset, or a visit with D and my mom. I understand, now.

Growing up in a predominately white suburb didn't help my self esteem much. As one of the few minorities in my elementary school, I was the target of the other kids' cruelty. The 'N' word was often thrown at me. I was told that I was dirty, that I didn't bathe, that I had 'cooties' and that I was ugly. I had a lot of friends, but the amount of bullying I endured often overshadowed that. The worst time for me was in middle school. The kids were meaner and had figured out bigger and better ways to taunt me. I was always the girl with no boyfriend, without a date to the dance because it was 'gross' to date black girls. Blonde hair and blue eyes were perfection in my small town. Throughout my childhood and into my early teens, I accomplished a lot: I won local and National beauty pageants, I modeled, I acted in television shows, commercials and I even hosted a kid's show on a national television network; but in their eyes I was never good enough.

During my last few years in elementary school, the incidents started in which my Grandma J ended up in hospital a lot. First it was pneumonia, then a fall down the stairs; but I knew deep down that something wasn't right.

Things had started to change for Grandma J after she was laid off from a job she'd held for over 25 years. At first, being off work was good, because it allowed her to do things with me, like taking me to castings or pageants. But after a while, things didn't seem right with her; she wasn't happy anymore. She had taken on a babysitting job, tending a baby from across the street, but she seemed to lose interest in the things she used to enjoy. She slept a lot; in fact, she slept almost all the time. I hated seeing her like that and I didn't know what was wrong. She seemed sad all the time. Had taking care of me and doing all those things for me taken such a toll on her? All the incidents led up to a day in my life that I often try to forget, without success.

My Grandma J was supposed to take me to Toronto for a photo shoot, but at the last minute she decided against it. The parents of the boy she looked after had requested that she no longer take him on trips to the city. I was mad, but I went to school as usual. During afternoon recess, I had a very weird feeling; a feeling that to this day I can't explain; I just knew that something wasn't right. I went inside to call my Grandma J and asked her to pick me up and bring me home. She refused; she couldn't because the boy she was babysitting was down for his nap. I had a tantrum like any other kid who doesn't get what they want. "I hate you!" I said and slammed down the phone. I have always regretted behaving like that; I'll never know if that's what pushed her over the edge.

"Tonya we need to go. Pack up your stuff, let's go," said my Aunt T from outside the classroom door. I packed up my backpack and jumped in the car as she told me the bad news. "Your Grandma is in hospital," she said. I was very confused. I had spoken to Grandma just 45 minutes before my Aunt showed up at school. When we got home, my aunt sent me to pack a bag as I would be going to stay with my friend, Patti, for a few weeks. I still didn't understand what was going on; I was only told that Grandma J was sick. My walk through the house that day happened in slow motion. I entered the house to be overwhelmed with the distinct smell of gasoline. In the front hall, there were dirty footprints and water all over the floor; I could tell that there had been many people in my house. I wasn't allowed to go into the kitchen, so I proceeded upstairs to my bedroom. As I looked through my drawers for a few changes of clothing, something on my bed caught my eye; the dirty outline of a body. It looked as though somebody had been lying there, all dirty and wet. I didn't understand it. I looked at my pillow and had to stop myself from being sick; there was burnt hair all over my pillow. It was my Grandma's hair. I just wanted to get out; I grabbed my clothes and ran. I didn't want to know what happened, but it didn't take long for me to find out. It turned out that the older brother of one of my classmates had been the one who called the police. My grandma had set herself on fire in the backyard.

After months of treatment, skin grafts, and rehabilitation, my Grandma J was well on her way to recovery. While they treated her physical injuries, they also treated her for depression. She was on and off different medications and she got better, but every time she decided to stop taking her pills, she would relapse back into depression. The episodes still happen to this day. However, none have ever been as bad as that day.

Coping with the situation at home, while facing the teasing and taunting of kids in middle school made everyday life a living hell. Kids had heard about my Grandma J's problems through people who attended the same elementary school as I did and teased me about it. They called her crazy and the 'Fire Lady'. I didn't care what those kids said; my Grandma

J was the most important person in my life. She had saved my life and I felt like it was my job to save her life, too. I had separation anxiety; I was afraid to go to school or anywhere else because I was afraid that Grandma J would hurt herself while I was out. It made having a normal life extremely hard; I had to grow up fast.

High school was tough, but the best years of my life. I attended a new school, where people didn't know me. It was the Catholic school system and I had grown up in the public school system; this was a fresh start for me and it was wonderful. I met so many amazing friends and I soared. This was also the point in my life where all my goals became clear. I knew exactly what I wanted from life; and what I didn't want. I knew I NEVER wanted to disappoint my Grandpa and Grandma J. I wanted to make them proud. I never wanted them to go through the things they went through with my mother. I wanted to go to college to study Television Broadcasting and I wanted to work at the same Television Network where I had worked as a child. I knew that I wanted to cut all ties with my father and all negativity. I set these goals for myself, and one by one, I checked them off.

After D got out of prison, he tried to spend time with me, but I declined. I just wasn't ready; I no longer felt any connection to him. I didn't like him or anything he stood for. He was conniving and manipulative, and as I got older, I got wiser. Just because we were blood, as he always used to ram down my throat, I didn't have to like him. D is a horrible person. I see it now in the way he treated me. If I didn't do what he wanted, or see him when he wanted to see me, he would verbally abuse me. He called me the 'wannabe-white girl' and 'peach-skinned girl', trying to persuade me that I didn't know who I was. I knew who I was and I was exactly who HE was NOT. He was not honest, he was not genuine or loyal, and he was not a person I wanted to be around. He eventually remarried and had twins with his new wife.

My mother mostly stayed out of my life. Every once in a while she would call me, drunk; but other than that she concentrated on raising my brother. I always felt like the mistake she wishes she hadn't made. Sometimes it was hard, because it would have been nice to have somebody my mother's age to relate to. Relating to my Grandma J about certain things was difficult because of the age difference. It wasn't easy, though, trying to talk to someone who was constantly drunk and saying nasty things they didn't mean. When my mother told me that she wished she had aborted me, I drew the line. I don't need her when I have such wonderful and supportive grandparents and friends.

After high school, it was a big decision to move away for college. The problem was Grandma J; I was afraid to leave her. My Grandpa J would, of course, take great care of her, but I was so scared that something horrible would happen. I had to let go; if I didn't do this, I would regret it. I would be giving up the opportunity to make my grandparents proud. I needed to prove to myself that nothing could hinder me from being successful.

College was amazing. I moved to the big city. Toronto was so different and the people were so inviting and accepting. I learned to deal with being away from home and coping with the separation anxiety and issues that accompanied it. I visited home often to get my fix of small town life, but when the weekend was over I was back in the city.

I took the Broadcasting program that I had dreamed of since childhood and after an internship, I was offered a job at the same network that I had always wanted to work for. When I graduated from college, my Grandma and Grandpa J were there to see me. I was the first of their children or grandchildren to earn a college diploma. I was making all of my dreams realities because I believed in myself; I wouldn't allow anyone or anything to bring me down. After working in television for three years, I realized that I wanted to try something new. I love a challenge and I was still young, so I thought, "why not?" I have always had a love for writing and communications and I felt that Corporate Communications or Media Relations would be a good career move. I had no formal training in Corporate Communications, but I had a drive to do it. I believe that nothing is impossible. I applied for about 100 jobs, but eventually, I got the one I wanted. I was offered other jobs and I had interviews, but I didn't settle for anything less than my ideal job. It was a job that allowed me to move home to be close to my Grandpa and Grandma J; a job that encouraged me to learn and grow, while developing skills in the field; and a job that I was happy with.

I am 100% proud of the person I've become and the obstacles I've overcome. I've beaten the odds. Touring across Europe is something I would still love to do one day and as long as it is in my power, I will do it. Ironically, it's also been a goal since I was a child to write for a book. Nothing is impossible.

Lisa Bradburn

The document states in typeset letters that my transitory stay was of extreme quiet. Hands passed over my body to bathe, feed and change me, however it was not a home of love; it was merely a house to pass the time until a new family arrived to claim me. If a cry was heard in the night, no rush of anxiety was heard echoing down the hallway to wipe the tears; I learned at an early age to stay within my own thoughts.

Perhaps it was the tufts of curly, jet black hair, hazel eyes and rosy cheeks that drew my new parents. Possessing childlike beauty, it seems, helps one to become adopted; even more helpful was the lack of children available in the mid seventies which caused the young couple to remain on a seven year waiting list.

I once heard a wise woman say that children who don't remember much of their early years are those who've encountered a privileged time in their lives. My memories are sparsely mixed like discarded fragments of film kept in a scrapbook. Expanses of fields, tender kisses jumbled with so much time within me. Beauty can sometimes be revealed in impending tragedy. Before the departure, the grandest moment came in the form of a fantastical roar of fire seething into a giant hot air balloon, descending to a level where the world becomes absolutely still, gliding by the fresh May fields. Then the reel stops and only the loose tip of the film ticks around and around.

What seems as commonplace today as taking a car to the garage for an oil change, their separation and inevitable divorce occurred when I was twelve years-old. Two years prior to that, my mother started to suffer from innumerable illnesses I couldn't comprehend, except for living in fear that she would die. The reality was that she was killing herself with alcohol, yet she was able to hide the effects from me. Despite the past demons that continued to plaque her, she loved me intensely. While my mother lay in bed, a common theme emerged as ample time was granted to face inward; shy and awkward as the initial stages of my adult life were beginning to dawn.

In the fall she left us. The signs and words misinterpreted as my father filed for divorce without the realization that my Mother only sought a time limited separation to desperately pull her life back together.

"Will you come away with me?"

"I cannot, since you do not know where you are going."

Each path would present its own set of unique challenges and I couldn't undermine the attachment I felt toward our old rambling farmhouse. It was a very confusing period as my father struggled with his torrid emotions; ranging from periods of intense anger and desperation against the woman he still loved. There were moments when he would suffer an emotional breakdown and cry uncontrollably into my hair while clutching me for comfort. There was so much chaos in the lives of my immediate family members; I made a firm decision to remain calm and cool. I barely shed a tear and it wasn't long before I felt incapable of emotion.

My father's lifelong passion for hunting turned into an obsession; each night delivering a chilled silence to the old house. Perhaps it was all the memories contained within the farmstead that kept him at bay. Then the women came. He struggled with the idea of being alone and needed a new woman to fill the void in his life and become a replacement maternal role model for me. I craved my father's attention and believed a new stepmother would be counterproductive; if we were to find ourselves once again, we had to allow time to heal the wounds. For many years, a silent anger festered inside me, believing my mother's struggles were discarded far too quickly rather than being faced head on. Today, I still struggle and recognize that I must fully forgive in order to let go.

The inevitable occurred, no matter how much I begged to remain still. Our farmstead had acted as a fortress of protection and comfort. With a blink of an eye, it was gone, only to be replaced by the single most dreaded structure known to sink the heart of a young teenage girl; a trailer. I didn't ask for this, not any of this. Fear of rejection by my peers prevented me from emerging from the school bus at night, rather I'd slink off down the hill and walk steadfastly back. My burning desire was to not merely exist in this world and delve into complacency, but I wanted to fight like hell. Late at night under the covers in our tin box, I would scan the pages of Vogue bought secretly at lunch hour to fantasize about the new life I aspired to create for myself.

In light of dark situations, I cast aside my new stepbrother; however in time, my heart opened and I grew to love him. We were similar in that many circumstances were bestowed upon our lives by the adults around us. I never developed a fondness for my stepmother as she would lag around the trailer in oversized track pants, drinking coffee, while soap operas boomed loudly in the background. Her half finished cigarette butts littered the ashtrays, the tips covered in frosted fuchsia.

Could this have been a marriage of false expectations? As time lurched forward, my father's old habits began to resurface. Nights of stumbling around in the forest baying raccoons and tales of dogs getting in the way of porcupines were heard at breakfast, while attempts at real communication failed miserably. As the months inched closer to my sixteenth birthday, I began to take stock of my life.

I was tired of having a designated cupboard of special food for no particular reason. Enough of the accusations of smoking pot and engaging in sexual activity (I wasn't, yet). I needed an end to claustrophobic living quarters when all I desired was to be free.

It was time to take control and carve my own path. I could hear the wheels of her car smooth over the pebbles in the driveway. Great preparation had been made to pack all of my belongings prior to my mother's arrival and it was now a race against time before my father came home from work. I congratulated myself as everything had been arranged perfectly, my stepmother away for the evening. Then the plan fell to pieces. My father's oversized truck rolled in, as anger and hurt flashed upon his face when he saw what was transpiring before him. The last few moments were a whirlwind, a flurry of bitter words as a chase ensued around the kitchen table. I didn't want to be caught and yet I was, held so tight my breath was almost taken away.

The beautiful reality is that my parents possessed an exceptional love for me, albeit they were broken and could only function to the best of their abilities given the circumstances. With age, my harshness has softened as I understand their humanness; especially when visualizing my parents' own periods of immense growth post marital breakup. It can be a dangerous game to fantasize over who I would be if another couple walked into that waiting room so many years back. I am who I am through them, through thick and thin.

As my twenty-fourth birthday came to pass, I had lived with a man for three years. I believed I had achieved it all; an impending marriage to an intelligent, down to earth man, the corporate job and a nest egg beginning to accumulate. A longtime fascination with Ireland meant the castle and cathedral were booked for the ceremony and it would only be a matter of time before a new arrival would enter into this world while settling down in a shiny new shoebox of a condo.

Is this what we are programmed to do? As my mind focused on the finite details of the wedding, I was plagued with the notion that there was something relevant missing. Then it dawned on me; by centering on the present, I was ignoring the meaning of a future 'forever.' Anxiety levels began to rise. I felt an insatiable need to peel away my skin, to become more than I was; for my actions to be shocking and authentic. There were times I craved for my entire body to scream that I am a woman without ever having to say a single word; to shed the little girl tears and finally come into my own.

London was calling. For a week, I absorbed the sights and smells of this complex and riveting city with a best girlfriend. At the end of the second last day, I leaned over and looked at her intently,

"I'm moving"

That one decision charted an entirely new course in my life. The most gut wrenching part of hurting someone is observing emotional pain and being helpless to ease the suffering. I watched as he departed into the late grey November day. He was unaware of my presence. At that moment, I should have fallen apart; rather I became an anchored stone, cold and distant, waiting in grand anticipation for the future. That was the last time I saw him until my return.

One month prior to my departure, I received an important phone call.

"Ms Bradburn, this is the Children's Aid Society. You placed a search within our registry and we are calling because we have located your birth mother."

A lump became lodged in my throat and suddenly I felt nauseous. No preparation time is granted for such moments, although I silently waited. The agency asked several questions to measure my true intentions and ensure that I was stable enough to continue with the process. My mind raced in several directions; will we look alike, possess the same graceful mannerisms and mutually share a great passion for fine art and European history? How will our lives change after we meet each other?

The genuine response provided to the agency was a simple request to add a new friend in my life. No replacement could ever be made for the woman who had provided me with such unconditional love. Acting as an intermediary, the agency was able to express my ultimate gratitude to the brave woman who had given birth to me, in recognition of choosing life at a time when abortion could have been an option to a young girl who had aspirations of a university degree. One has to admire such strong determination.

Within two days, the agency called back. My birth mother had confided that her husband and children were not aware of my existence and to enter into her life would ultimately have devastating consequences. Certain people would crumple under the weight of rejection. However, it is impossible to lose someone when you have never known them. For this, I was not prepared to hurt her and to this day, the pursuit is over.

Moving to the UK in the dead of January without a job and possessing few acquaintances is not an enticing prospect and one I do not personally endorse. The high of a big adventure was still resonating inside me as I deplaned. Within a few weeks, I was suffering from a deep depression; my journey appeared to be doomed from the start. I recalled the day that my father had moved me from Benson Avenue. Like so many times before, the tiny blood vessels in his neck would pulse and a wave of anger would flash and gradually climb to his cheeks and come to rest in his forehead. I recognized the generational gap between us as the words streamed from his mouth, "Good Lord, girl, why would you leave someone who can take care of you?"

There are times in our lives when a fork in the road emerges and the route you take will help to define who you are going to be as a person. Usually the toughest choice is the right one. Sitting in a dingy, cramped flat in up-and-coming Fulham, my remaining $200CDN sat on the table, peanut butter crusted to one side. With absolutely no employment prospects and living in one of the world's most expensive cities, the stench of desperation overrode the sweet smell of Persil detergent.

Fuck it. It was my decision to move to this damp, miserable city and I refused to leave without an honest fight. I selected an appropriate crisp, navy blue and white pinstripe suit and my senses intuitively guided me to Hammersmith, where I assumed big American and British corporations awaited my arrival. In an age where resumes were emailed to a giant black hole known as 'Human Resources,' walking the dirty streets of London with photocopied synopses of my life seemed archaic. Naturally, the rejections followed, along with closed doors and stares of disbelief. The English, it seems, do not behave in this manner.

Dampness enveloped my body and there I stood shivering, hair disheveled, as evening began to set in. My eyes were full of tears and the thought of another 'no' left me gasping for air. A young man stood in the front entrance of a large telecommunications company, enjoying a cigarette. After smoothing down my skirt and running my fingers through my hair, I approached him. Within three days, I found myself in the realm of the employed once again.

Fate led me to him one morning as solemn people stood on the rickety train approaching Westminster Station. Our bodies touched as a whirlwind of activity swarmed around us, moving on and off the train. I was reminded of the small charcoal minnows that flow together in the coldest depths. It was a typical misty day when the weather remained undecided; the grey clouds hung low, the heavy breath of tube riders rose up, steaming the windows. I inadvertently glanced up and my heart thudded against my chest. He was the most handsome creature I had ever laid eyes upon. The train became hot, hot, hot! Beads of sweat trickled down my back from the muggy heat. He was engrossed in a thick novel, his brilliant olive eyes moving quickly over each word. With the station fast approaching, I knew I had to get him to notice me before our ways parted forever.

"Erm, hello. Your book looks very interesting, what are you reading?"

What followed was the most important love affair of my life. In a city of nine million people, this fascinating man lived within a stone's throw of me. From my third-storey flat, I could peer down upon the grey line of row houses and see his shared accommodation. His singsong northern Irish accent was like delicate music to my ears and we looked beautiful together. Somehow, I became a woman, self assured, very present, blossoming and alive.

After a year of living in Fulham, a deep darkness came to rest upon the great city once again. I pointed my pale face towards the sky and a large red maple leaf emblem flew by with a dull roar to the west and suddenly, I felt a pang of sadness in my heart. It was time to go home.

Back in Toronto, the winter thawed into spring. One day as I strolled down the street, I spotted a wedding party exiting the church up ahead. Suddenly, my past firmly confronted my present. There he was, tall, proud and dashing standing beside his new bride and surrounded by friends and family showering the happy couple with blessings. Our past mutual friends gathered around in celebration of the special, intimate moment. I immediately felt as though my presence cheapened their sacred space. A few people glared over in my direction, but this accidental mishap was a matter of being in the wrong place at the wrong time. I straightened my posture with a sense of purpose and empowerment; all I could do was stare straight ahead and keep walking. After passing the scene, I let out a huge sigh of relief and smiled for the new couple. That could have been my day, but it wasn't and that was just fine.

After nearly a year apart, there were times that I missed him so terribly it felt like little knives were cutting holes in my heart. Our long distance relationship slowly dissolved into broken promises, long pauses of silence and time lingering further and further from phone calls. The separation was unbearable and our once loving relationship was on shaky ground despite my unwavering desire to push on.

It was a chilly, November evening when I stopped at the crosswalk in front of the Royal York Hotel. The season brought salted slush on the pavement and giant flakes of snow spat down from the sky. Shivering at the corner, I peered down to see an exquisite pair of Italian leather shoes.

"Your shoes are too fine to wear in this weather."

The man looked at me intently and as my gaze moved up his finely tailored length, I noticed a face of androgynous beauty as if made from porcelain. Formal hellos were exchanged. In a thick, foreign accent he explained that he was a representative of the Czech government attending a political convention. I was overcome with his intoxicating presence. An invitation was extended to me for the following night to discuss a potential business opportunity as I was seeking employment as a Project Manager. That night I called London and requested permission to meet this prospect and with slight hesitation, a decision was made.

What started as innocent flirting somehow led to Russian vodka in his embellished suite. What started as a simple toast to prosperity led to strewn clothes and muddled memories, devoid of passion or feeling. I felt utter deception. He proposed that I become his companion when traveling on business to Toronto and through a pounding headache, I declined. There was no excuse; what remained was great pain and internal suffering that wouldn't depart.

"Did you sleep with him?"

"Yes."

Somehow through it all, we managed to stay together and I returned to London on my twenty-eighth birthday to smooth over our differences, only to find a chilled reception. It was over. My heart was numb; shattered into a million pieces because everything that once was, was no longer. His face and the evidence found in his flat gave it all away; long strands of jet black hair stared up from the bathroom floor while two empty wine glasses rested on the kitchen counter, lipstick smudged on the rim of one. An empty cake box mocked me from the top of the garbage bin. The final slap in the face came in the form of a used form of a used wrapper roughly dropped by the edge of the bed, a corner poking outward asking to be revealed.

"Do you have something to tell me?"

"No."

"Are you sure? I have something to show you."

Where some women would flee home, I remained in a state of agony, a plea for reconciliation. As the lush, patchwork hills rolled on towards Belfast, the intuitive voice inside me whispered this would be the last time we would see each other. The lines blurred between love and hate. He no longer reached in the night; his subconscious mind spat cruel words in an attempt to push me away. As a gesture of goodwill, his family had provided us with a quaint, grey limestone seventeenth-century cottage between the isolated, jagged hills and wild, northern sea. We walked in silence. Gurgling brooks brought the first hints of spring as dozens of new tadpoles spawned, turned and gushed forth. One day, under the frozen sky, the most brilliant rainbow emerged and like children, we ran to the top floor to peer at its beauty. For a long time it remained and then the colours melted into each other, gradually fading away. I wanted time to stand still again, but it was all a grand illusion.

My soul fell from the sky and dropped into the chilled Atlantic, giving way to self loathing. Like an old deck of cards flicked to the floor, I discarded my friends and faced inward to cope with the loss. Death would have been easier; instead he coexisted with someone else leaving me with faded replacements. At night, I collected fragmented physical attributes and personality traits from men who vaguely resembled what once was in the hopes of rebuilding him again. Little dabbles began to resurface as frequent dirty habits. A bitchy, self-absorbed side of me emerged as more and more was shoveled up my nose and I collapsed into a dank well of despair. The inducement surged forward, and the boundary pushed too far as my heart crashed and banged against my body, echoing in my ears. Time beckoned my departure. I laid there for three days, sweating and dispelling filth into my soaking bed sheets when a thin ray of light streamed down toward my body, bringing hope and forgiveness in the form of my mother. Her maternal instincts had known that I needed her and she had telephoned every couple of hours in her most gentle, understanding and loving way. She understood me.

Today, I thank God for every day that I wake up on this earth. Others suffer far worse fates and sink to the bottom for unspeakable amounts of time. This is not a part of my story.

Every day, when the hands of the clock smoothly glide to the position of 11:11, my eyes automatically shift to acknowledge the time, no matter where I am in the world. There is no explanation, except that in the AM or PM, it has become a part of my routine. I have come to accept that it is my maker revealing his presence in a discreet relational manner and in return he requests a friendly acknowledgement.

Where the valves were once shut tight as a barrier to entry, I am learning to open the door to allow strangers a fighting chance. The meek, half flat smile has blossomed into a large, toothy grin, present in the moment. My unwavering faith in a higher power combined with self belief has saved me from a great fall, despite the fact that I will always be a half finished canvas. I accept that true perfection will never be achieved and real beauty lies with acceptance of our personal flaws. Ethnic origins become irrelevant when we peer into the mirror and recognize that we are all comprised of human flesh and bone; capable of opening our forgiving hearts to ourselves and the world around us.

Francesca Ortepi

Based on appearance, I seem like a typical 29-year-old woman. I appear to have a lot going for me; beauty, a great career and wonderful family and friends. But appearances can be deceiving.

I was raised in a strict Italian household; the youngest of three girls and Daddy's last chance for a son. Yes, that's right; I was supposed to be 'Frank.' It was pretty tough growing up; my older sisters could do no wrong and they never tried to challenge my parents' discipline; as a rebellious child, I was on my own. On top of all that, my middle sister hated me. I was fortunate to have good looks, smarts and an outgoing personality. I was never afraid to take risks or suffer the consequences. I had no worries, no cares about anything. I just did as I pleased and didn't think about who I may be hurting or any other repercussions. My sister hated me for that.

The problems began when I started dating a popular guy in high school. This guy was in my sister's grade and he was also in ...oh yeah... A BAND!! That meant *sex, drugs & Rock n' Roll* and for a 14 year-old girl just entering high school, I thought I was on the right track to a great four years. My sister's jealousy only increased, however. The relationship with my rock star was ill fated, but we remain friends to this day.

I skipped years of high school classes, except for music, drama and English; I needed to keep my creative juices flowing. I misbehaved and abused drugs and alcohol. I woke up in my final year and said to myself,

"What the fuck are you doing with your life, Francesca? Get a grip and make some changes!" So I did.

I straightened up and graduated from high school a term earlier than most of my friends and classmates. After graduation, my father insisted that I either get a job or go to university. Who was I kidding? Mine was a creative mind; I wrote short stories and poems, I painted, modeled, traveled and did whatever else I pleased. I honestly didn't think my attention span could handle university. Don't get me wrong, I don't knock post-secondary education, but after seeing both sisters put four years toward a diploma with little effect, I was in no hurry. It wasn't until my best friend's mom, Rosanna, said to me,

"Well, you have to be educated. A woman must be able to support herself. Even if there's a man in your life, you should depend on yourself." That was it, the light bulb went off in my head and back to school I went.

What would I study? Believe it or not, the Dental Assisting and Office Management Programme in Community College. That's right, the rebel was now the loose cannon in scrubs. People might have thought I was like a bull in a china shop, but I'm like a chameleon and I adapted to my new environment as effectively as I usually do.

I ended up loving my chosen field and it felt good to be back in school with some discipline. I got a hands-on education and graduated with honors. What followed was a career that opened up a lot of doors and led to many adventures in the years to come. So it was scrubs and 9 to 5 in an office; who would have thought it?

But time passes quickly. Ten years later, I'm still in the field, but managing offices. I now have the luxury of selecting the days or offices I wish to work in. It's pretty sweet! Lately, though, I've become a bit tired of the 9 to 5 routine, so I've found pleasure in working a few evenings outside the office at a Martini and Wine Lounge in the heart of the city.

My life doesn't sound all that bad, does it? Actually, it isn't...anymore. Of course, I have gone through hurt, love, hate and loss and some major hurdles, such as open heart surgery at nineteen. They say you can never be too sure about your friends, but your family is always there for you. I never knew how true that was until my unfortunate series of events occurred.

A few years ago, I ended a long, drawn out relationship of six years. It was definitely a relationship of sex, drugs & rock n' roll. But I was blinded, not by anything as romantic as love or even lust, but by *comfort*. I was confusing love with complacency. Years went on and it had become very one sided. I had put all my ambitions on hold for this man. I'd been in the relationship for so long and was so young that I didn't see what was happening with me, how I was losing myself because of this guy. It wasn't until some friends and loved ones started actually pointing out how unhappy I was that I woke up. Because I was unhappy.

For a while, the lifestyle was great. I traveled, met some amazing people and saw some really awesome musicians play first hand and close up. But I have asthma, I've had heart problems from birth and I'm a smoker. I know I am an idiot, but I also know the rock n' roll lifestyle wasn't helping any.

So, all things come to an end. When my relationship did, it was painful.

I thought I was going to die and my world was going to crumble beneath me. But, as I realized and have heard over a million times before,

"No one has ever died of a broken heart." So true and spoken like a light shining down upon me from the heavens, I realized I can't wallow in my own self-inflicted sorrows forever. I decided I would take what I could learn from the relationship and move on. I could never *hate* him for what had happened; hate isn't even a word in my vocabulary. I'm a firm believer that everything happens for a reason and you take what you have learned to make the next experience better. Like a step up my imaginary staircase of life. Once I took that step, there was no backing down or looking back. It's either a flaw or a unique quality of mine that I can easily walk away from something and not look back. Once I took that step, I knew everything was going to be better. But life threw me another curve ball and I kept thinking I could catch it.

The people who know me can attest to the fact that I'm a very giving and nurturing person. I'm the type of person who would give away the shirt off my back and the last five bucks in my pocket. But for some, give them an inch and they want a mile. Nothing is ever good enough and kindness is mistaken for weakness. I call these people '*feeders.*' Feeders steal your positive energy and if you're not careful, they'll suck the life out of you.

This feeder was like a sister to me; she knew me inside and out. I'd been having strange feelings and vibes, but I never thought it would be her. If only I had known that I was about to get stabbed in the back. She managed to take me for a loop for a year, but I would always turn a blind eye and give her one more chance to redeem herself for her wrongdoings. Hey, don't call me stupid; I really thought she had a good heart. But, it was slowly dawning on me that this feeder was trying to destroy my world.

This woman was trying to step into the footsteps of other people's lives, including myself. She started running her mouth off to people about stuff I apparently said to her that wasn't true. She turned out to be a lying, conniving chameleon with another acquaintance of mine. Then tried to pass the buck and say it was me.

Rumours spread and people were hurt. It turned out; she had lied to us all. She never thought I would find out, nor do anything about it. She even had the nerve to try to mend the friendship after I reamed her out. I do hope she is well though, as I've never wished harm on anyone I've ever met. I hope she grows from that experience.

So let's fast forward to today. I haven't spoken to that feeder since. I couldn't be happier with my family and friends. I have my ups and downs, but I focus on my ups over my downs. The next steps in my staircase are becoming more visible and I'm not afraid to take those steps to where ever they may lead me, knowing I have amazing support and security around me. My family is my world. I still have two best friends and I cherish them. Dating is going well; I'm very happy with the guy I'm with. I'm loving every minute of my days as I look forward to the next; happy, healthy and blessed with positive people around me!